AUTISTICS IN ACADEMIA

Embracing neurodiversity, *Autistics in Academia* amplifies the voices of thirty-seven autistic academics from around the world, unveiling their unique perspectives in academia. Sandra Thom-Jones, an academic and advocate, spotlights overlooked contributions, addressing challenges veiled by stigma. The book aims to dismantle barriers and foster a more inclusive academic landscape. Drawing on first-hand narratives, this work not only raises awareness but also provides insights into how non-autistic individuals can actively contribute to the success and enrichment of autistic academics. This book is an essential resource for those seeking to understand, support, and champion the contributions of autistic individuals within the academic world, and for anyone interested in building a more inclusive academy.

SANDRA THOM-JONES, honorary professor at the University of Wollongong, most recently served as Pro Vice-Chancellor, Research Impact at Australian Catholic University. She now works as an independent autism researcher and consultant. Thom-Jones is also the author of *Growing into Autism* (2022).

AUTISTICS IN ACADEMIA

Narratives of Work, Adversity, and Achievement from Around the World

SANDRA THOM-JONES

University of Wollongong

Shaftesbury Road, Cambridge CB2 8EA, United Kingdom

One Liberty Plaza, 20th Floor, New York, NY 10006, USA

477 Williamstown Road, Port Melbourne, VIC 3207, Australia

314–321, 3rd Floor, Plot 3, Splendor Forum, Jasola District Centre, New Delhi – 110025, India

103 Penang Road, #05-06/07, Visioncrest Commercial, Singapore 238467

Cambridge University Press is part of Cambridge University Press & Assessment, a department of the University of Cambridge.

We share the University's mission to contribute to society through the pursuit of education, learning and research at the highest international levels of excellence.

www.cambridge.org
Information on this title: www.cambridge.org/9781009374064

DOI: 10.1017/9781009374057

When citing this work, please include a reference to the DOI 10.1017/9781009374057

First published 2025

A catalogue record for this publication is available from the British Library.

Library of Congress Cataloging-in-Publication Data
NAMES: Thom-Jones, Sandra, author.
TITLE: Autistics in academia : narratives of work, adversity, and achievement from around the world / Sandra Thom-Jones, University of Wollongong, Wollongong.
DESCRIPTION: New York, NY : Cambridge University Press, [2024] | Includes bibliographical references and index.
IDENTIFIERS: LCCN 2024012507 | ISBN 9781009374064 (hardback) | ISBN 9781009374033 (paperback) | ISBN 9781009374057 (ebook)
SUBJECTS: LCSH: Youth with autism spectrum disorders–Education. | Children with autism spectrum disorders–Education. | Inclusive education.
CLASSIFICATION: LCC LC4717.5 .T46 2024 | DDC 371.94–dc23/eng/20240422
LC record available at https://lccn.loc.gov/2024012507

ISBN 978-1-009-37406-4 Hardback
ISBN 978-1-009-37403-3 Paperback

For Don

Thank you for never letting me think I couldn't be an academic.
I wish you were here to read this.

Contents

Figures

Tables

Acknowledgements

Thank you to Stephen Accera for your ongoing support and enthusiasm for my idea, and willingness to answer all of my questions, from my first tentative approach to Cambridge University Press to the reality of this book.

Thank you to Jeff, Austin, and Lincoln for your never-ending belief in me as a writer, for listening to my ideas, and for all the cups of tea. Thank you to Chloë van der Reijden for once again being able to turn my thoughts into beautiful illustrations.

Thank you to the many wonderful colleagues, bosses, staff, students, and collaborators I have worked with over the years who have taught me that autistic people can thrive in academia in the right environment, and to the ones who have taught me that we can be destroyed by academia in the wrong environment.

Most importantly, thank you to Dr Amandine Catala, Dr Dave Caudel, Dr Patrick Dwyer, Dr Laura Gilmour, Jessica Harrison, Fiona Lee, Dr Dora Raymaker, Penny Robinson, Phoenix Shetty, Sarah Thorneycroft, Dr TC Waisman, and twenty-six other anonymous autistic academics for sharing their reflections. Each of these thirty-seven has provided insight into their lives in an effort to help non-autistic readers understand what it is like to be us, and autistic readers to realise that they are not alone. These people are so much more than study participants; they are my collaborators and comrades. Many of them have committed additional time to reviewing drafts of the chapters within this book to help me be confident that I have comprehensively and authentically represented the group's perspectives.

Author's Note: Why This Book?

Growing up as an (undiagnosed) autistic child, I didn't 'fit in' in many places, but I loved books and knowledge. I imagined that the ideal career would be a university professor, spending every minute of my working life gaining new facts and sharing them with like-minded colleagues.

As a (diagnosed) autistic adult, who still didn't 'fit in' many places and still loved books and knowledge, working as a Pro Vice-Chancellor and autism researcher, I began giving talks at universities about how we could be more autism-inclusive. I was surprised at the number of people who came up to me afterwards, or emailed me when I was back at the office, and said things like, 'I really enjoyed your talk today. I'm autistic but I haven't told anyone at the university. Can I ask your advice about . . .?'

I could understand why so many of us were entering academia; all those books in the library and no library fees, all that knowledge at our fingertips. I had an inkling why so many of us were leaving academia and those aspects of the job that weren't part of the respected and admired 'eccentric professor' stereotype we grew up reading about and aspiring to. I wanted to know what were the things that were working (and not working) for autistic people working in academia; what were our successes and challenges, our motivations, aspirations, our high and lows; and how could the person-environment fit be improved so that more of us could remain and thrive in academia.

I decided the only way to find out was to ask. So, I designed a study. My initial plan was to recruit six to eight autistic academics, ask them a few questions, and write a paper. Instead, I recruited thirty-seven autistic academics, asked them a lot of questions, and wrote this book (and a few papers along the way).

A Bit about 'How'

I obtained approval for the study from the Human Research Ethics Committee (Institutional Review Board) and shared information about the study aims and how to access more information via my Facebook page (Autistic Professor) and social media groups for autistic academics (such as the Facebook group Autistic Researchers Researching Autism).

A total of forty-two people enquired about the study, and thirty-seven went on to participate. Over the period of a year, I emailed them a reflection topic at the beginning of each month, and they had until the end of the month to return their reflection. Each topic included a series of prompts, but participants were encouraged to write on any aspect of the topic that was of interest or relevance to them. As participation in each round was optional and based on the relevance of the topic to their personal experience and interest, participants were included in the sample if they completed and returned the consent form, statistical data sheet, and at least four reflections. The majority of participants (twenty-seven) completed all rounds; thirty at least 75 per cent; and thirty-two at least 50 per cent.

Reflections were saved into a consistent format and imported into NVivo for coding. An inductive approach to data analysis was utilised, allowing the themes to emerge from the data. The analysis process was iterative, with initial codes created and then a visual map produced to identify overlapping and intersecting codes. The codes were then refined and merged with constant reference to the content of each lower-order code to ensure that all included text was relevant to the over-arching theme.

Participants were asked to provide their preferred pseudonym for analysis and reporting. This ensured that the data was anonymised but that each individual could easily recognise comments and quotes attributed to them when reviewing the draft findings, which they were all invited to do for the papers and for the chapters that constitute this book.

Some Thoughts on Intersectionality

The prevailing stereotype of autism is a white cis-gender male; this stereotype dominates both media representations of autism (Aspler, Harding, and Cascio 2022; Jones 2022b) and society's perception of what autism 'looks like'. The diagnostic criteria were developed based on the way that autism presents in this cohort (Navarro-Pardo, López-Ramón, et al. 2021), and there is considerable evidence that assigned female at birth (AFAB) autistics are under-diagnosed, mis-diagnosed, or late diagnosed (Gesi, Migliarese, et al. 2021; Lockwood Estrin, Milner, et al. 2021). In addition to sex at birth, there are discrepancies in diagnosis rates among autistic people as a function of race and ethnicity (Goldblum, McFayden, et al. 2023). Autistic people of colour are less likely to be diagnosed or to receive appropriate supports and services (Morgan, Rodgers, and Tschida 2022), and experience cumulative discrimination (Davis, Solomon, and Belcher 2022).

When I commenced the study, I collected very limited demographic data on the participants (age, gender, country of residence, diagnosis/identification, whether they held a PhD, and years in academia). The decision not to ask for more detailed information – such as race, ethnicity, sexuality, or religion – was difficult to make from an intellectual perspective but essential from a credibility and safety perspective. As you will discover reading this book, many autistic people have not disclosed their diagnosis, and many of those who have disclosed still hide aspects of themselves from their colleagues, due to systemic stigma and discrimination. How could I assure these individuals that their identity would be protected and have them feel comfortable sharing personal reflections with me if on day one I collected enough demographic information that their colleagues could readily identify them, even with the use of a pseudonym?

As the study progressed, and the participants became familiar with the study and with me as a researcher, they increasingly shared information on these aspects of their lives, and you will see references in the quotes and discussion to aspects of race, gender, sexuality, ethnicity, and religion. However, I cannot definitively state the proportion of participants who fall into various important groups, and I acknowledge this as a limitation of the data. I wish this was not the case, and I wish we lived in a world where I could ask these individuals to explicitly state all their complex, inter-connected identities without fear of consequence. I can say that the representation of people of colour is limited but not nil, that the representation of people who are an ethnic minority in their country of residence is small but significant, and that the representation of gender identities and sexualities is more diverse and representative.

I encourage those who want to know more about autism in academia, and particularly how to make their institutions more inclusive, to read some of the excellent work that has been written on autism and intersectionality (Botha and Gillespie-Lynch 2022; Lopez, Nicolaidis, et al. 2022), and particularly about the absence of people of colour in autism research (Lovelace, Comis, et al. 2022).

Some Final Thoughts

I am extremely grateful to these thirty-seven people who so generously shared their thoughts and experiences with me (and with you). They did this for the same reason that I wrote this book: because we all want to see academia become more understanding, supportive, and inclusive, and for our many current and future autistic colleagues. As I will remind you many times throughout the chapters, the autistic people you meet in academia (or anywhere else) will not share all the traits, characteristics, strengths, challenges, thoughts, behaviours, and experiences that are represented in these reflections. However, while we are each unique individuals, we share some common types of challenges and strengths – and we have so much to offer to academia.

CHAPTER 1

Who Are We?

*I play board games often, and Dungeons and Dragons most weeks with a group of friends I got together, I host and run the games which is fun because the host (aka the Dungeon Master [DM] or the Game Master) is a part of the group but also the leader but not a part of team. The role and dynamic is hard to explain but the important part is that it gives a structural reason for me to be a part of the group without feeling fully part of it and the same as everyone else – the team works together to overcome the obstacles, puzzles, challenges and scenarios that the DM designs (all as part of a story you create together), which makes it natural that I'm not a part of the "how do we beat this puzzle" conversations, I'm not a part of the problem-solving because I'm the one to set the problems. This means that I am a valued member of the group – the most valuable because sessions can't physically happen without me. I know I'm important to the group, that I matter, because I'm needed, and I know I'm liked because otherwise they wouldn't want to come and play. But I'm still not in the thick of it, part of the team – which disguises the constant feelings I have, as an autistic person, of being a perpetual outsider. I think being raised NT [neurotypical] when I'm not, and also masking, in a neurotypical world has given me a powerful case of imposters' syndrome, so I never really feel included, welcome, or valued by a group of people unless I'm totally absorbed in something (e.g. a game) or I've been told that the group wants me there and values me. So as DM I know that I have to act, conceal my reactions to people suggesting the correct solution or a totally ridiculous and silly solution to a puzzle or problem, because my pokerface is important to the game. So masking is normal. I know I have to prep things ahead of time and that the sessions make my brain tired because it's intense decision making, so taking breaks and finishing when *I* need to is normal and accepted. I'm a part of the group, but as DM I'm not part of the team – so my feelings of being involved but not always included are right, accurate, and also totally normal and not a reflection on me or on whether or not I'm wanted there. There are a lot of ways that DnD feels like the perfect environment for me to spend time with friends, because it aligns so well with my needs relating to being autistic.*

(Evelyn)

This book explores the experiences of thirty-seven autistic people working in academia (thirty-eight if you include the author). As you read through the chapters, you will learn a lot about the experiences of these individuals as they navigate the university workplace, about the challenges they face and the value they bring to higher education and research.

In this chapter, I will tell you a little bit about these people beyond their work roles and employment experiences. In a different world I would introduce each of them to you by name and tell you about their unique personalities, interests, and gifts. However, we live in a world where autism is still very much stigmatised, and where disclosure comes with significant risks to career progression and social inclusion. Thus, many of my participants have asked to remain anonymous, and I will share their combined stories in a way that gives you a sense of their diversity while maintaining their anonymity.

Throughout the book, the participants are referred to by the pseudonyms of their choosing, and Table 1.1 outlines the age (at the commencement of the project) and gender identification of each individual. All other demographic information – such as country of residence, years in academia, or discipline – will be discussed in the context of the group to avoid the risk of individuals being identified by colleagues.

Of the thirty-seven participants, at the time of the study thirteen were living and working in Australia, eleven in the United States, five in Canada, five in the United Kingdom, and three in Europe. The majority (thirty-two) had a formal autism diagnosis; two were undergoing a diagnostic process (and received a diagnosis prior to the completion of the study); and three self-identified as autistic.

Approximately one-third (twelve) had a doctoral qualification, thirteen did not, and twelve were currently studying for a doctorate. Their duration of employment in academia at the commencement of the study ranged from one year to twenty-three years, with a mean of 8.7 years (median eight years).

Contrary to the stereotype that autistic people cluster in information technology, the group were employed across a vast array of disciplines, with many in multi-disciplinary roles or concurrently holding roles in more than one discipline (see Table 1.2). The predominant discipline groups were social sciences (including psychology, sociology, social work, human geography, gender studies, child protection, and linguistics) and humanities (including philosophy, history, and German studies).

A significant number are in education (including primary, secondary, and higher education, as well as specialist areas such as educational psychology, music education, special education, and languages). Some are in the physical sciences (including engineering, physics, systems science, environmental science, environmental archaeology, and urban sustainability) and the health

Table 1.1 *Participants in the study*

Name	Gender	Age	Reflections
Alex	Non-binary	34	4
Amelia	Female	23	12
Amy	Female	39	12
Ava	Female	50	3
Baz	Male	32	12
Betty	Male	32	12
Charlotte	Female	37	12
Dave	Male	46	12
Dee	Non-binary	47	12
Ella	Female	36	12
Emma	Female	30	12
Eva	Female	n/s	12
Evelyn	Female	28	10
Flora	Female	32	12
Henry	Male	39	6
Isabella	Non-binary	57	12
Jade	Female	27	11
Jane	Female	38	12
Kelly	Non-binary	51	12
Liam	Male	52	6
Lisa	Female	51	5
Louise	Other	42	12
Marie	Female	43	12
Mia	Female	57	12
Moon Man	Male	58	6
Morgan	Female	38	12
Olivia	Female	44	12
Proline	Non-binary	26	12
Psyche	Female	41	12
Ruth	Female	40	12
Saskia	Female	50	12
Scarlett	Female	37	12
Scott	Male	25	12
Sophia	Female	41	12
Sunny	Other	49	12
Trevor	Male	48	12
Trina	Female	42	12

Table 1.2 *Disciplines of participants*

Social science	**12**	
Sociology		2
Psychology		7
Social work		1
Human geography		1
Gender studies		1
Linguistics		1
Child protection		1
Education	**10**	
Primary/secondary education		3
Educational psychology		1
Higher education		1
Music education		1
Special education		1
English as a second language		2
Foreign language teaching		1
Health	**6**	
Public health		2
Neuropsychology		1
Biostatistics		1
Speech pathology		1
Allied health (disability)		1
Physical sciences	**6**	
Engineering		1
Environmental science		1
Physics		1
Environmental archaeologist		1
Urban sustainability		1
Systems science		1
Business and law	**5**	
Leadership		2
Employment		1
Marketing		1
Law		1
Humanities	**4**	
History		1
Philosophy		2
German studies		1
Arts	**4**	
Artist		1
Creative writing		1
Film studies		1
Writing studies		1

sciences (including public health, neuropsychology, biostatistics, speech pathology, and disability services). Others are in arts (including fine arts, film studies, and creative writing), and in business and law (including leadership, employment, and marketing). This is consistent with the (limited) data on autistic university students; for example, in a survey of 102 autistic university students in Australia and New Zealand, fewer than one-third were undertaking a STEM major (Anderson, Carter, and Stephenson 2020).

Of the thirty-one who engage in research, eight are specifically focused on research into autism and five on research that includes autistic people as well as other groups. The remaining eighteen undertake research with no, or minimal, direct involvement with issues related to autism (although that is not to say that they do not engage in autism research in their 'spare' time).

Home Life and Relationships

Approximately two-thirds of participants are living with their partner, with the majority of the remainder living alone. A minority live with parents, other family members, or a roommate, either for companionship or to receive or provide support. Some also live with their dependent children, and approximately half have pets in their home.

The participants ranged from very introverted individuals with few social connections to very extroverted with large friendship networks. Those who reported few if any social connections included some who find social interaction draining and need the isolation to recharge, some who prefer to spend their time with family, and some who would prefer more social interaction but find it challenging to make and maintain friendships, a situation exacerbated at the time by the COVID-19 lockdowns.

> *I know not all autistics are introverted, but I really do need my time to myself to recharge.* (Scott)

> *I am fairly introverted, so I am quite contented on my own. In other countries I've lived and worked in, I often do befriend co-workers and spend a lot of time with them outside work. Here in [country], that is not really a part of their culture. And, [country] has been on a strict lockdown since December, so I cannot really go out and spend time with people in person. Currently, I am by myself 95% of the time.* (Trina)

> *He [the narrator's partner] is pretty much the only person I spend time with outside of work. I trust him and I do not have to play a role with him.... I also love my*

mom but unfortunately she lives really very far away. So I talk to her on the phone very often but I haven't seen her in the last two years. And I miss her. (Sophia)

I always love seeing friends, but I often find that I seem to like their company more than they like mine, and I always still find myself sidelined for other, better friends. (Psyche)

Unfortunately, the biggest thing about the non-work me is my health and disability. I, like many autistic people, have Ehlers-Danlos Syndrome plus over a dozen chronic conditions that come along with it. Honestly, these days my health is the prominent facet of my life.... Unfortunately, a lot of autistic women have a similar circumstance. (Jade)

However, the majority reported spending their time with their families and/or a small group of friends. This was not a function of the common and inaccurate stereotype of autistic people as isolated loners in their own worlds, with no desire for human contact. Rather, it was a combination of the quality and quantity of interpersonal interactions that we seek. Participants reflected on deep and meaningful connections with their partners, children, and close friends, and the enjoyment they experienced in spending time with people they felt comfortable and relaxed with. They also discussed the need to manage their energy levels due to the (social) exhaustion of work, education, and daily life in general, which will be discussed in detail in subsequent chapters.

I don't really like socializing outside of work. I prefer to spend time with them [family] when I'm not at work. (Trevor)

I live with my partner and my kid, who like 99% of the time are the only people I spend time with outside work. I don't really want or need much social contact and after spending almost all my energy on work, family and myself there's really not much left over. (Morgan)

We have some friends we enjoy seeing, but for the most part we enjoy spending time just the two of us (mostly talking, watching documentaries, going on outings, traveling when we can). (Amy)

We are not extremely social people, but we do have a small group of friends. We have one couple that we spend a bit of time with out of work (maybe one or two days/nights a week) and some other friends we see on occasion. We try to manage the amount of socialising that we do during the week and on weekends, so that we don't end up exhausted. (Scarlett)

A common thread in the reflection on friendships was the foundation in shared interests, with many individual friendships and friendship groups focused around a hobby or special interest. This is consistent with the findings of a recent review of the literature on autistic friendships, which concluded that autistic people, more so than non-autistic people, define friendship based on homophily and propinquity (Black, Kuzminski, et al. 2024). Related to this was a view that strong connections do not necessarily require face-to-face contact but can be equally fulfilling if they are electronically mediated. Those with children in particular commented on the 'safety' of friendship groups consisting of other neurodivergent people.

> *I also lead a writing group, so the four other folks involved in that I spend a lot of time with – we meet every other week, but also enjoy writing together. I have an intermittent knitting group with another set of friends. And, well, just spending time with friends. I've always had a lot of amazing friends, and they're really why I'm alive at all. Community is an enormous protective factor. My friends are all weirdos like me – I'm a pretty firm believer in just being authentic and letting the people who will mesh well with that in, even if it looks different from mainstream. I love them dearly.* (Sunny)

> *My friends are a mixture of academics and people who are simply creative with a good sense of humor. I would say all of my longterm friends fit the creative personality even though not all of them are academically inclined. My shared hobbies with my friends include debating or discussing science or world issues, sharing digital art or playing online games, swimming and hiking, and spending time with my animals who are also some of my best friends.... I will still probably use text or email or the phone 90% of the time to talk to my friends but those in person lunches or swims 6 or 7 times a year mean a lot even for an extreme introvert like me.* (Eva)

> *I keep in touch with my close friends via text and sometimes phone or Zoom. Some people think that's impersonal but most of them are Autistic and we have a really close bond.* (Ruth)

> *I find the most safety with other parents of autistic kids, and other adults (parents or not) who are neurodivergent. They understand that some people behave in unexpected ways.* (Saskia)

Hobbies and Interests

The group members' hobbies and interests are as diverse as their academic disciplines and, again, demonstrate the inaccuracy of the myths around autistic people. By far the most common category of hobbies and interests was creative pursuits, ranging from painting to knitting to jewellery making and everything in between. Evident in participants' descriptions were the many functions that engaging in these activities serve for autistic people, providing an outlet for stress, sensory input, repetitive movement (stimming), and providing a sense of safety and security.

> *I'm currently building a bed from scratch – wood and screws and a drill etc. I love having hobbies, I sew and crochet and scrapbook and design things, I am*

getting into basic interior design.... I want to learn to watercolour, make my own art and maps for DnD, I have a 3D pen I want to learn to use. I want to build my own furniture or at least upcycle it. (Evelyn)

I really like making things and can't remember ever not being like that – when very little, I wrote books, stories, poems, I drew detailed pencil drawings and I really liked origami. Crafts continued throughout adult life, and I got into modular origami, model making, I made greetings cards for a while, I made jewellery and chain maille, paper cutting, colouring, Lego building and collecting, and all manner of arts and crafts with my daughter too. I also learned a bit of coding, have kept up my spreadsheet passion, learned to design websites and do graphic art and design for various jobs I did, and I got pretty good at Photoshop. (Louise)

Oooh so many! A love of beads and making jewellery is something I've done since I was about 10. Absolutely love it, love colours and collecting shiny things! I've been crocheting & knitting for about 15 years now – I feel safe if I take my project with me where ever I go. I suppose it's the grown up equivalent of taking a teddy everywhere. Even if I don't do it, I like to hold it. (Olivia)

I really enjoy woodwork and playing music but I don't do that much of either these days. Both have been a passion since adolescence. I find the methodical nature of working with wood and doing something with my hands quite calming. (Ruth)

Contrary to the myth that autistic people lack creativity and imagination, in addition to these craft-related activities, many participants reflected on their enjoyment of writing fiction and poetry (including at least one famous novelist in our group). While early understandings of autism included the misnomer that autistic people have impoverished creativity (Craig and Baron-Cohen 1999), more recent research – alongside the increased recognition of autistic authors, actors, and artists – has demonstrated the fallacy of this viewpoint. In fact, recent studies have shown that autistic children do not lack creativity but have a unique creative cognition profile, including a greater capacity than non-autistic children to generate creative metaphors (Kasirer, Adi-Japha, and Mashal 2020), and that autistic college students enjoy fiction writing more than their non-autistic peers and write at a higher reading level with fewer grammatical and spelling errors (Shevchuk-Hill, Szczupakiewicz, et al. 2023).

I still regularly write poetry as an outlet and have a few folders of writing somewhere. I keep meaning to start writing creatively more often but at the moment I don't write enough for my PhD so I can't justify it. (Louise)

Writing (Fiction, Poetry, etc.) – I have been interested in writing from the time I was 11 years old. I love to play with stories, explore ideas, and make discoveries as I write. I also like the way that many different subjects, memories, and ideas can build to form one story. It feels like a conversation with ideas. (Marie)

I have so many hobbies and interests outside of work that it's really difficult to find time to spend on them all! I love engaging in all of the arts, but particularly writing and visual art. I have drawn and painted since I was a very small child, and have written poetry, prose, short stories, stageplays, and screenplays. I use the arts to express myself, as I find it so difficult to express myself adequately through speech, and find it so difficult to be heard, seen and understood by others. By pouring my heart and soul into various art forms, it seems to be easier to communicate to others these parts of me that otherwise remain so invisible so frequently. In this way, I can ease some of the loneliness of being me. Music and dancing are more selfish . . . I indulge in these arts mainly for my own benefit. Both have been solo activities for me for most of my life, although I have had flurries of social elements in each over the years. (Psyche)

Other indoor activities that were commonly noted as hobbies and interests included reading, music, games (predominantly strategy games), and cooking. Again, participants articulated the function these hobbies served in their lives – including helping them to find an escape from their problems and place in the world where they could 'fit in'.

I have always loved reading fiction since I was a toddler (I think was hyper-lexic) – I ALWAYS have to have a book on the go otherwise I feel naked. It is also a wonderful escape for me, the best escape. I love fantasy & science fiction for that reason but I also love psychological thrillers and crime novels because I love the puzzle aspects of them. (Olivia)

At age 9, after discovering the concept of what-do-I-do-now books and the idea that one could design a system to run a simulated adventure – exploration, combat, conflict-resolution – I began what has become my greatest and most-rewarding passion – gaming. From designing my own game systems to play by myself, to having middle-schoolers ask to play in my games, to developing close friendships through my gaming, this passion has had a profound impact on my life and most of my social skills and understanding of humanity. A good game session is like a work of art, like a good book, but the group is involved in the telling, each member adding to the complexity and dynamics of the narrative. One could say that my later obsession with physics should have been an obvious career-choice – I love rule systems, and physics is the rule system of reality itself – much more complex and imaginative than anything a human could devise. To this day, I game twice a month, and much of my free time is spent crafting and designing the next game session. Check in with me in another 40 years, if I'm alive you'll likely find me in a retirement home gaming with some old friends. (Dave)

Participants also reflected on more active hobbies and interests, including bushwalking and hiking, exercise (from walking to highly competitive sports), gardening, and animal care. Some engage regularly in a variety of active hobbies, for example, Charlotte who regularly participates in both day and multi-day hiking, cycling, and stand-up paddle boarding. For others, it is more about being at peace in nature.

> *I think part of the reason I like walking in the countryside so much is because I'm looking at all the detail. I love the way the raindrops flash with sunlight on the trees, thousands of sparks of light, and I love the colour of the leaves when the sun shines through them, and I love the varied colours of the hills and fields. I think the walking motion is also soothing to both me and my husband. I love every change of colour in the sea and sky, and watching clouds and weather fronts moving in or past, and watching flight behaviour and wing shape and colour to distinguish the different birds, and looking at the changes in the sea that tell you where the fish will be massed, which in turn tells me where to look for dolphins and gannets. I love when there is no sound but the wind and the call of the occasional chough or oystercatcher or raven. That quietness is so important to me. Walking in the countryside is a special interest that I share with my husband; it's as intense as the imaginary world games I played when I was a kid. Sharing a special interest is the most amazing feeling in the world.* (Mia)

> *I've been a martial artist since I was a teenager, although I haven't always been actively training with a school.... During the pandemic the school offered classes over Zoom, which really helped me deal with the stress of both the pandemic and grad school.* (Dee)

> *Past hobby = cycling. I raced time trials on my new road bike in 2007, and started track cycling at the end of that year. I got my AusCycle coaching accreditation, and was assistant (female) coach of the Thursday evening cycling group for juniors and started training & racing myself.... I raced in a few Victorian Masters championships, and the Australian Masters Track Championships.* (Jane)

Our eclectic group of participants had an equally eclectic range of special interests beyond those discussed above – including photography, cyclones, dance, bees, food, Lego, medical procedures, perfume, languages, real estate, spirituality, and many other topics.

Two aspects of autistic interests that were commonly addressed in participant reflections were the distinction between 'hobbies' and 'special interests' and the potential overlap between interests and work. Special interests are intense, immersive, and often lifelong, bringing great joy and meaning to an autistic person's life (and often referred to by others as 'obsessions'). Hobbies, on the other hand, are activities that we dabble in that may be fleeting or engaged in at a superficial level.

> *Non-work me is 100% a photographer! When I photograph, I can get absolutely lost in it for hours. I forget to eat and drink and go to the bathroom. It becomes*

my world. My mind is quieter, and my focus is purely on what is in the little frame in front of me. It's a beautiful experience of utter flow, and photography is one of the only places – actually, the only place – where I experience that feeling. I forget about the world and all the difficulties I face and the horrible aspects of much of reality and simply feel pure joy. It's my meditation – my spiritual practice. I'm tearing up right now just thinking about how special it is to me!. . . [whereas] Both of these (craft and cooking) are 'hobbies', not special interests, as differentiated by the very different level of passion! (Ella)

I collect perfume. I've been doing it for 35 years. I am interested in all aspects of the process, from the molecular structure of the scents to their combinations to the marketing of them. (Saskia)

The autistic passion for reading and learning results for many in a synergistic relationship between 'work' (or study) and special interests, something that is reflected on in more detail in later chapters. Conversely, some reflected that their academic career had led them away from reading as a hobby, particularly those whose relaxation reading had always been non-fiction rather than fiction books.

Outside of work, I like hanging out with my dog, exploring interest areas (many of which are work related), and reading/listening to podcasts. (Amelia)

This question is a fun one. I would say a lot of my special interests revolve around academic stuff and I often spend time reading journal articles for fun. For instance although I am an education researcher I love reading articles on genetics and neurobiology for fun including genetic factors in autism and some of the studies on Covid19 genetics. (Eva)

Outside of work, I am an extremely passionate autism researcher, currently working on my PhD. That's my passion, my hobby, and my work to hopefully make some small improvement in how my people (autistic people) are treated in society. (Jade)

I used to read, I used to read a lot but after I got into academia, I don't do that anymore. Because I read so much as my job, the last thing I kind of wanna do is read. And that's because the only books I read are non-fiction books, so it's just . . . At the end of the day, you just don't really wanna take in more information. (Charlotte)

Would They Be Surprised?

When asked whether they thought there were things about their non-work identities that would surprise their colleagues, only three of the participants responded that they thought this would not be the case.

Many felt that their colleagues would be surprised by the nature, focus, or depth of their special interests. This was in a few cases the result of a deliberate decision not to share this information with others – for example, due to previous experiences of being belittled for having interests that were seen as childish or inappropriate – but in most cases due to a belief that others simply would not be interested. Others mentioned specific aspects of their life or experiences that they thought would surprise colleagues, either because of the preconceived ideas people have about 'autistic lives' or because of previous reactions from others to the revelation of personal facts (often that they themselves thought were unremarkable).

> *I don't tend to talk a lot about my special interests at work and if I do it's in fairly general terms so I think a lot of people would be surprised at how deep and broad my brain goes on them and how much time I spend focused on them.* (Morgan)

> *I think they would be shocked at the range of previous jobs I have done and interests I've had. I do know other people that switch things around as often as me but I do find autistic people tend to know more about every interest they've had.* (Louise)

> *Things I think will surprise people they think are totally obvious (like my fountain pen collection) and things that I think are totally bland people will think are amazing (like when I went through a short phase of knitting fractals).* (Sunny)

> *I think much of what I do outside of work would surprise my colleagues. There is an assumption that as a minoritized Autistic person, my life must be difficult and economic security must be difficult. Safety in general as a minoritized Autistic person is an issue but I am privileged to be living a good life.* (Kelly)

A consistent theme in many of the reflections was that colleagues would be surprised to see them being their 'autistic selves' at home, that is, acting and being in ways that felt comfortable. These authentic selves are often very different to the neurotypical masks that autistic people are forced to wear in workplaces and other social settings in order to fit in and be accepted (discussed in subsequent chapters, and the consequences are explored in detail in Chapter 7).

> *I think most of non-work me would surprise my coworkers, including all the stimming I like to do at home.... Maybe the thing that would surprise them most is all the mental health stuff.* (Amelia)

> *I think pretty much everything about the non-work me would surprise my colleagues. I am very different in my life at home. I dress totally differently on the weekend. I can stop playing a role and wearing a costume.* (Sophia)

> *I function very well at work, but I think my work colleagues would be surprised at how low functioning I am outside of the work environment.* (Trevor)

One thing that does relate a little more to work: I think people at work see me as an organized person. They might be surprised at the amount of work it takes for me to show up to meetings on time and remember regular tasks. They might also be surprised at just how much studying and reading I have done, to create the organizational systems that I use. (Marie)

I think people would also be surprised how different my home life is to "normal people" – we're a house of three autistic people who really aren't interested in following the rules or the status quo. I get the feeling people would be surprised/horrified to see some of the ways our neurodivergent little household happily runs. (Morgan)

I can imagine that colleagues – e.g., my editor or academic supervisors with whom I'm not yet as close – may be surprised that I'm autistic. I feel like most people would be surprised that I'm autistic! There are some very pervasive stereotypes around autism that are ingrained in people's minds, and they most certainly don't look at a [physical description] who masks like a trooper and think to themselves, "that's what autism looks like". So much of my experience is very much an invisible disability – the struggles I face and the challenges I've had to overcome are internal and hidden in interpersonal interactions. (Ella)

Other aspects of being autistic that participants felt would surprise their colleagues were co-occurring conditions and (the ongoing impact of) past experiences of trauma.

There are many parts of my life I keep private, mostly in relation to what I consider to be the abnormal or stigmatised aspects of my life that I have lived with forever. In the rare event I do disclose what my life is like or was like during my childhood I am always met with an odd amalgamation of shock and pity and sadness and praise for being so 'resilient'. (Flora)

They may also be surprised to hear that in all my life I have never felt safe, or known what it feels like to be accepted in the community. I seem to exist outside of my human body, and outside of the human race. (Psyche)

Some Final Thoughts

The aim of this book is to give you some insight into the experiences of these thirty-seven people. What they have in common is that they are autistic, and they are working in academia. This means that they share many of the same challenges and frustrations, as well as many of the same strengths and successes. However, what I hope this chapter has also shown is that this is a diverse group of people, and they are representing a wider cohort of autistic people working in academia who are equally diverse.

Stereotypes surrounding autism are pervasive and harmful. The stereotypes perpetuated by news and entertainment media typically portray

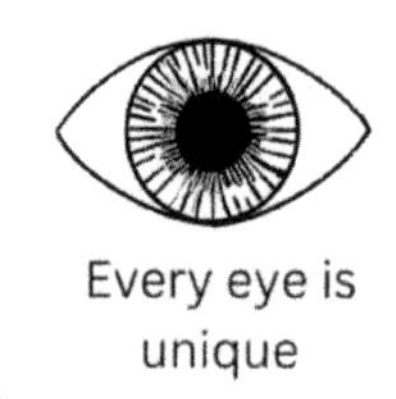

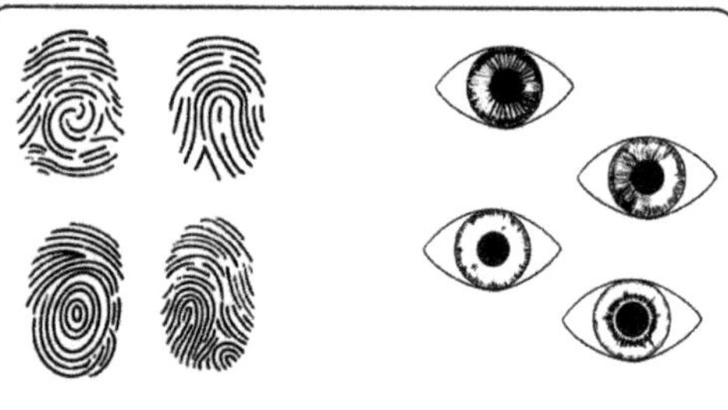

Figure 1.1 Autistic people are individuals. Source: Art by Chloë van der Reijden.

autistic people as white males (Aspler, Harding, and Cascio 2022; Jones, Gordon, and Mizzi 2023), or as children or adolescents, and assign us to roles such as a victim, a danger, a burden, or a savant (Gaeke-Franz 2022; Jones 2022b; Mittmann, Schrank, and Steiner-Hofbauer 2023; Yến-Khanh 2023). Such stereotypes, and the continuing use of the word 'autistic' as a pejorative (Patekar 2021), contribute to social exclusion and discrimination of autistic people (Hamilton 2019; Fontes and Pino-Juste 2022).

The reality is that autistic people – while sharing some key characteristics – are as diverse as non-autistic people. Throughout this book, I will often refer to strengths and challenges of 'many autistic people' or as 'common among autistic people', but beneath these generalisations are individual people who are each unique in their own constellation of autism and their identities and characteristics as individuals (Figure 1.1).

CHAPTER 2

How Did We Get Here?

> *... my current research area [employment experiences of autistic women], the thing that attracted me was obviously because, hey, I'm on the spectrum, and I have had the shittiest work history in the freaking world ... I'm hoping that my research will change things for other people on the spectrum and make their work lives so much more enjoyable and a lot easier.*
>
> (Charlotte)

This chapter explores both the literal and figurative answers to the question of how the participants became autistic academics. From the literal standpoint, this includes pragmatic aspects such as the courses they studied and career pathways they followed, as well as the obstacles and successes they experienced in applying for positions in academia. From the figurative standpoint, it focuses on how and why they chose their particular disciplines and areas of research.

At the time of completing their reflections, the group were employed in a range of roles across universities and related institutions, with many holding two or more concurrent part-time roles. Thirteen were employed in teaching roles, ranging from part-time teaching assistant positions to full-time tenured lecturers (faculty). Fourteen held early to mid-career research positions, ranging from casual research assistants to postdoctoral positions to part-time and full-time tenure-track roles. Five were in senior leadership roles, including director or associate director of research centres or university departments. Three were working in university administration, and two in unpaid university roles. Three were self-employed, undertaking work in collaboration with or on contract for universities or research entities; two had recently left the sector; and two were in between roles. Eleven were enrolled in a PhD program.

Two primary reasons were given for holding multiple part-time roles. One related to the unstable nature of academic employment and the need to take on whatever work was available to ensure financial survival. The other related to the heavy demands of full-time academic roles and the incompatibility of these demands with the reality of the autistic experience, particularly for those with co-occurring conditions.

> *My current role is quite mixed is the simplest way of describing it and I would say my research interests are more so driven by community needs than where the dollars are and that I have received minimal funding other than one small grant for this current project that covers partial expenses. If I was doing this for hopes of becoming rich I would have left 10 years ago. However, I do hope to earn enough to get off of disability as due to my perceptual and motor issues I can't go work at a pizza place or a grocery store so academia or related consulting work is my only option for gainful employment.* (Eva)

> *For example my teaching role – I set my own hours according to my needs, I have flexibility to cancel and work around other work and my mental health constraints, and I can do it from my home which helps to alleviate the anxiety of being out and about, using public transport and being around others. I also don't have to answer to a boss about how I do things so micromanagement just doesn't exist in my life. I've worked roles in the past where every detail, the minutia of the role, is strictly micromanaged and that caused a lot of anxiety and exacerbated my depression because of how I was constantly self-monitoring and self-censoring to fit the expectations of others.* (Evelyn)

While some had taken a very direct route to their current career – undergraduate degree, postgraduate degree, into an academic role in the same discipline – many described complex journeys that led to their current roles. For some this was a function of exploring different disciplines and finding the right 'fit', moving from one area to another as opportunities arose and interests changed. However, for many it was a result of situational, social, and environmental challenges that resulted in them needing to change directions or take significant career breaks. These included personal and family physical and mental health challenges, as well as workplace bullying and discrimination.

> *I started out in university as a landscape architecture student. After a year in the studio I realized I was more analytical than creative and switched degrees to political science. I started an interdisciplinary MA after several years of thinking of going to Law School, and I wound up taking a geography class somewhat by accident and discovered there was a discipline that allowed for the study of pretty much everything, and I chose the discipline for my PhD.* (Liam)

> *During these department seminars I felt like I was watching a documentary where lions tore gazelles apart without the excuse of survival. I saw many colleagues and students torn down in front of a room full of people who claimed to be their peers. It was disheartening and anxiety provoking to say the least to watch others cry while their research was belittled.... After a year of fighting I would wake in the morning without the will to live ...* (Flora)

Survival. Being undiagnosed, black, and female in the late 70s early 80s, survival in schools with over 2000 students was my incentive to learn about leadership. (Kelly)

What Attracted Us to Our Roles?

Despite the range of roles, disciplines, and locations, there were remarkable consistencies in the reflections on what attracted these autistic academics to their current roles and professions. The four overarching – and somewhat overlapping – themes were empowering autistic people, social justice, understanding the world, and intellectual stimulation.

Not surprisingly, most of those employed in autism research roles commented that they were attracted by the opportunity to make a contribution to the well-being of autistic people. For some this was inspired by wishing to protect future generations from the harms they themselves had experienced, for others by seeing others being marginalised or mistreated, and for a minority by a reflection on their good fortune at receiving support and understanding.

As far as my application into autism and mental health/disability services intervention research a lot of it is rage, actually. I would like to find ways to improve these systems, as well as the broader social context they exist in, so that future generations won't have to go through some of the stuff I, and my generation did. We are only where we are because of the work done by previous generations, and I feel it's important to be part of that lineage, including in academia. The relationship between knowledge and power is for real. (Sunny)

I was diagnosed as autistic at age 22 while I was studying my undergrad. in psychology. I didn't really know anything beyond the stereotypical idea of autism at the time. I then quickly became connected with the autistic community and became heartbroken to hear their stories of being mistreated throughout their lives due to being autistic. I felt like I had, in a way, been able to skip being mistreated due to all the misconceptions of autism because I was diagnosed so late. When I saw how misunderstandings and stereotypes had contributed to the mistreatment of my people, I decided to dedicate my budding research career to making things better for my people, for the autistic community. (Jade)

Being autistic I wish to pass on the good fortune I had in receiving needed support from toddlerhood to the present. (Moon Man)

This passion for social justice was not limited to concern for their own neurotype. Many of those working in other fields were driven to choose those areas because of a commitment to the well-being of others, particularly those experiencing marginalisation and discrimination. Words like 'oppression', 'injustice', and 'struggle' were common throughout the reflections on what attracted these people to their current roles and their lifetime's work. Some entered academia in the hope of researching answers to problems they had seen in previous 'real-world' careers, and others were career academics, but they shared a desire to find ways to advance outcomes for those most in need.

> *I worked in the out of home care sector as a youth worker for 6 years prior to research, I saw a great need for research to be conducted in the sector to improve child and family outcomes.* (Baz)

> *If I was doing this for hopes of becoming rich I would have left 10 years ago.... I hope to leave behind something whether I end up as a faculty member or an adjunct with consulting work. For one less child to be bullied in school, one less immigrant or indigenous family to have slurs shouted at them on a bus or a park, one less internet troll celebrating the murder of a minority, for people with any differences not to fear store security or the police, for non-binary or LGBTQA individuals to go about life and not be treated differently. I know I can't change the world but if I can influence the attitudes of a few people who may go on to advocate for other people, I hopefully leave some seeds planted for a brighter tomorrow even if I'm planting one tree in a vast forest.* (Eva)

A common reflection among those in psychology, sociology, creative arts, and related fields was that they were attracted by a desire to understand the world – or, more specifically, to understand other people and (hopefully) themselves. For many this came from an inherent feeling of being different from other people, not fitting in, and not understanding why – a common experience for autistic people – and a desire to 'learn' more about being human.

> *By watching films and reflecting on them from a philosophical perspective, I could better understand myself: my inner world, my needs, goals and, in effect, other people and the society. In other words, films and philosophy helped me better navigate in a neurotypical world.* (Betty)

> *I was drawn to psychology as I found it difficult to understand people in my youth. I developed an enduring special interest in psychology in my twenties as I found it was a way to understand people through a scientific process rather than an intuitive one which suited my style of information processing.* (Trevor)

Not surprisingly, intellectual stimulation was a key attraction to a career in academia across all disciplines. For some this meant following a lifelong passion from a childhood hobby to a productive career, and for others a chance discovery during secondary school or undergraduate university studies that sparked a passion to learn the intricacies of a niche research area.

Other attractions to current roles and careers expressed by multiple group members that further demonstrate the inaccuracy of many of the stereotypes surrounding autism were a passion for language and a love of teaching. The love of language included both written and spoken language, participant's native and foreign languages, and the science of language acquisition and development. The passion for teaching (expanded on in Chapter 4) combined the joys of sharing knowledge and helping others to succeed.

Finding a Job in Academia

The process of obtaining a job in academia was described as stressful and exhausting by the majority of participants. While job-hunting is difficult for most people, and academia is renowned for its competitive nature and complicated recruitment processes, the process can be particularly complex for autistic people seeking roles in predominantly non-autistic environments.

By far the most challenging and confronting aspect mentioned in multiple reflections was the 'job interview' – that gruelling confrontation when we are judged on our suitability for a role, not for our skills and knowledge but for our ability to communicate in a context designed for neurotypical people.

> *It seems that people either love me (and I get the job right away) or I hear nothing back. I think part of the issue is that I don't really know how to 'behave' in interviews. I'm not very good at sucking up to people who I don't like, so it's challenging having to put on that mask when it feels disingenuous.* (Emma)

> *Horrendous! I am absolutely awful at interviews. I go blank. I think weird thoughts and because I know I've got to push them out the way, I can't and then I can't focus. I also need time to think and this comes across badly. And then (of course!) when I consider a question to be pointless, I get irritated but because I can't show my irritation, I go blank.* (Olivia)

> *I have applied for a couple of jobs over the years, and been through a couple interviews. Honestly, interviews do little more than evaluate your ability to talk yourself up and talk up your experience to a bunch of strangers who are evaluating you to make sure you're confident but not TOO confident *rolls eyes*. Just let us prove we can do the job and work well with the team. I've had "autism" moments in interviews that I'm sure contributed to my not getting a job that I'm fully qualified for. E.g., one the panel asked me something like "If you were collaborating with other team members, what would that look like?" I then proceeded to explain the visuals of us sitting around the table together to talk, before I realised they weren't asking for visuals at all.* (Jade)

> *I have historically been terrible at applying for jobs, academic and otherwise. I've often not made it past initial application stage or bombed at the interview.*

I once applied for a low-level, short-term desk monkey job at my old uni for some extra summer cash. I think they just interviewed me out of courtesy and I didn't make it past interview. It may have been because I stumbled when asked about interactions with clients. I stopped in my tracks, thought for a moment, and then said I couldn't answer the question because this is a university, we have colleagues, we have students, but we do not have clients. I don't think that went down so well. I've also left a few jobs and projects because I find it incredibly difficult to work with people whose ethics I find troubling. (Ruth)

Similar frustrations with the focus on social skills, difficulty interpreting ambiguous interview questions, and challenges in responding to questions due to the need for additional processing time have been reported in studies with autistic people in other employment contexts outside academia (Markel and Elia 2016; Nagib and Wilton 2020; Vincent 2020; Davies, Heasman, et al. 2023).

Several in the group commented on the significant impact that this process has on their physical and mental health, far beyond typical levels of weariness or disillusionment with the process. Despite this, they continued to battle through the process, with many demonstrating extreme levels of commitment to preparation and rehearsal to ensure they met the gruelling requirements of the process. Others in the group reported extended periods of unemployment, and ensuing periods of self-doubt and internal criticism, as a result of these experiences. The thirty-seven people sharing their stories in this book are extremely intelligent, capable, and highly qualified individuals; they are also survivors in a world where so many other autistic people have been defeated by systems that were not designed to recognise and nurture our potential.

I think a lot of interviewers would say they're looking for the "human" component, which often roughly translates to the "social communication that makes the interviewer feel at ease" component. I'm a pretty skilled masker, and I can successfully mask during interviews and perform the role as expected, but then that's one more thing I'm having to think about when already stressed. When mixed in with formulating answers in real time, it's just a lot to think about and a really overwhelming and stressful experience. It's hard for me to stay out of a mental health spiral when in that process. (Amelia)

The interview process for my current role was very difficult, even though I had already been working at the institution and working in this role as a part-time faculty member. After the initial application, there was a phone interview. Finally, there was a day of in-person interviewing, which included an interview with the university president, an interview with the full faculty, with the department, with the hiring committee, and a teaching demonstration open to anyone interested in attending. At each stage, I was judged not only by my performance or my answers to the question but by my demeanor and social skills.

> *It was difficult. My preparation for both the phone interview and the day of in-person interviewing was extensive. I hired a career coach who specialized in academic jobs to help guide me in knowing what to expect and how to approach questions and conversations during the interview process. I also prepared a 6-page document of potential questions I might be asked, as well as data to use in my responses. Luckily, I succeeded in getting the job.* (Marie)

> *Searching for jobs was very difficult for me. I was getting help from many different agencies, but still, it took a lot of time (more than 18 months, 575 days to be precise) to get a job after my PI told me that he didn't want to work with me anymore belittling me as he said, "You are not a kid. You are not an undergrad" etc. The problem with me was the intersectionality of my autism and transgender identities. The main obstacles for me had been hard to navigate the system. I perform well only if I have to do one thing at a time, not more. The success was that I was able to find a dream job at the end with [organisation].* (Proline)

Other significant challenges to obtaining an academic position that were commonly mentioned included aspects of communication, social interaction, information processing, and routines that are characteristic of many autistic people. Differences in our communication and information-processing styles that make finding and applying for jobs difficult include things like interpreting job advertisements, which are often ambiguous, and following confusing social rules about when honesty is not appropriate or desirable.

> *Job searching is hard because I take things literally, so I don't know when it's appropriate to apply for jobs I don't meet the essential criteria for but which I might be suited for anyway. I struggle to know what terms to search, what roles mean/would look like.* (Evelyn)

> *Job searching, interviewing, and leadership have always been a challenge for me because there are such strong proscriptions against telling the truth. I'm not talking about issues where confidentiality is a concern; I mean even further than that. For instance, you can't say, "Yes, the department has a history of harassment, but we're working against it with anti-harassment and anti-racist initiatives." That's what I'd love to hear. But the expectation is to deny the problem in the first place. "What? Harassment here? Never!" It's an insult to all the people who have struggled in toxic departments and universities.* (Saskia)

Research has shown that autistic people are considerably less likely than non-autistic people to apply for roles where they do not explicitly meet all of the selection criteria (Markel and Elia 2016), even when they are equally capable of undertaking the role, as articulated by Evelyn (above), and less adept at 'tailoring' descriptions of their previous experience to meet the criteria (Davies, Heasman, et al. 2023). This very literal interpretation of job advertisements, and need for clarity of expectations and processes, can put autistic job seekers at a significant disadvantage.

The need for routine and stability that permeates the lives of many autistic people can also serve as a significant barrier to employment in academia. Many of us find the concept of moving away from our homes overwhelming, and the fear of the unknown prevents us from applying for roles that would require relocating. This can also limit our ability to apply for promotion to roles within our own organisations where these may require working across multiple campuses or engaging in frequent travel.

> *Fear – I cannot handle more of this sort of social failure. travel. Oh my gosh the thought of packing, selling and moving! And then finding a new place! I've done this a lot before but it now seems insurmountable in my current state.* (Isabella)

> *A couple of quite big obstacles I face are the fact that I can't relocate – I can function well at work, if everything else in my life stays consistent, and I also have huge executive dysfunction issues when it comes to 'life admin'. The thought of having to do everything that's involved in relocating is so terrifyingly overwhelming I can barely even think about it. According to everyone this means I'm shooting my career in the foot.* (Morgan)

Given the numerous challenges and obstacles experienced in the job-seeking process, it is perhaps surprising that the majority of the thirty-seven are currently employed and/or have been employed for substantial periods of time in the past. For many, this is due to perseverance in the face of repeated knock-backs. For others, success came from 'playing the game' and learning how to mask their autism in an interview.

However, for some finding the right fit was a smoother or faster process resulting from the synergy of a role opening up with someone who was familiar with their work and capability.

> *I fear I'm a very poor sample for this one – on the day they handed me my diploma, during the celebrations after the ceremony, my boss announced the creation of the [organisation name] and asked me to direct it. I'd been warned a huge opportunity was coming my way so I didn't look for any jobs. So yeah, my career was handed to me on a silver platter, I recognize how extraordinarily fortunate that was and how absurdly lucky I am, but long story short I didn't look for a job, and now it seems likely I will never have to.* (Dave)

> *I have been extremely fortunate in my employment in academia because I've had to do very little job hunting. I first approached my now-supervisor because I was hoping to volunteer with her to learn research skills in the field. She is one of the only people I've ever met who actually liked me from the start, and she hired me as a Research Assistant, then later as a Teaching Assistant. When she left that University, I went with her as a Research Assistant and the person who*

took over her role kept me on as a Teaching Assistant. . . . My supervisor has also been extremely proactive in telling all of her colleagues about how strong my work is, so they come to me to offer me work. This semester, I had so many job offers for Teaching Assistance work that I had to knock some back, and I'll be marking an extraordinarily large load of work. My Research Assistance role is also ongoing, as my supervisor continues to seek funding to pay me. I feel grateful for how relatively easy it's been. (Ella)

I was offered a research assistantship in my second year, after taking a seminar with the professor I now work for, and talking with him about the grant-funded project he is a co-principal on. I feel like a lot of that opportunity came out of my persistent interest in talking to him about it, as well as having made a good impression on him during the course of the seminar. I will be continuing that RAship for the next academic year, and he offered me employment this summer as well. And another faculty member, having worked with me on a small RAship last summer, also wants to work with me again this summer. (Dee)

I've always been more of a back-door person. Traditional ways of getting jobs have never worked well for me, but I have other ways in. I started as the community co-director of the collaborative and over time that opened doors and got me into networks of other people doing similar work, and linked me to mentors, and I shifted over to the academic side. When I completed my PhD, I was able to secure enough funding to pay for my own position. At that point the director of my institute (a major ally, role model, and mentor) was able to make a position for me as a Research Assistant Professor. I've been in that role now for five years and am up for promotion this year. (Sunny)

I think the thing that has worked for me is the fact I've stayed in the one small institution, and people's knowledge of my work has compensated for my lack of ability to play the recruitment game well (I've literally had someone say to me 'dude, you completely fucked that interview, but we're giving you the job anyway because we know you're good'). I think I've also been saved by the big fish in small pond effect – being in a regional university means positions often aren't very competitive. (Morgan)

Most of my academic employment (including paid work on committees, boards, and hiring panel and my research position) were positions I was invited to engage in, which, I recognize is a privileged position. (Kelly)

What really stands out to me in these explanations is the extent to which the group attributes their employment successes to luck, happenstance, or the kindness of others. The reality in the vast majority of cases (remember that I know the identities of these people) is that they are in these roles because they are uniquely qualified and competent. Dave was not 'absurdly lucky' to be appointed to the role of director of a newly established centre; they recognised his expertise and snapped him up before he was recruited elsewhere. Ella and Dee were not 'fortunate' that they were offered research assistant roles; they were sought out by senior academics who recognised their capability and commitment, so much so that colleagues of those academics also sought them out. Sunny and Kelly are not 'privileged' and Morgan is not in a less competitive area than other academics; these are incredibly accomplished and highly regarded senior leaders in their respective fields.

Keeping a Job in Academia

While Chapter 5 explores in depth the particular challenges we face as autistic people working in academia, I will touch briefly here on participants' reflections on the primary barriers to maintaining employment once they had made it through the recruitment process.

The casual nature of academic employment was, not surprisingly, a significant challenge for many. The need to regularly – and in some cases annually or more – 'audition' for the role they have been successfully undertaking causes a significant level of uncertainty and anxiety. While this is the case for many people working in academia, with its increasingly casualised workforce, it is particularly difficult for a cohort who have a fundamental need for stability and consistency.

> *The only frustration I experience in this area is the fact that these academic positions are now casualised, meaning that I have to reapply for them (especially the Teaching Assistance roles) every six months. This is time consuming, and it's also a bit nerve-wracking for a while because I never know if I will continue to have work.* (Ella)

Two terms that arose frequently in the reflections were 'work-life' balance and 'burnout', with the tension often exacerbated by high self-expectations and fear of failure, leading to working excessive hours. Autistic burnout is not well understood in academia, and has only quite recently been identified as distinct from traditionally recognised burnout (Raymaker, Teo, et al. 2020; Arnold, Higgins, et al. 2023).

> *I've experienced autistic burnout and inertia, both of which have slowed me down in terms of productivity, contributing to feelings of impostor syndrome, not belonging, and self-doubt. Work-life balance can also be difficult to manage when you first start (and beyond if you don't pay attention).* (Amy)

Some Final Thoughts

Many of the participants reflected on the difficulties they had experienced in obtaining roles in academia, particularly in relation to challenges in the selection process related to writing applications and interviewing for roles. Similarly, several reflected on difficulties in maintaining roles and obtaining promotions due to communication barriers and the impacts of stereotypes and prejudices. Many of the 'considerations' they sought – such as having questions in advance of selection interviews, being provided with clear expectations and explicit instructions – are good practice that would benefit autistic and non-autistic employees alike.

> *I interviewed for a postdoc, I didn't know the work group, and they knew that I was on the spectrum. I was quite upfront about that and, yeah, I had asked for their interview questions in advance. And what's really interesting is I . . . 'Cause I was working as an RF at that point as well, so, and I was full-time and I was flat stick [going at top speed], and, yeah, they sent me those interview questions about, I think it was two hours before the job interview, like they emailed them to me. So, yeah, I didn't actually get a chance to see them properly and prepare before the interview because they sent them at such short notice. Yeah, so next time I knew, for that moment, next time that I need to specify in advance means X number, at least 24 hours or something like that so obviously they thought two hours was plenty of time, but yeah, it was not.* (Charlotte)

> *I do best when guidelines and expectations are clear and concrete, when I can get organized and pace myself, and when politics don't interfere with actual merit (which can be frustratingly rare in academia).* (Amy)

Those who had been able to overcome these barriers, typically because they had found allies in the workplace who valued their contributions, had survived and even thrived in academia. Clearly, there is a lot more that our academic institutions can do to attract and retain autistic scholars; and clearly there is a lot to be gained from doing so.

> *I have been tenured and promoted thanks to a small group of people who had my back and believed in my abilities, and I will always be grateful to them.* (Saskia)

> *So I feel like once people have worked with me, they appreciate my work, so keeping employment is less of a hurdle than getting it in the first place. And I actually just received a multi-year fellowship from the [funding agency], which will provide me with three years of funding over the next five years.* (Dee)

> *Maintaining employment in an academic role has been the easiest form of employment to maintain for me so far in life. I am most suited to academia, and feel that I am appropriately valued in this environment. I seem to mix well with other academics, and in academia my specialist knowledge is not only not unusual, but is actually a boon.* (Psyche)

CHAPTER 3

Apprenticeship

> *They need education about autism that is led by Autistic experts with lived experiences. They need empathy and unconscious bias training. They needed an accountability structure to ensure that no student falls through the cracks.... The cost is too high to wait for accessibility to move from the four corners of a policy document to positively impacting the lives of Autistic students in higher education. I spent decades of my life fighting and waiting for a time when blatant prejudice and ableism would not be tolerated in higher education. Action needs to be taken now by those of us who are able to make changes to the systems we live/work in so other Autistic individuals coming after us might have a better opportunity.* ***Who might I have been had I not experienced so many barriers to education?***
>
> (Kelly)

The journey to a career in academia commences with university studies. Autistic people continue to be under-represented in university enrolments, and even more under-represented in university graduations. In this chapter participants reflect on their university experience, including the transition to university. Topics discussed include interactions with peers, teaching staff, and administration; supports that were, or could have been, provided; and recommendations for improving the university experience for future autistic students.

Note: This book represents the voices of thirty-seven people who overcame all of these challenges to obtain a university education (and so many more to embark on, and remain in, a career in academia). It is important not to forget the many, many autistic people who were prevented from attaining a university degree due to similar challenges; a world of lost opportunities for them and for the profession.

Only six of the participants were diagnosed (or definitively self-identified) as autistic prior to commencing at university, and five received their diagnosed during their undergraduate studies. The majority transitioned directly from high school to university, although for many this 'first' attempt at university studies was challenging, and for several it was not successful.

> *My undergraduate degree took three program switches and 6.5 years to finish both to find the right career fit and a research mentor who recognized my strengths and was able to accommodate me.* (Eva)

> *My first attempt at higher education came directly after high school. . . . Due to disabling barriers in the classrooms (including mandatory group work, mandatory presentations, mandatory physical attendance), I quit college several times and re-entered hoping for better outcomes. It took me almost 9 years to complete a 2-year diploma in social service work.* (Kelly)

These experiences are consistent with the limited research on those who do not complete university studies (Cage, De Andres, and Mahoney 2020; Cage and Howes 2020), which cites lack of transition support as a key factor – including not knowing what university will be like, not knowing what is expected of them as students, and not knowing how to navigate systems and structures.

Among those who commenced university later in life, the predominant reasons for the delay were fear of failure, significant physical and/or mental health issues, and the impacts of abuse, neglect, or abandonment. This is perhaps not surprising given the considerable body of evidence that autistic people are more likely to experience neglect, emotional abuse, physical abuse, and sexual abuse than non-autistic people both as children (Hall-Lande, Hewitt, et al. 2014; Pfeffer 2016; Gibbs, Hudson, et al. 2021) and as adults (Weiss and Fardella 2018; Griffiths, Allison, et al. 2019).

> *I went to uni quite late in life. It was something I always wanted to do, but I think my fear of failure prevented me from taking that step. My mother had me Wechsler tested as a kid and I grew up being told I was clever. I think that created a lot of (mainly) internal expectations for me. After seven years working in universities, I'm only now getting my PhD underway and I think that was the same issue with confidence.* (Ruth)

> *I started my UG late at 35. My pre-university life was a mess, time spent going between transient jobs and being too depressed to function.* (Olivia)

> *I went from foster care into homelessness, including living in a tent for a while. I left school at 16, but I took the equivalency examinations and was awarded top marks in every subject. I went to university a few years later.* (Mia)

I Want to Go to Uni

What stood out for me across the reflections – and will become apparent to the reader as this chapter progresses – is how many challenges this group faced, and how tenacious they were in overcoming these challenges.

Why is getting a university education so important to us as autistic people? There is the pragmatic motivator of 'I can do this, and I should do this,' which is common to many people who have achieved good grades at school and are motivated to meet the expectations of themselves, their parents, and their teachers. It is likely that many of the participants would meet the criteria for twice-exceptionality (intellectually gifted students who [are] also neurodivergent or have a disability), thus struggling with the dissonance between their high cognitive capacity and their individual learning challenges (Gierczyk and Hornby 2021; Hamzić and Bećirović 2021).

> *I went to uni b/c I saw it as a pathway to gaining a career that I'd be interested in. It was expected by my secondary school teachers that I would attend uni also.* (Charlotte)

> *I had a strong sense that Smart People were supposed to Do Something With Their Lives and get Successful Careers through Going to Uni, but I had no idea what I wanted to be when I grew up and I kept switching desperately trying to find something I could tolerate the thought of a career in so I would not become A Disappointment.* (Morgan)

More than that, and consistently voiced in the reflections, is the love of learning that is inherent in so many autistic people (Anderson, Carter, and Stephenson 2020; Madaus, Reis, et al. 2022).

> *I decided to go to university as I wanted to use my brain and learn in that kind of way. I initially went to explore a range of different subjects and courses. Over time I found I was motivated by a deep sense of questioning, the "why" and "how" of knowledge pursuit. This led me to learn more about research and academia and sent me on my pursuit towards getting qualified in the area.* (Baz)

> *I had always wanted to attend university. There was just something so exciting about the prospect of higher education. Unfortunately, my experience wasn't the best and I feel that academia is extremely overrated at this point.* (Emma)

> *I knew I had untapped potential and always had a passion for academia and learning. I knew I wanted to create a better and more stable financial life for myself in the future. I also came to learn that because I was 21 at the time I was considered a mature age student and the fact I had not finished year 12 did not mean I could never go to university.* (Flora)

Can Someone Tell Me the Rules?

The 'hidden curriculum' (the unspoken or implicit rules, values, expectations, and social norms) is a well-known phenomenon of workplace culture, and is recognised to be particularly evident in academia (Raso,

Marchetti, et al. 2019; Barham and Wood 2022; Laiduc and Covarrubias 2022). While this is addressed in more detail in Chapter 4 in relation to challenges for autistic academics, it is noteworthy that this was also a common reflection in participants' recollections of their university experience.

> *They could have explained the "hidden curriculum." My own children will grow up knowing 100% more about academic culture than I did. I had no counselor to see except my academic counselor, whose job it was to see if I was making progress to degree, and mental health counselors, whose job it was to see if I was developing a mental disorder. Counselors designated to helping students, especially first-generation students, navigate university culture would be so valuable. I was eaten alive socially by sophisticated peers. Knowing the rules of the game is requirement #1 in playing the game with any chance of success.* (Saskia)

There is a need for more research into, and recognition of, the significant disadvantage that autistic students face in intuiting this hidden curriculum and the barriers it places to successful completion of their studies. Byrne (2022) provides a useful summary of some of the ways that autistic characteristic can contribute to hidden curriculum difficulties, as shown in Table 3.1.

Consistent with the (albeit limited) literature on the experiences of autistic university students, the challenges experienced by the group were not a function of their intelligence or their ability to undertake the work required for their degrees (Anderson, Carter, and Stephenson 2018). Rather, they tended to do well where expectations were clear – in terms of structure, participation, assessment tasks, and learning outcomes – and to struggle where these expectations were ambiguous or inconsistent (Gurbuz, Hanley and Riby 2019).

> *The main problems I have experienced as a university student due to my autistic nature have been being unable to find critical information and essential details related to assignments and deadlines, and once I have a lecturer who would only provide assignment feedback over the telephone, which was utterly traumatising to initially instigate (so I therefore left it to the very last minute to arrange a phone meeting with him), and completely unhelpful for personal reflection, as the verbal feedback style made me so anxious that I instantly forgot everything that he said to me the moment that I put the phone down, and was unable to make notes detailed enough to be of any benefit for my personal improvement.* (Psyche)

> *I had a lot of trouble. Mostly this was around seeking clarity of assessment task (AT) instruction (including clear feedback on ATs) – this was in a time before we had rubrics, extensive task instructions and feedback (other than a grade)*

Table 3.1 *Social characteristics of autism and their potential effects on perceiving the hidden curriculum (from Byrne 2022)*

Characteristic	Hidden curriculum difficulty
(1) Issues with intonation, repetitive behaviours and social-emotional reciprocity.	The way an autistic person presents themselves maybe misconstrued as disruptive or insulting by others. Resulting exclusion, or self-isolation due to negative experiences, could restrict social access and reduce overall exposure to the hidden curriculum.
(2) Restricted interests and an apparent preference for solitary activities from social disengagement.	Necessary, non-explicit cues that convey information on social expectations from within the hidden curriculum could be deemed uninteresting. These cues are then missed or ignored and relevant lessons from the hidden curriculum are missed.
(3) Difficulty recognising non-verbal cues, such as facial expressions or eye contact.	Information from the hidden curriculum related to appropriate intonation, expression and social action is left partially or completely unperceived. If these appropriate actions are not learned, this can also exacerbate issues with social representation in point (1).
(4) Impairments in verbal communication or initiating conversation.	Inhibits the ability to ask for further information or help when a social cue is misunderstood. As a result, the unspoken lessons from the hidden curriculum are less likely to be made explicit and aren't learned.
(5) Deficits adjusting behaviour to suit different social contexts.	Difficulty recognising the difference in nature between social interactions with peers and academic staff could inhibit access to the hidden curriculum. An inability to adjust behaviour between these contexts could lead to the expression of behaviours that with peers would facilitate hidden curriculum access, but are not as [effective] in a supervisor-supervisee context.

given to students. Further, it was never clear to me what we needed to read and how that related to learning outcomes, etc. As such, I never knew what it was I was supposed to do to keep on top of course content. I literally went to lectures, tutes [tutorials], handed in ATs and did nothing else. I also found the lack of structure was difficult to adjust to. (Charlotte)

It's Not Just the Content, It's the Context

However, the bigger challenges for the majority of the group were the social and environmental aspects of the university experience. While many were happy to remain on the fringes of the social milieu – seeing university as a place to learn rather than to socialise – others felt isolated and excluded. Sadly, for many this went beyond not being included in social groups to being deliberately excluded and targeted for harassment.

> *I don't remember a lot of interactions in class. In social settings, I was uncomfortable pretty much all the time. I was unsure of the rules of interaction. I often felt accosted by people who wanted to talk while I listened, but I didn't know why.* (Marie)

> *As for peers at University, I was socially clueless but always tried very hard to connect with others. I had strong acting skills and so was able to mask enough to get by and found some friends even if I experienced a lot of rejection. I'm a socially motivated person and seek out connection and friendship with others even when I found this exhausting.* (Trevor)

> *I did try to make friends and interact with other students. I reflect back now on how incredibly embarrassing many of those attempts were, I really didn't understand how to make new friends, I didn't understand the unwritten social rules of university.... I preferred friends at university who were studious. I didn't want to make friends with people for the socialising etc. I was more interested in people I could study with. In hindsight I found many fellow students at university intimidating, but I couldn't exactly say what it is that made me feel that way. I think to some extent I tried to keep to myself.* (Scarlett)

Previous research has found that autistic students tend to be socially isolated and struggle to make friends at university, and that, while active bullying may be less prevalent than in secondary school, social exclusion due to stereotypes around autism can be pervasive (Goddard and Cook 2022).

The environmental aspects of university can be very challenging for autistic people (O'Connor, Jones, et al. 2024; Waisman, Alba, and Green 2022). The vibrant, dynamic nature of university campuses that make them appealing to many neurotypical people can also make them extremely hostile for us as autistics. The constant and synergistic sensory stimulation, the crowded environments, the constant social interaction, and the necessity for frequent movement between locations can combine to create an overwhelming environment that is physically and emotionally exhausting.

> *[University name] is famously hard to get through, and by the end I was both academically and socially burned out.... I don't think I fully realized just how hard of a time I was having.... But the amount of work to keep track of, on top*

of living on my own for the first time, plus the social environment and nearly constant presence of other people really pushed me to a breaking point.... By the time I graduated, I was really burned out on school, so it was a long time before I was ready to even think about pursuing an advanced degree. (Dee)

I dropped out and went back to University several times. I felt terribly ashamed of my permanent state of anxiety; we were expected to participate in intensive discussions, which were marked, and which took place several days a week (we had about 24 hours a week of lectures and seminars). The idea of speaking in a group would cause the room to go dark, and I felt like I was going to pass out, but failure to speak up meant poor grades. (Mia)

More generally, I found university very challenging as an autistic person. I found the campus impossible to navigate and was constantly lost, despite having worked there for some time before my degrees. The squares were constantly busy and loud and I don't know how I would have coped without my own work office, it was completely inaccessible as a campus for an autistic person. There was hardly anywhere that was properly quiet.... Lectures were awful – there were often technical difficulties with microphones squealing, people were always muttering and talking and eating stinky food, I was often late and then had to either walk past everyone to get in (which I couldn't do) or I would just not go in. My notes from lectures made absolutely no sense. I felt like most lectures were a complete waste of my time. Luckily most lecturers did lecture capture, so I could watch them back later, and I found that worked much better for me as I could pause things and write notes properly. (Louise)

What Did We Gain?

There was fairly unanimous agreement that, like non-autistic people, we gained a qualification that served as a 'ticket' to what comes next, whether that was a subsequent degree or a career opportunity. For many this was accompanied by a perception of growth in knowledge and expansion of world view from interaction with fellow students, teaching staff, and teaching materials. Previous research has found that autistic students find the academic side of university to be more central to the experience than non-autistic students and have a strong sense of self-determination to succeed (Lei and Russell 2021). There was also the sense of accomplishment that comes with the successful completion of an important step in the transition to adulthood (for those who attended university directly from school) or other forms of independence (for those who returned to university later in life).

Ironically, I think my autism is what helped me through college. I had a horrible time socially but the academics were excellent. Learning from people whose special interests were as strong as mine kept me feeling like I wasn't alone.

> *Of course, I couldn't hang out with my professors, so this didn't help my social life, but studying and being in class were affirming experiences for me.* (Saskia)

> *It was nice to move on from when I graduated. And it was nice to graduate in general. Aside from getting involved in social justice things and autism-related things, I had experienced my first romantic relationship (and subsequent emotional/sexual abuse and heartbreak) and had a lot of similar experiences that have made me who I am now and were probably beneficial in some ways, but it was nice to leave things like that behind too.* (Amelia)

We Found Our Tribes (and Perhaps Ourselves)

For some, university was the place in which they first met like-minded people and found a community where they felt they truly belonged. Typically, these connections came from shared interests, shared values, and/or shared neurotypes.

By its very nature university study brings together people with shared interests (into disciplines and courses) and provides a platform to deepen and share their knowledge of and passion for their subject area. This makes it in some ways the ideal environment for a group of people whose intensely focused interests can make them outcasts in other contexts (Ghanouni, Jarus, et al. 2019; Bury, Flower, et al. 2021). Autistic people also tend to have strong moral values and a commitment to social justice, and universities (particularly certain disciplines) attract and encourage those with a commitment to social change.

> *I gravitated a lot toward leftist spaces. Some of the people I'm closest to now are people I met in those spaces. The spaces (and many of the people in them) were often of the belief that all kinds of people live in the world and so the ideal would be for the world to accommodate all kinds of people and all kinds of needs, which felt (and feels) comforting in a way that I hadn't had much experience with prior to college.* (Amelia)

> *Among 30–40 students who enrolled, I engaged regularly with a group of 5–7 students. They were my friends throughout entire studies.* (Betty)

For others, university was where they connected with other autistic people and developed their confidence in being themselves and in expressing their autistic identity.

> *Halfway through 1st year, I found out another of the students who hung around [campus facility] was autistic too. This was the first autistic student I'd met – I was jumping up and down from excitement in the middle of the busy campus centre at lunchtime!!!* (Jane)

After a few years, I got diagnosed with autism. I went through that whole journey of self-understanding. I met my people. I met fellow autistic students and autistic people outside of uni. This meant I had a space inside and outside of the uni where I was totally and completely able to be my authentic self without fear of rejection or ridicule. These spaces allowed me the opportunity to realise that I AM ok. People can and do like me for who I am, autism and all. After I developed that friendship base of my fellow people (neurokin), I was much more confident to put myself out there and interact with my peers. (Jade)

Stick with It, It Might Get Better

The group's reflections on graduate/post-graduate studies further demonstrated the importance of social, structural, and environmental supports. For some, the transition meant more acceptance, more flexibility, and greater recognition of their strengths. For others, it meant the loss of the (albeit limited) supports that had been available during undergraduate studies.

Those who had a positive experience at graduate school typically reflected on a combination of more personalised supports and greater access to services alongside their greater ability to ensure their needs were met based on having a diagnosis and the confidence to advocate for themselves.

My experience in graduate school was different because there was a mentoring program and a women's group in my department, which made it very easy to meet people and make friends from the first few weeks I entered my PhD program. We saw each other quite often: we had study dates, movie nights – it was fun. (Amy)

By the time I began my second graduate degree in 2018, I found a great deal of support at [university]. I believe this was likely due to the shifting culture of acceptance and inclusion, particularly in a state like [state], and also due to the size of [university] as a public research university. Prior to this, I'd only attended small, private institutions. I had an autism diagnosis and was able to register with the campus office for disabilities in order to get an accommodation letter. I had already been issued a temporary disability parking permit which allowed me to avoid large, brightly lit parking structures on campus (these caused me to become dizzy and disoriented). Faculty on the campus accommodated me by dimming lights in classrooms (if possible) or giving me flexible attendance consideration when necessary. (Trina)

By grad school I had gotten proficient in self advocacy, so for the most part many of my peers were accepting, though in some instances many conversations were needed before they internalized my struggles and accepted them as real.... As an open self advocate, I'm fortunate that I've gotten proficient in effectively

> *explaining/describing my accommodation needs, though it took years of failure to reach that point (and evolving attitudes in general).* (Dave)

Conversely, those who reported negative experiences at graduate school typically reflected on inflexible systems and structures, as well as pervasive lack of understanding of autism and the needs of autistic students. Several of the group also described experiences of outright discrimination by university staff. The tenacity of this cohort was evident in the number of reflections that described these experiences in the context of 'first attempt', 'second attempt', 'third attempt', and so on at post-graduate studies.

> *I stayed at the same university for my masters degree, and this was a different experience because I'd got my diagnosis in the summer prior to starting it. In a lot of ways this was harder – not just because the work was a step up from what I'd done before, but because there was so much stigma and misunderstanding around autism and I felt like I had to spend a lot of time educating people. I remember telling one lecturer I'd been diagnosed and he looked at me, aghast, and said "do you think it was a mistake? I mean, you're not mindblind! You respond to my feelings and everything"…. My dissertation supervisor was initially sceptical about my autism but he was a very frank and open man and we had lots of long open conversations about autism, hyperlexia and dyslexia (his own research interest) while working on my dissertation project. I have some lovely memories of that time, though again at times it was very hard, and I remember crying more than once when he made flippant comments about autism which showed he didn't really understand it.* (Louise)

> *I started a coursework masters, then transferred to a research masters, then upgraded the research masters to a PhD. This was 2–3 years' worth of (part time) effort and I still didn't have anything completed to show for it…. Still had the same issues with engagement and success but at least managed not to fail anything. I got HDs in special topics units where I could define my own work program and assessment, and passes in topics where traditional models of learning were expected…. (PhD attempt 2) Finally I got in and did really well at the research development program (a year of pseudo-coursework), but made everyone very uncomfortable by continuing to be "too innovative", too left-of-centre, not good enough at following rules. I wrote my proposal, did my Confirmation of Candidature presentation, then I got the list of conditions I had to address before they approved it and I more or less fell in a heap. I just couldn't do it – I couldn't play their game on top of working full time, studying part time, having a family and managing chronic illness and neurodivergence.* (Morgan)

> *In the last iteration of my studies (doctoral program 2017–2020), I experienced prejudice from an instructor…. My doctoral supervisor attempted to discuss the issue with the prof to mitigate any challenges,* ***however the instructor insisted that there was no place in graduate school for Autistic individuals.***

I made a formal complaint and the vice-dean agreed that the professor was in clear violation of my human rights. The university supported my request to be marked by another professor for my final papers. I got the highest mark in that class. (Kelly)

The Ideal University

The Ideal University Knows What Autism Is (and What It Isn't)

A common theme across the reflections was the lack of autism awareness evident among university staff and systems. This was more than just the absence of knowledge (i.e., not knowing what autism is or how to support autistic students), but in many cases the presence of inaccurate knowledge. Participants regularly commented on stereotypical perceptions of autistic people (e.g., white, male children) and the ways that autistic people think, interact, and learn. This is consistent with recent research with autistic university students that has identified autism training for staff as one of the major recommendations for improving support (Scott and Sedgewick 2021).

For some this lack of understanding resulted in being offered 'supports' that were less than helpful, including those designed to make them appear less autistic, consistent with research into university students' reasons for dropping out of university (Cage and Howes 2020). For others, this resulted in a reluctance to ask for supports or to disclose themselves as autistic.

> *... specialized/disability services should really know what autism is (and is not) and do their homework to help these students as best they can.* (Amy)

> *Some basic education about neurodiversity can go a long way. Assuming everyone has your perspective and viewpoint is a faulty, entitled, and frankly false assumption.* (Dave)

> *University communities need to be educated more on neurodiversity, and it is a slow change. I do see the change happening though, and this is very encouraging. I do feel that Christian (evangelical) colleges and universities (in the US at least) have lagged behind institutions they would regard as "secular", and this is very concerning to me.* (Trina)

> *Some understanding of ASD might have helped, and some clarity on the assignments. Having said that, the tutors were really open to helping individual students, and there was plenty of help there,* ***if only I hadn't been so afraid of asking for it.*** (Mia)

This lack of autism awareness likely contributed to the common experience of teaching and administrative staff not noticing that the students were struggling – whether that was with the academic coursework or with social or environmental aspects of university.

> *[I wish they had] Paid attention. Noticed my struggles – I'm bright, I knew the content well enough most of the time, and my work wasn't BAD but I was clearly much more intelligent and capable than the work I produced or the exam grades I received. I didn't know study skills that worked for me and my autism, dyslexia, dyspraxia, ADHD.... I didn't know a lot of things that it was their job to notice. I didn't see the point of the tutor meetings unconnected to my course so I never booked any, but that's because the boundaries weren't articulated so it seemed like they could/would do literally nothing, and since I didn't know what or why I was struggling, there was nothing to confide. I wish my tutor had made more of an effort to be someone I could talk to, or communicated the purpose of having a tutor.* (Evelyn)

> *I guess a more personalized approach during my studies would have been very helpful.* (Sophia)

Some of the group completed their university studies more than two decades ago, some less than two years ago, but their experiences were nonetheless similar. They are also consistent with recent research which consistently finds that autistic university students report that their teachers and their peers don't sufficiently understand their needs or accept their differences, which can lead to isolation and anxiety (Gurbuz, Hanley, and Riby 2019) and/or discontinuation of their studies (Cage and Howes 2020).

The Ideal University Explains Things to Us

Group members reflected on the need for greater clarity of communication in order for university to be accessible and achievable for autistic students. This covered all aspects of university studies and all forms of communication. One common request was for clear, accessible, online content, laid out in a way that can be understood and navigated by autistic brains.

> *[University name] should have a more cohesive approach to how they provide information to their students. Currently, they have multiple web pages relating to different aspects of university life, and how they operate is akin to the left hand not knowing what the right hand is doing. This can result in many many lost hours trying to navigate webpages looking for essential information, being led round in circles, or trying to decipher essential details that are unclear. This does not seem to bother the neurotypical students as much as it does me.... I would love to speak to other autistic students to find out what their experience of the [university] online platforms are like. The result for me is that I am often the very last student to find out critical information and can endanger my studies by potentially missing important deadlines or details that are essential for*

completion of the qualification. A simple fix for this could be to consult a team of autistic people who attempt to navigate the webpages to ensure that the system is also clear for atypical students. It could also be helpful to have an 'autism translation service' for autistic students, in the form of an autistic university employee(s) who could translate the neurotypical instructions and online systems for them. (Psyche)

The lack of clarity in written information – subject outlines, assessment rubrics, and so on – was a common concern and an 'easy fix' for making universities more autism-friendly. The group reflected on the need for information about subjects and assessments to be provided in a way that was explicit, non-ambiguous, and supported by access to a human being for clarification. Related to this was the common experience of our non-neurotypical information-processing styles and our autistic ways of receptive and expressive communication being interpreted as lack of intelligence. Our brains are wired differently, and two-way communication requires both parties to work towards shared understanding.

Well if someone doesn't understand a thing it does not make them entirely stupid. Find another way to explain things. Being explicit helps enormously too. (Isabella)

The Ideal University Is Sensory-Friendly

It is no surprise that the group commonly reflected on the need for university campuses to be more sensory-friendly if they are to attract and retain autistic students. This is not an artefact of the time since these academics were students, with our recent research finding that sensory issues on campuses continue to pose a significant challenge for today's students (O'Connor, Jones, et al. 2024). A systematic review of twenty-four studies of intervention for autistic post-secondary students from around the world identified no interventions that included aspects of targeting sensory sensitivities, suggesting that these were not isolated experiences (Anderson, Stephenson, et al. 2019). While I recognise that it would be a costly and resource-intensive exercise to retrofit current campuses with dimmable lights, soundproofing, wayfinding, and many other features that would make them more accessible, these should be fundamental considerations for new buildings. In the meantime, all universities should provide ready access for autistic students to sensory-friendly spaces to enable them to escape from the sensory overload of campus life.

From an environmental perspective, there is a desperate need to create more sensory-friendly spaces on campus. Ideally, these spaces would also be developed by (or at least in partnership with) autistic students. (Ella)

> *. . . spaces where autistic people could go to escape the hustle and bustle and noise of uni, but still feel a part of the community – instead of needing to escape and just go home in isolation.* (Baz)

The Ideal University Assesses Our Knowledge

The few members of the group who had received adjustments to assessment criteria (a proportion of the small subset who knew, and had disclosed, their diagnosis) had typically been provided with an extension to submission deadlines. This is a useful, and often necessary, adjustment – but not sufficient in isolation, and never an adequate replacement for ensuring the autistic student understands the task (see the section 'Can Someone Tell Me the Rules', about expectations).

The group had a number of other suggestions around how assessments could be more autism-friendly, with the most frequent relating to oral presentations and groupwork. Oral presentations can be extremely stressful and intimidating for autistic people, especially when we are being judged on the performance aspect of the task rather than our knowledge of the topic. Autistic people who are offered options such as pre-recording their presentations or presenting to a smaller group will have a much better chance of demonstrating their learning successfully.

Group assignments are a constant struggle for autistic students (Irvine and MacLeod 2022). We hear your argument that university is meant to prepare us for the workplace and thus working in teams, but I would counter: How many workplaces stick you in a group with people you have never met before, each of whom has different values around the required quality of the final product; provide no ground rules about the frequency, location, and duration of your interactions; and judge you all equally on the outcome regardless of your input? Consider options such as clear ground rules for groupwork, allocating team members based on GPAs, or allowing the option of working in pairs or alone.

> *I know that groupwork is totally amazing (sarcasm) and collaboration is what we are trained to want our students to do, but I have always hated it. Groupwork for me takes twice as long. I do better work by myself. Allow us to do that.* (Olivia)

> *Generally, more flexibility and options would be helpful, especially around groupwork.* (Scott)

The Ideal University Provides Necessary Adjustments

There is a growing body of data that reports that many autistic students do not apply for or utilise the 'reasonable adjustments' offered by universities, thus administrators may argue that perhaps the problem is the students' lack of motivation to use the resources made available to them. However, the literature also shows that the primary reasons autistic students do not utilise these adjustments are (1) they don't know they exist and how to access them and/or (2) the adjustments offered aren't actually the ones they need (Anderson, Carter and Stephenson 2020; Fabri, Fenton, et al. 2022).

These factors were clearly evident in the groups' reflections, with their recommendations for universities including not only flexibility in the types of adjustments offered to students, but also a request for dignity and respect in response to students' needs.

> *Been respectful about adjustments and made it easy to get them. Have assumed the student knows what they need and isn't just trying to weasel out of work (especially at a graduate level!) and just make it easy to happen. As someone who provides plenty of reasonable adjustments for my interns and mentees, it's really not that hard to listen, be respectful, and find a solution that works well for everyone.* (Sunny)

> *I think the formal accommodations process in US universities is not terribly effective, and often isn't well-suited to autistic students. If I'm overwhelmed by the constant exposure to fluorescent lighting and crowded lecture halls, an individual accommodation isn't going to fix that. They might allow for me to take tests in a quieter location (which would have been great during my undergraduate years), but the bigger issue is the day-to-day buildup of stress and sensory overload that just builds to a breaking point. Autism affects so many things in a person's life, and can vary so much between individuals, that it's hard to address with some boilerplate accommodation policy that might help in some limited circumstances (like during a test) but not the larger environment.* (Dee)

> *University more generally could have been a better place for me with assigned quiet and sensory spaces, all lectures recorded and no obligation to attend in person, added times in exams (I've never had this), lecturers to have been trained on autism and actually understand it so there are no "but you don't look autistic" comments. I struggled immensely with group work and seminars and often tried to avoid these which went against me a little.* (Louise)

A significant barrier facing many autistic people in transitioning from 'student' to 'academic' is the rigidity of requirements around doctoral studies. For example, many autistic people who have the academic grades and intellectual capacity to be extremely competitive for a PhD scholarship are constrained by the requirement for full-time enrolment, which is not feasible for many of us. Similarly, standard provisions such as shared workspaces, 'hot desks', and inflexible attendance requirements can prevent otherwise very capable autistic scholars from completing their doctoral studies. This was evident in the number of group participants who were reluctant to undertake doctoral studies or had commenced but discontinued.

> *Also, we have to register for "full-time" just to get full scholarship which is unfair because it can be hard for autistic people like me to register full time, not to mention that we shouldn't have to choose between scholarship and mental health.* (Proline)

The Ideal University Has Autistic Staff

The lack of visibility of openly autistic staff employed in universities poses a significant challenge. As will be discussed in a subsequent chapter, many autistic people (including a number of the study participants) do not disclose their diagnosis to their employer due to the very real fear of discrimination and marginalisation that follows disclosure.

The immediate, pragmatic benefit of autistic staff is that students have access to people who understand their ways of thinking and communicating and who can better support them in navigating university, as well as increasing autism awareness and appreciation among non-autistic university staff. The longer-term benefit is that by seeing their neurokin accepted and valued in these roles, the next generation of autistic students and scholars will begin to develop a sense of optimism that academia does value their unique strengths and is a safe place for them to build a career.

> *There also needs to be a company-wide strategic plan focused on hiring, accommodating, and retaining autistic staff at each university. Representation matters, and having staff representation could change how people perceive and respond to autistic students.* (Ella)

> *My main thinking in this area has been revolving around building autistic and cross-disability community and culture within academia. If things are harder for us because of the way things are structured, at least we can collectively acknowledge that and maybe work to change it. Knowing now that I'm autistic has helped me put a lot of what I went through then in perspective; I think it would have helped to have that kind of peer support at [university], even if I didn't have institutional support.* (Dee)

Some Final Thoughts

These thirty-seven academics reported numerous significant environmental, practical, cultural, and attitudinal barriers to university study. Despite these barriers, they continued into a career in academia driven by a passion for gaining and sharing knowledge. However, the consistency, extent, and impact of these barriers demonstrate the point with which I commenced this chapter: that the reason for the lower postgraduate education completion rates of autistic people does not reflect lack of capacity or commitment but rather systemic barriers to inclusion.

Universal design for learning (UDL) is increasingly being discussed and promoted as a framework within which universities and other higher education institutions can make education more inclusive for people who are currently disadvantaged and marginalised by the system, including autistic people (Lubin and Brooks 2021; Hamilton and Petty 2023). While UDL has clear benefits for autistic students, as with other cohorts UDL does not replace the need for individualised services (Griful-Freixenet, Struyven, et al. 2017). In addition, there is a need for broader neurodiversity-affirming practices to be implemented in our institutions. While institutions should consult with their own autistic students and alumni to ascertain specific barriers and facilitators on their campuses, the participants have provided some initial recommendations for university teachers and administrators to consider.

> *In short, lecturers, tutors, and university administrative staff can make university a more positive experience for autistic students by challenging their own ideas/ableism about autism and being open to learning about what it is and how it presents from autistic students, then making the required interpersonal, systemic, structural, and environmental accommodations to make our lives easier.* (Ella)

CHAPTER 4

Strengths

I think being autistic is also a strength when studying sociology, because I feel like I've always had to study people and social behavior. Sociologists often remark on how much of social behavior is so ingrained that it becomes taken for granted, but most of it hasn't felt that way to me. So I feel like it's often easier for me to observe what's going on and notice the details than for someone who maybe learned social expectations more unconsciously and has to learn to look at them consciously.

(Dee)

This chapter explores the bi-directional strengths of autistics in the academy: the strengths that autistic people bring to their role and the strengths of the university environment as a workplace for academics.[1] Key strengths of autistic people that are beneficial in academic roles include focused interests, attention to detail, pragmatism, and many other aspects that may not be evident in common stereotypes of autism. Strengths of the academic environment as an autistic workplace include the cerebral nature of the role, structured interactions, and the value placed on in-depth knowledge. Combined, these bi-directional strengths are expanded on below in the context of the resulting capacity for autistic people in academia to learn, teach, work, help, and connect.

Autistic Strengths in Academic Workplaces

While much of the focus of the literature is on the challenges and deficits of autistic people, there is growing recognition that autistic people also have many strengths and assets that they bring to the workplace. Recent studies with autistic employees (Anderson 2021; Cope and Remington 2022) and with employers of autistic people (Scott, Jacob, et al. 2017; Grenawalt, Brinck, et al. 2020; Friedfeld Kesselmayer, Ochrach, et al.

[1] Note: A subset of the data in this and the following chapter was published in S. C. Jones (2022a), "Autistics Working in Academia: What Are the Barriers and Facilitators?," *Autism* **27**(3): 822–831.

2022; Phillips, Tansey, et al. 2023; Wen, van Rensburg, et al. 2023) have identified key strengths in cognitive aspects as well as personal qualities such as honesty, reliability, and productivity.

Cognitive Skills

The most commonly identified cognitive strength across the reflections was the autistic ability to (hyper)focus on a topic of interest. This, combined with our ability to memorise large amounts of information, provides a competitive advantage in the fields of research and teaching. We do not want to learn just enough about a topic to be able to pass a test or meet the expectations of [a] reviewers; we want to know every aspect of the topic. This is consistent with previous qualitative and quantitative research with autistic people across a range of employment contexts that identified the ability to concentrate or 'hyperfocus' on one task to the exclusion of all else as a significant benefit at work (Russell, Kapp, et al. 2019; Cope and Remington 2022). This includes a high degree of tenacity or perseverance, not stopping in their pursuit of knowledge despite internal or external challenges. As Wong, Donelly, et al. (2018) note, autistic people tend to avoid 'wasting time' on activities that do not contribute to the outcome, such as unnecessary socialising.

> *My ability to focus on a topic, challenge, or problem is my strength. I can research a topic for years and in some cases decades without ever feeling burned out by it. For example, I have studied leadership in a formal capacity through my master's degree and through my doctoral degree without fatigue. Informally, I have studied leadership in the systems around me all of my life.* (Kelly)

> *My biggest strength is probably the depth and intensity of my interest in my work. I don't just work in the autism space, I live in it. I study autism at work, then I go home and catch up with the autistic community on social media, keep contact with my autistic friends, check in with my autistic family, go to bed with my autistic partner, and go to sleep in my autistic brain.* (Alex)

> *I do have an immense visual and auditive memory about materialistic things, which makes me good at identifying objects and remembering where they are stored or remembering situations. . . . I am very involved in what I do, and I usually do not give up. I will brute-force and find pleasure through tasks that could drive most people off, and will not take shortcuts if that work is actually needed to get to relevant/new results.* (Henry)

> *Memory. I remember the topic schedule for one of my subjects, which makes linking between different weeks very easy & natural.* (Jane)

This thirst for knowledge and for a deeper understanding of all aspects of an area of interest relates to the acknowledged strengths of autistic people in systems thinking and pattern recognition. While we most commonly hear of this in the targeted recruitment of autistic people to careers in cybersecurity and technology (Shein 2020; Badhwar 2021; Qeshmi, Batchelor, and Burch 2023), it was also evident in the reflections from autistic academics across a broad range of disciplines.

> *I really love research, especially that feeling of being absorbed in a topic or technique. My ability to hyper-focus on a subject of interest really comes into play as does my ability to see patterns and connect dots across details.* (Dee)

> *The way my mind works is really ideal for systems science. I was frequently bemused during my training when coursework focused on ways to help non-autistic people gain better skills at thinking about things in ways that my mind has always done naturally. For example, being able to see through multiple perspectives at once and understanding the relationship between wholes and parts and feedback loops. Systems science is a lot about understanding patterns and complex causal relationships, and I'm a natural at that. Some of my professional training was in the category of "methods and skills-building to help people think more like autistics" LOL.* (Sunny)

> *My ability to see patterns, which I think is autism related, is also helpful because I see little details and repetitions between academic papers, especially between disciplines, that other people might not notice.* (Louise)

The bringing together of ideas from diverse disciplines to find novel solutions was also commented on by a number of the participants. For some this meant finding great joy in collaborating with colleagues from other discipline areas, whereas for others it meant obtaining qualifications in seemingly disparate fields in order to cultivate the skills and knowledge to solve the problems they were tackling in their research.

> *I take joy in creative problem solving and collaborative work to solve problems that can't be solved by a single individual. I am catholic (lower-case c) in my reading and take inspiration from a variety of sources. Human innovation is thrilling to read about and I like to apply it to local problems.* (Saskia)

> *My many special interests are essential to my well being, and having a job that makes use of these special interests is important as otherwise I would feel that I would give up in little time because of boredom. . . . I feel that I can bring a lot to my job and to my colleagues, not only because I am a paleopalynologist, but also because I am an electronic engineer, artist and graphic designer. I can facilitate multidisciplinary collaboration and be the interface to bring people that have different skillsets together and solve problems.* (Henry)

Attention to detail and its troublesome sibling, perfectionism, were mentioned in many of the reflections. A common reflection was on our ability to spend endless hours formatting a manuscript for publication, marking assignments, or proofreading course outlines, and for many to actually experience enjoyment from the process. The focus on detail that is common to many autistic people means that many of us have strengths in tasks that require spotting even minor variations and inconsistencies in our own and others' work. While previous research has identified this attention to detail as an asset across a broad range of employment roles (Russell, Kapp et al. 2019), the ability to focus on details, and to sustain that focus, is a definite asset in a profession such as academia where there are rigidly defined rules and processes to be followed.

> *I really enjoy designing figures and expressing concepts visually, and I am very proficient with Adobe Illustrator. I tend to be detail oriented, for some things it can be quite extreme, like on graphic design: I can spot slight difference in color hues, irregularities in the spacing or centring of objects, or objects that are not exactly parallel or perpendicular, double spaces in text, formatting issues in spreadsheets . . .* (Henry)

> *I feel being autistic makes me better at my job since I have to spot keywords in the database which I find it easy being a detail-oriented person.* (Proline)

> *Being autistic means that I am hyper detail-oriented and extremely organised, both of which serve me well in my current roles. I am an exceptionally good proof-reader, very good at distilling information, and love presenting information and feedback in clear, accessible ways.* (Ella)

> *I also have a good head for both mathematics and language, grounded in my high attention to detail. When I worked as a grader for undergraduate classes last year, my attention to detail and ability to focus also came into play when I was grading exams and essays.* (Dee)

An important caveat about the perfectionist tendency of many autistic academics is that, while it can make them ideal employees from the perspective of the quality and quantity of work they deliver, this is often at significant personal cost. A recent study with university students found that while (contrary to the stereotype) autistic university students demonstrated more advanced writing skills and higher nonverbal intelligence than non-autistic students, they faced challenges overcoming perfectionism (Gillespie-Lynch, Hotez, et al. 2020). It is important that employers are aware of this and ensure that the autistic academics in their team are able to set boundaries around their work commitments.

> *. . . a commitment to conducting very high quality work, and also a commitment to continuously improving. Good enough is not good enough for me when it comes to my work. If I'm doing a study and I don't have the methodological skills I need to conduct the most rigorous study possible, I will take the time I need to learn those skills so that my research can be of the highest quality.* (Jade)

> *My strengths are that I really spend a lot of time preparing my class and I want every one of them to be high level. Because of the pandemic, I have to teach some classes online this year and I am spending my last holiday time making sure the recording of my courses are of professional level, not only in their content but also in their looks. I spent a long time getting dressed so that it looks good on the camera. I try to have a perfect tone of voice, not too loud but loud enough; I mixed it with numerous video resources to make sure it is understandable and pleasant to follow. . . . So this strong will to always try to make it the best I can, no matter how much time and energy it takes, even if it is a big obstacle for my personal life is probably my biggest professional strength and my biggest challenge on a personal level (my partner sometimes doesn't quite understand my working hours although he is a very big worker as well).* (Sophia)

While many will be familiar with the stereotypical portrayal of autistic people as lacking in imagination and creativity, there is growing evidence that many of us are actually very creative and have the capacity to generate novel solutions to problems. Some of the great writers, actors, and artists are autistic, as are some of the most innovative scientists, inventors, and entrepreneurs. Many of the participants reflected on their 'out of the box' thinking, their curiosity, and their willingness to question accepted ways of doing things. This creativity and innovation were also identified as key strengths of autistic employees in a UK survey study, particularly those in caring professions (Cope and Remington 2022). Some of the participants also commented on how this characteristic improves their teaching by enabling them to reframe complex concepts in ways that facilitate student understanding.

> *I am also able to 'cut the crap' and get directly to the issue/problem. I never thought before that I saw the world in a particularly different way, but I have discovered that I am better at problem-solving than my colleagues. I often come up with solutions which seem obvious to me, but my colleagues will say that they hadn't thought of it like that. I think this is part of being autistic.* (Olivia)

> *I have creative, out of the box thinking, which likely needs a better outlet. I was doing backwards design and not testing way before it became a thing – people don't take tests on jobs and students forget what they memorized for a test as soon as they walk out, so why is there such a focus on lower order learning?* (Isabella)

One autistic characteristic that I think makes me good at teaching is I can think of things from a lot of different angles. As such, if students aren't understanding a concept or if I want to provide a different way of approaching a concept I can do so in useful ways. I think I can be a bit of an over-thinker, but as a consequence I think this means I think of things in quite detailed ways and the students benefit from my ability to break things down and simplify them. (Scarlett)

Some of those in management/leadership positions reflected on how their autistic ways of thinking and communicating contribute to their ability to innovate and lead change. This is consistent with previous research with autistic women who had achieved career success that found that they saw themselves as 'agents of change', able to develop strategies to manage difficult work situations (Webster and Garvis 2016).

I think in ways that others don't – I'm particularly good at orthogonal thinking and systems thinking, making connections and drawing things together in ways that other people don't or can't (or won't). Because I've never had the luxury of experiencing things intuitively or acting without very intentional thought, and constantly have to analyse everything carefully, I'm very good at saying things that normally go unsaid and making things explicit that would normally be tacit. This is particularly useful when it comes to organisational culture and why we do things the way we do. I also constantly question everything, including the status quo and why we do things the way we do. This means I'm an excellent innovator and change agent, and I'm also very good at getting things done outside traditional structures and models. (Morgan)

The critical thinking skills and analytical non-judgmental information-processing style of many autistic people, which flows on from this 'out-of-box' thinking, was also mentioned by several participants as an asset in academic roles. Group members commented on their objective search for truth and ability to analyse data without being constrained by pre-existing perspectives. Previous scholars have hypothesised that autistic individuals' lack of concern over what others consider to be 'fashionable' and their lesser susceptibility to social influence may lead to greater originality in their work (Happé and Vital 2009).

I am pragmatic through-and-through. I crave simplicity when resolving challenges and therefore start with the obvious and move from there. In academia this is a strength because I am able to see data for what it is without needing to have an opinion about it. I collate data into categories and themes and withhold any judgement regarding how they may appear or whether they 'fit' with my image of them. I work pragmatically through data collection, collation, and results and then sit back to explore what I have. Much like building a puzzle one piece at a time (without a picture) and then sitting back once it is almost done to determine what is appearing in front of me. (Kelly)

I know I think very differently than other people do, which means I come up with innovative, new ideas easily. I attribute this to autism, because autistic people are less likely to care about norms, to assume that the way things are done is the way they SHOULD be done. Autistic people are less bound by the status quo, partly due to lack of awareness of it maybe, and partly due to it not being important.... If we can improve it, then the status quo isn't a good enough reason not to. So for me, I come up with new ideas, ideas for refining or improving existing systems, procedures, research, literally anything I set my mind to, because I don't care for the neurotypical status quo and I don't see why I should. That makes autistic experts trailblazers. (Evelyn)

I think the biggest strength I've brought to my work in academia as an autistic person is strong critical thinking skills and a willingness to go against the grain (even just internally). (Amelia)

Many autistic people are early and avid readers, and it is the image of the early-reading autistic child that gives rise to the portrayal of autistic children as 'little professors'. Several of the participants commented on their ability to read and process information more rapidly than their non-autistic colleagues, and how this is a considerable asset in both the teaching and research components of academic roles. Note that while some participants used the term 'hyperlexia', they are referring not to the clinical definition of hyperlexic language disorder (HLD), which presents as a combination of advanced word reading skills and a reading comprehension disorder (Macdonald, Luk, and Quintin 2022), but rather to hyperlexic traits that have found to be associated with language abilities in a subgroup of autistic children (Solazzo, Kojovic, et al. 2021). In this context the reference is being able not just to read quickly but also to absorb and retain the information that has been read.

I also have hyperlexia as part of my ASD diagnosis, and I can read and score student essay exams very quickly and properly. This reduces workload for my colleagues. (Trina)

More senior academics have complimented me on my writing and speed at which I am able to complete tasks, for example a literature review or review of policy (Flora)

As a child I was hyperlexic – this is something that people talk about as if you grow out of it, but I taught myself to read aged 3, and still in adulthood I am a very fast and fluent reader. I process writing so much faster than any verbal information and my brain has less tendency to skip and forget things. This really

> *helps me with my PhD because of the amount of reading and assimilation of data I need to do, often over short periods of time.* (Louise)

Personal Qualities

The personal qualities cited by the participants could be grouped broadly into two categories: those that are stereotypically associated with autism (such as honesty and candour) and those that are commonly misperceived as being deficient in autistic people (such as empathy and people skills).

Honesty and integrity are recognised strengths of autistic people (Nocon, Roestorf, and Menéndez 2022), including in employment contexts (Cope and Remington 2021). While some participants noted that this tendency to be open and honest in our communications can have some negative outcomes – in the context of social structures that at times value half-truths and exaggerations – on the whole our predilection for truth and clarity is an asset in the workplace. This is particularly so in research roles, where data integrity is critical and both careers and scientific advancement depend on strict adherence to truth.

> *I'm honest. (See this pop again in challenges.) I make sure everything I propose is based on data that anyone in the department can access. I enjoy being helpful and of service. Maybe a lifelong drive to be included has led me to approach it as "being useful." I don't like to waste other people's time (again, see challenges).* (Saskia)

Hand-in-hand with honesty comes integrity and a commitment to equity and fairness, another common theme in the reflections. As Wong, Donelly, et al. (2018) note, many autistic people are intensely responsive when made aware of injustice, and advocate for underdogs, victims of bullying, and members of oppressed groups. This included ensuring fairness and diversity in collaborations with colleagues, not being driven by hierarchical structures and 'politics' where these had the potential to harm or disadvantage junior staff, and focusing on universal design and inclusive practices for students. In the research space, it also extended to inclusive research practices and prioritisation of research projects that advance equity and social justice.

> *I develop all my research to be accessible to as many needs as possible (universal design) as a natural way of ensuring inclusivity and diversity. Representation from diverse groups is critical to the development of equitable solutions to any issue being studied.* (Kelly)

> *I'm also a better manager for being autistic, because I don't (or at least I try not to) perpetuate the status quo that harms many, and I care a lot about justice and fairness and equity.* (Morgan)

> *My commitment to fairness means that I form good relationships with colleagues. I'm not competitive, nor do I seek credit where it's not due. While I appreciate the need for critique in scholarship, I don't engage in the one-upping or dog-fight type behaviour of criticism for criticism's sake. Often this is to my own detriment as there are a lot of publications out there that really should have my name on them, but I feel that I work fairly in project teams.* (Ruth)

While there is a pervasive stereotype that autistic people are lacking in emotion and empathy, there is increasing evidence that this is not the case. For example, studies with parents of autistic children have found that the most commonly endorsed positive traits include love, kindness, and happiness (Cost, Zaidman-Zait, et al. 2021) as well as intelligence and creativity (Warren, Eatchel, et al. 2021); and autistic adults report honesty, loyalty, and empathy as their key personal traits (Russell, Kapp, et al. 2019). This high level of compassion and empathy was particularly evident in participants' reflections on their strengths as teachers.

> *Having been bullied my whole life, I am also extremely empathetic toward my students, especially those who are struggling.* (Ella)

> *I am so incredibly empathetic and can often (sometimes I need a nudge) see some things and react in ways others won't. I am way better at coming up with meaningful student work than my colleagues stuck in the lecture then test mode. I am more creative with extension too but am ostracized from that side of my university.* (Isabella)

> *In terms of teaching, I think my strongest areas are my commitment to my students and the level of reflection I apply to my approaches. I know that I spend a lot more time doing individual consults and pastoral care type stuff than many of my colleagues. I try to prioritise student emails so that they never feel that they don't have guidance or can't ask for help.... even though it's hard to see my students struggle, I'm glad that they feel they can talk about it.* (Ruth)

An important related concept was the desire to be inclusive and welcoming to all people, which many acknowledged likely stemmed from their own experiences of being excluded and rejected. Consistent with this, group members commonly referred to themselves and their interactions with others as being non-judgmental.

> *A concern to include everyone and to make everyone feel welcome and comfortable and not mocked (e.g., in class discussions, or when new people come to a group where most people already know each other). I think this is connected to having often felt like I'm not really welcome or fitting in, and wanting to avoid that for others.* (Amelia)

I'm a good listener, and I do not easily make judgements or assumptions about the experiences of others. . . . I think I'm good at demystifying the rules of academia for students who struggle or are unfamiliar with them. . . . I seem to work well with students who other faculty members simply "cannot work with." I'm often surprised, in these instances, that other instructors had difficulties. (Marie)

While communication challenges are an acknowledged aspect of autism, and indeed one of the key diagnostic criteria, many of the participants commented on their communication style as a key strength that contributed to their success in academia. This apparent inconsistency stems from the fact that many autistic people are clear, literal communicators; we do not pad our verbal communication with unnecessary words or phrases that obscure meaning. While some may find our communication blunt, this style can be an asset in explaining concepts and processes to students or colleagues. Some also commented that a lifetime of having to adjust their behaviours and speech patterns to suit the expectations of others meant that they had developed high-level skills in adapting communications to different audiences.

I'm good at supervising PhD students and dissertations at all levels, as I am better at telling students why they should or should not do something/write a particular way than most of my colleagues, who just speak their own white British middle-class academic language and expect everyone else to know what they mean. (Liam)

Like most autistics (I think), I am visually based. This visual orientation helps me create engaging powerpoints and related educational material. (Moon Man)

My chameleon tendency means I'm really good at adapting communication to different audiences, and because I've had to think really intentionally about it, I'm good at articulating the 'how' of things that most people think about in really fixed 'you either have/do this thing innately or you don't'. (Morgan)

I find that I can often communicate more effectively in writing than in speech, so I can write easily and write well (when I can actually find the time to fit it in!). I'm very logical and detail-oriented, so I'm generally quite good at analysing and synthesising information to pull out meaning. I'm also fairly good at explaining processes and ideas in accessible ways. (Alex)

Autistic researchers Aimee Grant and Helen Kara recently published a reflection on their strengths as qualitative researchers, expressing that their autistic ability to hyperfocus meant they were able to get large amounts of work done in a short space of time; their attention to detail was useful for planning research, managing budgets, and coding data; their creative thinking was particularly helpful when analysing data, identifying patterns and links; and their autistic empathy enabled them to support colleagues, participants, and other stakeholders in the context of participatory and emancipatory research methodologies (Grant and Kara 2021). The reflections of the thirty-seven academics in this group clearly support this perspective on the strengths of autistic researchers.

The Strengths of Academia as a Workplace for Autistics

A Place to Learn

The cerebral aspects of the role were reflected on as major attractions to and benefits of working in academia. This included both the ability to focus on an area of interest and the more general intellectual components of the role. For those fortunate enough to be in research or teaching areas aligned with their areas of interest, academia provides a rare environment where autistic special interests are seen as valuable expertise (rather than as 'weird obsessions', which is how they are often denigrated in wider society).

> *I am being paid to conduct research that I am personally and professionally enamoured with. Call it a special interest or weird obsession or whatever other people may label it but for me there are some days I cannot believe I am as lucky as I am to be in the position I am in. I am also aware how hard I have worked to be in this position but that is somehow lost on me, I don't really consider what it took to get me to where I am unless it is in a negative sense.* (Flora)

> *I like that my job means I'm able to talk about my special interest and help people.* (Trevor)

> *I love being able to talk about topics that interest me – and to continually learn more about these topics.* (Marie)

The academic environment provides an opportunity to exercise many of the cognitive strengths of autistic people, including our intense focus, capacity to recognise patterns, and ability to generate novel solutions (Russell, Kapp, et al. 2019). It also values personal characteristics that may be undervalued in other careers, such as perseverance, perfectionism, honesty, and attention to detail (Cope and Remington 2021).

> *Oh my, where do I even start? It's not like I do this work out of coincidence; it's full of things I love and skills I enjoy honing and using. I love to learn. I love complexity. I love puzzles and investigations. I love not knowing things and the discovery of science. I love the creativity of the job.* (Sunny)

> *I feel that I am finally using my brain properly.* (Olivia)

> *I am happy that I can explore the unknown and come up with innovative solutions, bring people from various disciplines and bridge disparate approaches to solve complex problems.* (Betty)

A Place to Teach

The participants' reflections expressed great enjoyment and satisfaction in sharing their knowledge with others, and this was particularly evident in the comments about teaching. This went beyond the direct transmission of knowledge, reflecting not the stereotype of 'info-dumping' on others but the value of sharing information in a way that helps others to learn.

> *... student's face when they finally get something after they've been struggling to understand it. (i.e. "light bulb" moment) spec con student finally competing subject or sitting exam, etc.* (Jane)

> *Imparting large amounts of insight to smart students fast, giving them the tools to navigate the world better once they get out there.* (Lisa)

> *My favourite part of my role is teaching and talking about my favourite topics. I like helping people to understand new concepts and I think this is the part I do really well.* (Scarlett)

> *What I like the most about my job is feeling helpful. When some students come to me and tell me that they came to my course about special needs education thinking they wouldn't learn anything they already know and then changed totally their way of seeing things and of teaching thanks to my course, it could make me cry. I feel so happy and useful. Very often I get some nice compliments or emails and even some presents at the end of the year from my students and I feel like the way I am doing my job is ok. That is the biggest relief for me.* (Sophia)

Equally evident in the reflections was that a very positive aspect of teaching for autistic academics is the ability to help and support students. Participants commented on the enjoyment of watching students succeed, whether this was the short-term success of completing an assignment or the longer-term completion of a research degree or commencement of employment. This was particularly the case in relation to assisting students who experience marginalisation and/or disadvantage.

> *Being able to share my experiences with students and save them the feeling of being lost as an undergraduate. For me my goal is of course to prepare students to get the best mark they can in that subject, but my favourite part is to share tricks of the trade and break things down in a way I wish someone had for me rather*

> *than trying to de-code what is expected of students and why – when I explain it in simple steps the penny drops.* (Flora)

> *I've also found it very rewarding and gratifying to see my students' research projects develop and to see them do well in applications for scholarships, summer schools, or PhD programs.* (Amy)

> *. . . and I loved it when students would thank me for teaching them. I also loved the student reviews; I got good reviews for my teaching, and I was really proud of that. I was also the Welfare Officer for a few years, and a number of students told me that I changed their lives through my counselling and support. In the end, that is what has stayed with me and buoyed me up the most.* (Mia)

> *I would say my favorite aspect of ed psyc autism research is being able to help develop content and programs so students can be supported and accepted for who they are versus the standard they are expected to conform to while also learning survival skills and sometimes getting to witness the impact such as in the elementary classes I did a pilot project in this year.* (Eva)

These findings are consistent with those from a study of autistic teachers in the United Kingdom (Wood and Happé 2023), demonstrating that the ability to connect with and support students – particularly those experiencing marginalisation or disadvantage – is both a strength and a benefit of this career choice. Academia provides a unique setting to utilise our enthusiasm for sharing our knowledge with others and providing others with a nurturing and supportive learning environment.

A Flexible Place to Work

There were a number of aspects of the job roles themselves that participants discussed as what they like about working in academia. The most commonly mentioned aspects were flexibility and autonomy. References to flexibility included the flexibility of where to work, and particularly the option to work at home; when to work, including the ability to schedule work around energy levels; and how to work, notably the flexibility around how and how often to engage in social interaction.

> *I like that my job allows flexibility to carry out my role however and whenever I see fit. Being an academic means no set days or hours so long as I get the job done.* (Trevor)

> *You can work from home and work by yourself a lot of the time, while still maintaining some degree of social interaction for teaching or meetings.* (Amy)

> *Flexibility, definitely, the flexibility is what I like the most. It's really a godsend. I don't think I'd be able to keep up the level of output that I have been able to if*

> *I didn't have the flexibility, just I would be far too exhausted. Like I remember being in a regular workplace prior to academia and just commuting an hour each way, plus my full-time job on top of that. I was absolutely exhausted every single night and every single weekend.* (Charlotte)

> *I also like that my current roles are work-from-home (even prior to COVID-19), which suits me very well. I like being able to choose my own hours and work in my pyjamas with my cat on my lap, and I like not being exhausted from interacting with people at the end of each day.* (Ella)

The concept of autonomy and independence had some overlap with flexibility. As noted above, the flexible nature of many roles in academia provides opportunities to control when and where participants complete their work. Other aspects of autonomy that are highly valued by participants include the capacity to make their own decisions, to focus on areas of research and/or teaching that are of interest to them, and to work in ways that suit their cognitive processes and sensory needs.

> *I like the level of independence I have and I like being able to make my own decisions.* (Olivia)

> *I have control over my own schedule and immediate surroundings. Because I think differently from others and have different needs, I find this level of control is absolutely essential.* (Scott)

> *What I like most about my work would have to be the freedom I have to decide on my own research area. I've been given the freedom to do advocacy through research by conducting research aimed to improve the lives of the autistic community by addressing misconceptions, stereotypes, etc., about autistic people.* (Jade)

Other positive aspects of job roles in academia that participants discussed in their reflections included the potential for career progression and job stability, being able to follow a routine, visible indicators of success such as winning grants or having papers published, and employment conditions such as generous leave provisions and superannuation.

A Place to Help

A strong motivator and positive aspect of working in academia reflected on by a number of participants was the ability to help others and to make positive changes in the world. This is in addition to helping students, which was discussed above. Academia can provide an opportunity to undertake meaningful research and advocacy and to fight for social justice, an area of importance for many autistic people. This included those who are working in the autism field – contributing to research, teaching, and practice that improve outcomes for autistic children and adults – and those working in other fields that enable them to contribute to the well-being of those in society who experience marginalisation and/or disadvantage.

> *My research administration job allows me to contribute to research that will inform practice and hopefully help to improve the lives of autistic children, which is the main focus for my career and aligns perfectly with my interests and passions.* (Psyche)

> *I love the opportunity this work gives me to make a difference in people's lives and create systems change that could make the world better for the next generations of autistic people and people with other disabilities or intersectional identities.* (Sunny)

> *The feeling that I'm actually doing something that is having a big impact on people's lives. The refugees are being prepared to sit the GED exams, which are a school leaving equivalency certificate that can be taken anywhere in the world, at any time.... At the same time, I'm putting structures in place to better support new teachers and better retain the teachers we have, and helping to make teaching easier and more enjoyable for the teachers.... The conversation sessions are bringing joy to all the participants – the facilitators and the students. I'm helping people connect with each other positively. It feels pretty good.* (Ava)

A Place to Connect

Social connections are important for all people, but as autistics we can experience considerable difficulty in making and maintaining these connections. Participants reflected that academia presents opportunities for connection that enable us to utilise our strengths, be recognised as equals, and participate in a way that is meaningful. The ability to connect over shared interests and goals provides a structure for social interaction, and the recognition of a need for a range of expertise allows us to be recognised for our strengths rather than our challenges.

> *I enjoy working in a field where I can play to my strengths, working autonomously, working in a field of my interest, and working with other academics (and therefore 'fitting in' a little bit better), which I find I am most able to do as a PhD student, although sometimes this is also the case in my position as research administrator.* (Psyche)

> *What I love about my job, weirdly enough, is the connection with people. I love sharing a special interest with someone and watching the lightbulb go on as they "get it" and appreciate how fascinating it is. Shared fascination is like shared awe: a singular, bonding experience. As for the nuts and bolts, I love data*

analysis and especially plotting data in a way that makes sense visually. Data analysis and making graphs and charts is a "flow" activity for me. I lose track of time. (Saskia)

Some Final Thoughts

The life of an academic is one of deep engagement with areas of interest and where comprehensive knowledge of a specific topic is seen as a strength rather than an anomaly. Autistic strengths – such as intense focus, capacity to recognise patterns, ability to generate novel solutions, perseverance, perfectionism, and attention to detail – can come to the fore in academia in a way that makes this an ideal profession for our neurotype.

My autistic brain is a problem-solving brain, which in cognitively-demanding jobs is a good strength to have. (Dave)

I don't think "outside of the box": I don't even see the box. (Lisa)

For those fortunate to have supportive colleagues and employers, and to work in an institution that understands and addresses the needs of autistic people, the life of an academic has many other positive aspects. These include flexibility in working style and location, autonomy and independence, predictable routines, visible measures of success, and good employment conditions. Additionally, academia provides the opportunity to make a meaningful contribution to others – from teaching an individual student to researching solutions to world problems.

Maintaining employment in an academic role has felt easy as I enjoy the work and lifestyle. Successes in an academic role include attention to detail, ability to work tirelessly for extended periods of time, enjoy working at odd hours, and I find the work intellectually stimulating (most of the time!). (Baz)

Most of my successes in terms of searching, maintaining an academic role, they have actually just . . . They've just been some, just some really wonderful people, I suppose, really understanding, caring, just genuine sort of people, who are also quite switched on and competent, in their role. (Charlotte)

CHAPTER 5

Challenges

> *I've started admitting I am autistic and wow – what a mixed bag that is. I have people who insist it is a mental illness, people who insist I am not and cannot be because their son is, to people who either pity me or shun me more. I abhor pity. I don't at all care for being ostracized and shunned either. So communication is a challenge. Work environment can be – the physical. The emotional work environment is hugely challenging. I never had such issues before, and am quite frankly traumatized by things that have happened to me here. So I am now alone. I never was alone before.*
>
> (Isabella)

This chapter explores the bi-directional challenges of autistics in the academy. Many of the challenges experienced by autistic people in academia are similar to those experienced in other aspects of our lives – dealing with sensory challenges, different processing styles, social interaction, and communication. Other challenges that are inherent to academia include the breadth of activity, the performance and competitive aspects of the role, and complicated institutional politics.

A 2020 multi-country study found that stigma, communication challenges, and lack of understanding of autism were key barriers to successful employment for autistic adults (Black, Mahdi, et al. 2020). A survey of 249 autistic teachers in UK primary and secondary schools (Wood and Happé 2023) identified the key challenges for that cohort as lack of (autism) understanding and support, including limited flexibility and work accommodations; sensory overload, change, and unpredictability; mental health issues such as anxiety, fatigue, and burnout; and the emotional toll of observing poor treatment of autistic pupils.

Recently we have seen a small number of papers reflecting on ways that academia could be more inclusive and supportive for autistic people, typically from the perspective of an autistic scholar contemplating their experiences. For example, Taylor and Johnson (2020) reflect on the first author's experiences as a doctoral student in geosciences and suggest ways that the field could be more inclusive, and Raymaker (2017) reflects on being an insider-researcher in a community-based participatory research setting.

Going beyond the experiences of one individual, Martin (2021) reports on a questionnaire study that explored the experiences of twelve autistic researchers (doctoral students, part-time researchers, and other non-permanent roles) and 'revealed barriers at every stage of the employment journey for autistic academics and highlighted relatively straightforward ways of circumventing them based on principles of Universal Design' (p. 14). A recent autistic autism researchers' roundtable (Dwyer, Acevedo, et al. 2021) reflected on several topics, including the importance of autistic and intersectional identities, ways in which autistic autism researchers can enhance the quality of autism research, tensions and conflicts that we face as autistic autism researchers, and ways in which inflexible institutions and practices can impose barriers that restrict autistic involvement in academia.

This group of thirty-seven autistic people working in academic institutions around the globe identified a range of challenges and frustrations. Aspects of social interaction, interpersonal communication, stigma, and discrimination were frequently raised as causing tension within the workplace, as well as leading to anxiety and distress for the autistic employee.

Social Interaction Is Complicated

Social aspects of the role were by far the most frequent topic of discussion in the reflections. This theme was dominated by the complexities of social interaction and the challenges it poses for working in academia, including the energy required for constant masking of autistic traits to 'fit in'. Other commonly mentioned social aspects were politics and negative behaviours of others in the workplace.

Difficulties with social interaction are a common characteristic of autism, so it is not surprising that many members of the group commented on the emotional energy required to manage the nature and frequency of social interactions. This included both 'work-based' interactions, such as meetings, and 'social-based' interactions. Understanding and following social rules, interpreting others' actions and reactions, masking autistic behaviours, and combining 'professional' and 'personal' interactions are effortful activities for many autistic people. Some of the aspects that non-autistic people find relaxing and enjoyable (such as morning teas and after-work drinks) can be the most challenging aspects of the workplace for autistic people.

The thing I like the least about my work would have to be the social game. It's stressful. I am extremely skilled with my research. I am great at my work. But I can't help but feel like a bumbling fool sometimes when I'm trying to work through an unexpected social thing. (Jade)

I also don't like all the socialising that seems to be required. Being constantly socially accessible (coffee, lunch, meetings, etc) is difficult for me. I am used to working in roles where I can sit in my office and eat lunch or go for a walk on my own and it never seemed to be an issue, but networking seems to be a pretty huge component of being an academic. (Scarlett)

I have been in academia for a long time not knowing I was autistic. And I kept on wondering why I didn't quite fit in. My first year was very pleasant and as I started knowing my colleagues a bit better, trouble started. They thought I was pretentious, hard to work with. I didn't understand it because I was trying very hard to be nice and polite and to do my work perfectly. I was respecting all the rules although most colleagues weren't. But I didn't feel comfortable going to after work meeting at some colleague's place although I tried a few times. But that was very stressful for me. I didn't understand how to act professionally and casually at the same time. That was to challenging for me. And of course I never invited anyone to my place. The main issue I had in my work was the relationship with my colleagues. (Sophia)

The constant social interaction and the need to 'fit in' imposes pressure on autistic employees to mask aspects of their autism, which impacts physical and emotional well-being and career outcomes. There was frequent reference in the reflections to the sheer number of meetings that take place each day in academia. In addition to the energy required to participate in the conversation, there were frustrations around the management of meetings and the time that is wasted when there are more efficient ways of achieving outcomes.

I find meetings to be highly stressful and exhausting (in a way that teaching is not). It takes a lot of work to get through each one, as I think about how and when to participate, where to look, and what is expected. (Marie)

I also hated the meetings, which were often badly managed. In my last job, minutes were taken but never written up and circulated, and there was no summing up at the end of the meeting. This meant that half the people who were present went away believing certain rules or procedures had changed, while the other half were convinced that nothing had changed, and those who were not present were left completely in the dark. (Mia)

Data dump meetings. This is where we spend an hour to an hour and a half receiving information from administration that could easily have been read. (Moon Man)

The transient nature of academia adds to the intensity of the effort required to maintain social interaction. While we may have a consistent group of colleagues (as in other professions), the academic year brings new cohorts of students, and conferences and meetings bring new 'colleagues'.

> *I also find some social aspects of the job to be tricky; sometimes it's easy to connect with others over shared interests, but I'm often unsure how to read a situation. And again, with new classes and new work assignments every semester, I'm constantly having to navigate new groups of people and figure out how we're going to work together.* (Dee)

Some also noted having prosopagnosia (face blindness), a condition more common among autistic people than non-autistic people (Minio-Paluello, Porciello, et al. 2020), and the additional challenges this brings to social interactions.

> *Prosopagnosia. Difficulty in remembering faces. It takes me almost an entire semester to begin to recognize my students. As a result, I advocate for myself by indicating that I need to employ students name tents [folded paper tents on students' desks] to help in being able to refer to my students by name.* (Moon Man)

Social interactions take time and energy that is needed to complete work, creating an ever-present need to balance the work we are paid to do with the social expectations of colleagues. The tendency of autistic people to be intensely focused on the activity they are engaged in can be mistaken for rudeness or hostility. Lack of assertiveness and difficulties with spontaneous communication can be mistaken for disinterest or lower capacity.

> *Sometimes I want to just get into and on with work without social "niceties" – this can upset people, as people often take things personally, or then worry that I am upset or something happened or is wrong, no – I just want to do my work.* (Baz)

> *The challenges that I am facing are also multiple, as people that have peeled the outer layers appearances tend to appreciate and value me, first encounter situations can be difficult to handle. I find difficult to fit in certain roles that are expected from scientists, like being curious and collegial. I often find it very difficult to ask or answer questions on the spot, unless I have previously built a lot of prior-knowledge of the topic. Not being assertive and vocally participant in meetings and conferences can often be seen as not being interested or lacking intellect, curiosity. I can't engage in small talk, or sustain some conversations, which depending on people, can be a major issue.* (Henry)

For some, this social aspect went beyond the energy requirements of social interaction; they also had the ever-present worry of exclusion or hostility from colleagues.

> *One thing I dislike about working in general is the need to be around people. They make me anxious and uncomfortable because I don't trust them not to treat me badly for being autistic, or different. This means that a person has to be quite warm and prove themselves to me before I can even begin to feel comfortable in their presence. . . . While I am accustomed to being the weird or different one, or a pariah to some extent, I still feel uncomfortable with the treatment I receive as a result of being different.* (Evelyn)

> *I also find I get bullied more than most people. This has been the case since my childhood, but has continued into adulthood. Sometimes, some people quite simply take a disliking to me. It doesn't seem to matter if I mask and perform as many of the expected neurotypical elements of social interaction as I'm capable of – they just don't like me. In group settings, this leads to my being excluded and has a strong negative impact on my mental and emotional wellbeing.* (Ella)

The political nature of the workplace was a common topic of reflection in relation to the challenges of academia. At is simplest level, 'politics' in this context refers to understanding the hierarchical structure of the organisation, the nuances of power and alliances, and the need to intuit the hidden meaning behind communications.

> *Politics and the general unwillingness of people to behave like decent human beings. I resent having to spend so much energy navigating other people's feelings and their commitment to maintaining the power dynamics of the status quo. I know it's a means to my desired end, so I put up with it, but I wish it wasn't the case.* (Morgan)

> *I find office politics difficult to navigate and when people don't say what they mean and my having to decipher what they mean without looking like a clueless idiot.* (Trevor)

However, as Marie noted, this lack of awareness of and engagement in organisational politics can have its upside as our neutrality and integrity mean we are seen as fair and equitable.

> *Adjusting to my new role was difficult. The social world of faculty meetings was (and still is) mysterious to me, and I constantly felt as though what was unsaid was more important than what was said. This has been one of my obstacles and has ironically, also contributed to some success. Because I am often unaware of interpersonal tensions during faculty meetings, I have gained a reputation for being fair and generally pleasant to work with. At the same time, without realizing it, I have sometimes said the wrong thing and have upset colleagues.* (Marie)

By nature autistic people tend to be honest and direct, to be uncomfortable with deception, and to have difficulty detecting deception in others.

This can put us at a distinct disadvantage in a work context that is fundamentally competitive. There is constant competition for positions, for funding, for promotion, for publication, and – sadly – like high school, there is competition for popularity and social status.

> *I also find the social politics of academia to be challenging sometimes. I've been in the autism research space for long enough now that I have a good idea of who's who (at least in [this country]). I've developed fairly extensive networks, and I think I've developed some level of insight into the "lay of the land" regarding the various social-political alliances and fractures that exist between the different players. But, I know that I simply don't have the skills or the capacity to play those nuanced neurotypical games of interpersonal snakes and ladders, and most of the time I'm completely unaware that they're even going on.... I know that I'm likely missing out on opportunities because I'm not able to access the social politics of academia, and that's sometimes frustrating.* (Alex)

> *I thought that I might be exempt from politics in academia compared to the typical, general sort of mainstream workplace, but definitely not. And unfortunately, because of the politics, I do see a lot of questionable behaviour. Dare I say, people adding people or themselves to papers where they really don't deserve authorship, for example. And that's all sort of politically driven, but you know, it is what it is. You take the good with the bad, so ...* (Charlotte)

The interaction between the politics that appear to be inherent in academia and some of the inherent aspects of autism (anxiety, perseveration, perfectionism) results in considerable strain on some autistics working in academia, with negative outcomes that extend across and beyond the workplace.

> *What I like the least are the plots of university politics. You never know whom you can trust. Some people make alliances with people they have been very aggressive to in the past; some people will only help their allies no matter how bad they are in their jobs and how unfair it is. Some colleagues are recruited in a very unfair way. I don't understand all those unwritten rules and that makes me feel very unsecure in my professional environment. I am very cautious because of that and that makes my relationship with my colleagues even harder. I am seen as very cold and distant. But I can't fake feeling comfortable when I have the feeling that most people are playing a game I don't know the rules. And even if I start understanding a little how it works (to try to understand the rules, I took some higher responsibilities), I don't think they are fair and I don't want to play this game.* (Sophia)

> *I also find interpersonal politics extremely stressful. Even if difficulties are with only one person, that experience overshadows everything else. I get so stressed that I get migraines that can last a week. I also stay awake at night, anxious. It doesn't matter if there are dozens of other experiences that have been*

positive. My sense is that this is the dark side of my autistic capacity for hyperfocus. (Ella)

What do you like the least about your job? Dealing with the adults: academia is full of posturing and just bullshit in general. I have no time for that. (Lisa)

Frustration with the lack of commitment and competence of others in the workplace – both colleagues and students – was evident in many of the reflections. Those who place high expectations on themselves and work very hard to achieve these find it difficult to understand and accept the lackadaisical attitude of others.

Sometimes I let my disappointment bother me if I feel that the students aren't trying; I'm learning about different cultural styles, and am disappointed that for some people, unless you tell them "you must do this or you can no longer attend classes", they won't do the simple steps that you ask them to. I just don't like being bossy, but it turns out that l sometimes have to be. I like people to have autonomy, and to use it. (Ava)

My work is a very high standard and I share my resources and work freely amongst colleagues. I do not like it when other people do not share. I really hate it when I delegate a task to someone and then when I look at it, it has mistakes in it or they haven't formatted it consistently. Also it really annoys me when people can't do basic things then they ask me to do it – I only know how to do things because I have taken the time to understand how things work, have experimented and figured things out for myself. (Olivia)

This lack of understanding of the hidden curriculum, disengagement from institutional politics, and inability to 'read' other people has a range of negative implications for autistic people in terms of both their day-to-day well-being and their career progression. Participants reflected on feelings of anxiety and uncertainty from not knowing whether they are meeting the expectations of their colleagues and supervisors, or the negative outcomes from misunderstanding these expectations. They also reflected on their inability to understand and navigate aspects such as workload, promotion, and salary negotiations, because they do not 'read between the lines' of departmental policies and processes. Related to this was a sense of reliance on the goodwill of others, particularly their immediate supervisors, for their success and even survival at work.

Because I do not have explicit feedback from chairs and colleagues, I don't always know if I'm doing a good job, and there have been times when I have been uncertain of my value as a worker or what is expected of me. (Marie)

Another huge issue I've had is being completely unable to navigate the social transactions around salary negotiation. I've had several instances in my time where I naively believed everyone was getting paid the same, because everyone is under the enterprise agreement, and we were in the same roles starting roughly at the same time, but I didn't realise other people had negotiated increments and were getting paid more than me. It's something I get angry about – the entire system is specifically designed to punish neurodivergent people for not getting the same handbook as everyone else (Morgan).

I am currently being considered for department chair, and this will be my biggest challenge, finding ways to acknowledge and manage the truth without being blamed for "causing" friction that is already there simply by agreeing that it's real. ***My successes really depend on who is in leadership above me.*** *I have a dean who says she deeply appreciates my honesty. I think she is genuine. I hope so, anyway. The truth will only set you free if the people in power can handle it themselves. Autistic people are truthful to our own peril, because those in charge, especially in academia, are not always virtuous. (Saskia)*

It would be easy to assume that these social challenges are only experienced by those in the early stages of their career, but similar themes were evident in the reflections of those with lengthy careers in academia and those in leadership roles.

Leadership is really really expensive, from a cognitive and emotional energy point of view. I also really struggle with being one of only a few people who advocate for change in all sorts of domains and the fact that most people generally aren't too concerned with being decent human beings (i.e., I struggle with resentment a lot). I also have to expend huge amounts of energy existing in an ableist system that wasn't built for people like me. But then because I'm quite good at doing this and mask well and have crafted a 'competent professional' persona, my challenges are generally invisible unless I choose to expend the emotional energy to talk about it. I go back and forth on this one, some days I do talk about it to make it visible, other days I just don't have the spoons [a metaphor for limited emotional energy]. Same goes with asking for accommodations/asking for what I need – sometimes I can do it, and some days I can't and then after sucking it up for too long I end up in shutdown/meltdown. (Morgan)

I also really dislike having to remediate personnel issues. I'm a poor micromanager and not particularly good at working with people who need a lot of supervision, who are doing a really bad job, who are not engaged in the work, or who disrespect or dismiss my expertise. (Sunny)

There's a Lot to Juggle

There are a number of aspects of working in academia that are widely acknowledged as challenging for all neurotypes, but exacerbated for autistic people working in this field. These include job insecurity, low salary compared with many other careers, high workload, and the competitive nature of academic environments. Other aspects of the role itself that can be particularly challenging for autistic people include rigid processes, breadth of activity, lack of autonomy, and the 'performance' aspects of many roles.

While academia is seen by many as a privileged and relaxed work environment, the reality of modern universities is increasing workloads and reduced job security (Cannizzo, Mauri, and Osbaldiston 2019; Steenkamp and Roberts 2020), to the extent that a healthy work-life balance is difficult to maintain (Cannizzo, Mauri, and Osbaldiston 2019). The lack of job security that is inherent in the role of early career researcher or teacher is particularly problematic for people who struggle with uncertainty and change. The casual nature of the workforce means that there is ongoing uncertainty for those who do not have tenure, and concerns about career progression and future income are common.

> *The worst thing would be the high pressure environment and the lack of job security. I've been casual for six years and I earn less than a full-time supermarket employee.* (Ruth)

> *My position is 75% teaching, 23% extension and 0% research so I cannot get research grants or even get teaching grants + I am contractual versus tenured. All of it puts me at a disadvantage for grants, for doing any form of research, for feeling secure.* (Isabella)

A number of the reflections addressed aspects of their autism that exacerbate, or are exacerbated by, their ability to manage the heavy workload of academia. The former included underlying levels of generalised anxiety, perfectionism, and information processing. The latter included environmental, social, and communication challenges. While many of the group reported being able to meet, and even exceed, the expectations of their colleagues and supervisors, this was achieved at considerable cost to their own physical and mental health.

> *I accept that I function with a base low level of anxiety – this can increase quickly when certain communication, environmental and social factors are at play.* (Baz)

> *While I do value sharing knowledge, and like to engage with the public and students, I am suffering from a lot of social anxiety. Doing a two hour lecture feels like running a marathon: preparing the lecture takes me ages, as I struggle from filtering what information is relevant and should be delivered, from details that may not be essential. I do redraw every single figure I use for the*

PowerPoint presentation, so that they look beautiful and convey the exact point I am talking about. This does takes an incredible amount of time. I feel physically sick before delivering a lecture, and usually need to recover for hours or days afterward. (Henry)

Not good at asking for/taking time off. Also not good at switching off. (Jane)

I am a perfectionist (which could be seen as both a strength and a weakness). As such students often comment on how well delivered or presented my topics are, however this leads to me burning out and experiencing extreme anxiety and overwhelm (usually around Sept/Oct each year). (Scarlett)

Rigid processes and protocols were discussed by many as challenging aspects of working in academia. While this may seem counter-intuitive for a condition that is associated with a need for rules and routines, it is the adherence to inefficient or inappropriate rules and processes that they struggle with.

I think academic culture is, in many ways, incredibly hidebound and rigid. It is also slightly absurd that autism researchers can – entirely unconscious of the hypocrisy – so confidently accuse autistic people of being rigid and inflexible. I do sometimes find it frustrating – perhaps I might even say vexing – to be part of this culture. (Scott)

The thing that I like the least about my job are daily protocols which include sending email to my managers when checking in, going for lunch, coming back from lunch and checking out. Surprisingly, the part of job that many neurotypical folks find easy like following daily protocol is the hardest for me. (Proline)

Related to this is the resistance to change that appears inherent to academic institutions and the frustration that causes for autistic people when they have identified alternate processes that would improve productivity and increase the quality of outcomes.

Another challenging factor that affects me in both of my academic workplaces is adherence to rules that do not make sense. It does not take long for me to become unpopular because I like to question to the status quo, particularly if policies and procedures or ways of thinking seem outdated or illogical. All too often, I find that systems are in place simply because this is the way that things have always been undertaken, instead of there actually being a well-founded reason for their implementation. (Psyche)

Having to hold my tongue when I know if I did things my way there would be a better outcome for both the client the project is for as well as the material we would have available to publish from. (Flora)

While there is a focus on specialisation in many areas of academia, there is also an expectation of a broad range of skills and capacities that are assumed to be inherent in people who have been successful in gaining employment in academia. I can win a role because I am an expert in my field of interest, but to keep it I have to become at least competent in a range of other areas I was not trained for and that do not come naturally to me. For example, many roles require us to be able to teach *and* to do research *and* to undertake administration *and* to bring resources into the organisation *and* to understand and work with others *and* to lead and develop teams.

> *One of the challenges of academia is that it requires one be competent in many areas – one can't specialize and focus only on one or two little domains where one is especially skilled. One needs to be able to network, write papers, understand and implement research methods, hire and supervise other people, etc. Fortunately, I can at least function in many of these areas, but my sense is that autistic people frequently have an unbalanced profile of abilities that leaves us struggling to handle one or two aspects of the above.* (Scott)

> *More specifically, probably administrative work. It's annoying though necessary, I'm not very good at it, and it keeps me away from the science.* (Sunny)

The lack of autonomy in academia was noted as a challenge, particularly for those in administrative roles and junior members of research and/or teaching teams. Autistic people tend to thrive when given the opportunity to focus on an area of interest, and can struggle when asked to work on tasks that do not align with their area of expertise. Many discussed the disheartening impact of being allocated routine, repetitive tasks on areas that are selected by their supervisor, while not being able to focus their attention on their area of specialist knowledge. The lack of autonomy was seen as problematic not only in the choice of task, but also in the way that tasks are to be undertaken, with reflections on the frustration of being micromanaged and having to justify their ways of working.

> *In my latest job, I hated the sense of powerlessness. Academics in my institution were no longer allowed to exercise any agency; we were told what to teach by a management team, and all the creativity of academia was eroded. I had a lot of ideas for things I wanted to develop and teach, but I was not allowed to pursue these things.* (Mia)

> *I struggle to have others oversee my process of working. As an undergraduate student I was able to complete tasks and assignments and prepare for exams without having to explain my personal process of working with others.... It was not until my honours and PhD years that I realised how differently I work from other people and find it hard to articulate what I am doing and why.* (Flora)

However, as noted below by Amy, there are also challenges in academia that come from too much autonomy when this is operationalised as a lack of clear direction.

> *At times feeling paralyzed/frozen/inertia with the open-ended/unstructured aspect of academia and the freedom/autonomy that it brings (important to get organized, make plans, structure your time).* (Amy)

The performance aspect of the academic role was also reflected on in the context of conference presentations, media interviews, and other forms of public speaking. However, it was particularly of concern in the area of teaching (in the form of classroom instruction). While the transmission of knowledge is one of the most enjoyed aspects of academia for this cohort (see Chapter 4, section 'A Place to Teach'), the social aspects of teaching can be draining. This aspect of academia puts the onus of the communication on the autistic person (the 'teacher' who is there to educate and to entertain).

> *I find more and more that teaching drains me. It exhausts me. I really do like being with people from all different cultures, countries & disciplines but the interaction is exhausting. So when I would come home after teaching all day, I would hardly be able to speak.* (Olivia)

> *Lecturing is another. I have to read a script, as ad-libbing to slides just doesn't work as I go off on tangents. Also my stage presence isn't the most dynamic, so my student evaluations are polarized – strong students like what I do, and average students hate it.* (Liam)

> *. . . as a professor I am not much of a performer. I am excited by the work and by talking about it, but I am not flashy. I am not charismatic. I have been told that I'm intimidating. I go out of my way to be warm and friendly, but it doesn't come naturally. Students seem to expect entertainment as much as education these days, and I am not a natural entertainer.* (Saskia)

We Have Different Operating Systems

Information-processing styles were commonly mentioned as challenges in the predominantly neurotypical workplace of academia. Some related to communication and are discussed below, but many related to internal aspects of obtaining, retaining, and processing information. These included learning styles, information-processing speed, dealing with change, variations in information-processing capacity, and information synthesis.

Several of the group reflected on being a visual learner in a context where information is often presented verbally with no visual aids, such as in conferences and meetings. Working in a context where speed of information processing can be paramount was identified as a challenge. Academic environments often place value on rapid responses – whether that involves a snappy response to a question, a quick decision, or fast-paced marking of assessments. For people who process information carefully and conscientiously, with a focus on determining the most precise response, this expectation can result in missing out on opportunities or not being heard. The frequency of change in the academic environment, and the related expectation that we will be able to rapidly absorb and implement changes, was a source of stress for many.

> *Not always understanding/processing everything right away when there is a lot of new/unfamiliar information being communicated with no visual support (e.g., no handout or no Powerpoint at a conference).* (Amy)

> *The challenges of my job mostly relate to the anxiety produced by uncertainty and frequent change. Academic schedules change every semester, and at least as a grad student, my supervisor changes every year or semester, depending on the appointment. So new schedules and new expectations can be hard to get used to. I like some aspects of this frequent change, because it keeps things fresh and interesting, but I don't like the early stages of a new arrangement, when I need to figure out how to relate to my new supervisor, learn new tasks and orient to new expectations.* (Dee)

Some commented on the apparent paradox of being able to understand and work with complex information that others struggle with while concurrently struggling to process basic or fundamental concepts that appear almost intuitive to others. Similarly, there was discussion of the difficulty in identifying key points of information, separating the detail from the big picture, and knowing where to focus energy. This included various aspects of the academic role such as reading literature, writing for publication, reviewing others' writing, preparing lectures, and participating in administrative roles.

> *I find it difficult to catch up with the exponentially increasing amount of publication and literature.... Figures are catching my attention, but I often have to go through the text multiple times, otherwise I tend to catch the details and skip the overarching question and results. The reverse comes true as I find it difficult to write synthesis articles and find bounds as to what is appropriate to say instead of listing everything.* (Henry)

> *I struggle to focus with writing. *Everything* is important about a topic, because it wouldn't be what it is without all the details. So the advice when publishing in my discipline to 'tell us what's important, not what you know' is pretty much impossible.* (Liam)

Executive functioning challenges were frequently mentioned, and it was evident that these interact with the complex nature of academic roles. Reflections included issues of managing deadlines and requirements, organising data, staying on top of tasks, remembering things that need to be done, initiating activities, switching between activities, and maintaining focus. A common issue was working in a role that required working on multiple projects at one time and the cognitive load involved in managing the range of tasks, competing deadlines, and different task requirements. This is consistent with a recent study into employment experiences of autistic adults that found multi-directional associations between executive function, anxiety, and work performance (Woolard, Stratton, et al. 2021). Academia is an information-rich, rapidly changing work environment where there is a constant need to juggle multiple tasks and perspectives, which poses significant challenges for people with limitations on their executive functioning and working memory (Habib, Harris, et al. 2019).

All of those who mentioned executive functioning challenges also outlined the range of strategies they have put in place to address them, including writing copious lists, setting up calendar reminders, and using a range of physical and electronic organisation tools. Some compensated for executive functioning limitations by taking on part-time roles but working more hours than they were paid for, others by living with a constant feeling that they were not meeting the goals set for them, and others by pushing themselves to the extreme to meet the expectations of supervisors. However, it was also evident that managing their executive functioning challenges – while remaining model employees who consistently meet the demands of the role – has a significant impact on their well-being.

> *There are many challenges in my job. Time management is probably the biggest. Part of it is that I have terrible problems with executive function, and the only way I've found to manage that is to be militarily organised, as I mentioned before – which is exhausting. I have lists for everything, and they have to be on my phone, otherwise I lose them. Even tasks that need doing in ten minutes time – I have to write them down.* (Louise)

> *I can be very organised, but I am also wary that this organisation comes at a cost. In order to not become overwhelmed, I have to write a lot of to do lists, plan things out in a calendar and have a lot of organisational tools to manage my executive dysfunction. So what appears to be organisation and time management skills I think is just compensation for executive functioning difficulties.* (Scarlett)

> *Challenges include multitasking and managing executive function issues, so I stay organized and on task, otherwise I get quickly overwhelmed and stressed. Staying organized and on top of everything takes a huge amount of energy and I often come home exhausted, shutdown and nonverbal from the effort of socializing and organizing myself.* (Trevor)

The combination of these issues can make academia a particularly challenging environment for autistic people. As Psyche articulates below, rapid and frequent change combined with sensory and information overload combined with social exclusion can lead to missing important information.

> *Also, whenever there is a new function or procedure that the staff must perform in their work, rather than commit this new action to memory and incorporate it into their daily routine, my colleagues simply put up more notices that everybody ignores. It becomes very difficult to recognise when a new and important notice is placed up for us to take into consideration, as there are so many different notices plastered everywhere! Moreover, I am seldom included in the day-to-day socialising discussions that take place among my colleagues, so often these notices are the only means for me to glean new pieces of information, and my inability to notice new signs due to visual overwhelm has been responsible for me making many a mistake or missing vital information in the workplace.* (Psyche)

We Speak Different Languages

Communication in the workplace was identified as a significant challenge by almost all. This included both understanding others and being understood by others. Challenges in receptive communication included understanding questions from students and colleagues (e.g., in the context of questions from the class/audience following a presentation), understanding and following vague instructions from supervisors, and following conversations with others. As with non-work interactions, these issues are exacerbated by the energy required to manage the sensory overload that comes with interpersonal interactions, particularly in group settings. Challenges in expressive communication included difficulty finding the right words, expressions, and tone of voice; being expected to respond spontaneously; knowing how to start and end conversations; and a frequent feeling that others don't understand their communication.

> *I have also found it challenging to possess a different system for processing information, which is visual instead of auditory. I have to write all verbal instructions down, otherwise I lose track very quickly of what is being said as I'm so intently focusing on the social interaction, such as not making strange body movements and maintaining eye contact. This difficulty in following instructions is made considerably worse by the strange way in which my neurotypical colleagues fail to use the correct words to communicate their meaning.* (Psyche)

Many of these communication issues were associated with different ways of thinking, and being in the neuro-minority in the workplace. Group members described complex and high-level internal thinking processes, including making links between seemingly unrelated concepts, visual thinking, and being able to perceive and think in patterns. While these are common strengths of autistic brains and contribute to our ability to develop complex and novel solutions to problems, they can be difficult to explain to others. These differences in processing and communication styles also result in contributions being overlooked or dismissed, and a feeling of not being seen as a valuable member of the team.

> *My own difficulties in seeing the world as the neuromajority does – I've devoted my life to understanding how the every-day person sees the world and thinks, but it remains a complex, ambiguous, and baffling thought process. Physics wasn't easy, but it was easier for me to earn a PhD in physics than it was to figure out how people use language to communicate and how they perceive my words and deeds.* (Dave)

> *Exploding thinking – I think in exploding bursts of information, (think of throwing up confetti and being able to see each piece as it falls to the ground), often my thought processes goes from A to F.... When asked to explain reasoning behind something I have conveyed my brain can shut down and go blank as I search for a way to explain what I mean. Sometimes I talk very fast, like lighting is racing through my body. Other times I talk slow and disjointed taking longer to articulate and answer things. This frustrates and confuses people.* (Baz)

> *If it's not something I'm super passionate or motivated about, I often end up just being quiet all the time and trying not to take up any space because I know people don't want my input. I wonder if they think that suggesting improvements or alternatives equates to hijacking the project/task or taking leadership, rather than trying to help enhance the product. I don't know but I don't feel welcome participating in group work as a result. I'm unfairly disadvantaged when staff don't know about autism.* (Evelyn)

Difficulties in written communication are also problematic for autistic people working in hierarchical university environments, particularly learning the nuances of correspondence such as emails and formal letters. These skills are perceived to be intuitive to non-autistic people, and there is often a lack of awareness that as autistics we may need additional support and direct guidance to learn these complex social rules.

> *In academia, we have to interact with types of people we hadn't interacted with before, and in contexts and for purposes that are completely new to us. Things like emailing research participants, approaching people to seek permission to recruit participants, and the scariest, writing cover letters and emailing editors. I can't help but feel I was extremely underprepared to work out how to navigate the different forms of communication. It's all so unfamiliar. It's all so new.*

I know other people may not find it as difficult to work out what level of formality is required to email a research participant, or an editor, for example, but I also know that autistic people aren't the only ones who could benefit from some scaffolding here. (Jade)

Several discussed being sensitive to criticism from others, and being worn down by negative feedback from supervisors, colleagues, or students. There was a recognition that this reaction to criticism was in part due to over-sensitivity, but also that there was often unfair criticism due to poor communication from others or a tendency to attribute problems to them rather than to others due to their autism being seen as the 'reason' for problems arising. Several mentioned often internalising this criticism and perseverating over how they may have contributed to the communication issues or negative outcomes.

I'm also quite a private person, particularly as I have previously suffered domestic abuse, so being so public about my health and neurotype can feel quite scary and exposing. I worry all the time that I will be criticised, that I will say the wrong thing, that people will say I'm not autistic enough, or will undermine or ignore my work because of my diagnosis. (Louise)

I automatically take things to heart too quickly if I think that someone has criticised my work, particularly since I'm working my butt off and it's unpaid. I'm consciously trying to make myself change that automatic response, and instead consider whether communication could have been more clear, etc., and not take things personally. (Ava)

Lack of Autism Awareness

Almost all of the group members commented on the lack of awareness of, and misunderstandings about, autism. Many expend considerable emotional energy trying to correct these misperceptions, but find themselves frequently ignored or dismissed based on 'learnings' from media exposure or limited exposure to autistic people. A common concern was the impact of others' negative and dismissive comments about autism. Those who had disclosed were negatively impacted by ableist assumptions about their capacity, and those who had not disclosed by offhand insults and negative comments about autism from people who were not aware of their diagnosis. These challenges were in some ways greater for those working specifically in autism research, with constant exposure to literature that positions autism as a deficit and to practices that are harmful to autistic people.

HOWEVER, being an autistic autism researcher can be very hard. So much of the literature I have to read is, at best, incredibly ableist and, at worst, completely dehumanizing. People do not consider that I may be autistic when they meet me, and speak to me in ways that is often very upsetting and insulting about autism and autistic people. (Louise)

It can sometimes be difficult to work – as I do – in a field of research where autism is perceived as a clinical disorder with deficits. On a daily basis, I hear and read remarks about autism and other neuro-minorities that can be quite demeaning and insulting . . ., the remarks are thoughtless and inconsiderate, and if my self-esteem was anything less than rock-solid, I imagine they would be pretty devastating. (Scott)

It was extra difficult, given that my thesis advisor didn't really understand my struggles, so she was always disappointed with me when I told her I couldn't do various things (e.g., be a guest speaker for one of her courses or attend a conference as a presenter). I think part of my frustration is that one of my colleagues under the same advisor (also an autistic female) was able to go to all these conferences and speak in public, so I think my advisor thought I was making excuses or something because she saw that this other autistic person was able to do the things that I couldn't do. It's almost like as soon as people know you're autistic, they automatically assume every autistic person acts the same way, even though we don't (and when you don't live up to their standards of how an autistic person is 'supposed to be' somehow you're the failure!). (Emma)

Intersectionality poses additional challenges, with some of the group experiencing offensive and demeaning commentary about multiple aspects of their identity. Issues of discrimination based on gender, race, sexuality, and other characteristics are cumulative and contribute to feeling unwelcome or unsafe in academia. For some this created a hostile work environment that is both exhausting and damaging.

Although I'm pretty new to academia, I don't feel like being autistic is something people really understand. A lot of negative portrayals in the media make us look like heartless, unempathetic, self-absorbed control freaks and I think a lot of people buy into that. I am also aware that as a woman, women's voices are rarely heard or valued, or promoted in the workplace, etc., so adding autism to that makes for a challenging combination when it comes to commanding respect or demonstrating expertise. (Evelyn)

Often in academia, I will be corrected in my statements about Autistic culture, individuals, and language by those who are not Autistic. Faculty, and staff will tell me that I am incorrect given that they have family members who are Autistic and therefore they are knowledgeable about autism. Much like being Black (which I am) or Indigenous (which I am), there are nuances and swift growth/ changes from within the culture that cannot always be seen from outside of the culture. It is an added job for me to educate or re-educate those around me regarding autism. This is tiring. (Kelly)

I also experienced enough antisemitism in my academic career to make me feel terribly isolated. One of the problems is that I was never sure if people hate me because I am autistic, or if they hate me because I'm Jewish. (Mia)

Autism-Unfriendly Environments

Physical aspects of the work environment pose additional challenges for autistic academics, particularly those with sensory sensitivities. The most common concerns raised were bright lights, noise, and air conditioning. Several commented that this constant sensory input led to sensory overload and meltdown. This is consistent with findings from a recent UK survey of the experiences of autistic teachers (Wood and Happé 2023).

The sensory challenges were exacerbated by institutional policies such as who is 'entitled' to an office, lack of awareness, and lack of willingness to make necessary environmental adjustments.

I have sensory integration issues in classrooms and offices where bright lights are used. I also struggle with air conditioners and find it difficult to maintain my composure when a room is too cold for me. (Trina)

Doing any work during a sensory meltdown has always been a struggle, one I tackle in part by simply not doing much work when I'm in the middle of one and making up for it on my good days – a flexible schedule is key to success with this challenge. (Dave)

Sensory issues can make my role very uncomfortable and fatiguing. I need adjustment to my workplace to manage sensory issues and social demands, otherwise I become exhausted. (Trevor)

It is noteworthy that several of these reflections came from people who work in institutions that one would expect to be responsive to sensory issues, such as autism-focused research and training centres.

While many expressed frustration with the status quo, others seemed resigned to working in inappropriate conditions despite the evident cost to their well-being (and the minimal expense and effort it would require for organisations to address these issues).

And the office that they put me in for when I do go in to the office, pre-COVID, of course, it's quite bright, and they thought they'd try and help by removing a light bulb above my desk, but that doesn't really help. But it's the thought that counts. And they also seated me next to, like in sort of a shared office, and there's quite a bit of movement, which is quite distracting, but I guess they don't . . .

They didn't really sort of think about that, I guess. And yeah, I'm only in there once a fortnight, so there's no point in me making a fuss about it. (Charlotte)

Some Final Thoughts

While many of the social challenges are not unique to academia (North 2023), they are exacerbated by both the transient nature of social groups (such as student cohorts) and the complex dynamics between collaboration and competition. The competitive nature of academia, with its implicit motivators to withhold knowledge from others, is problematic even for neurotypical people (Hernaus, Cerne, et al. 2019) but is exacerbated for autistic academics, who typically have fewer social networks. A recent study concluded that a competitive psychological climate is associated with high work engagement and career success for people with high leader-member exchange (strong relationships between employees and supervisors), but with burnout and lower career success for those with low leader-member exchange (Spurk, Hofer, and Kauffeld 2021).

It was concerning to note the extent to which many participants accepted the challenges of working in academia as inevitable and/or requiring them to 'try harder' to navigate these challenges. As Martin, Barnham, and Krupa (2019) note, autistic employees can flourish in the workplace when provided with supportive working environments; employers need to be aware of, and willing to provide, the reasonable adjustments for autistic employees to achieve their potential.

Many of the challenges identified by the group – and echoed in the literature and in the lived experience of autistic academics worldwide – could be remediated by adjustments to the physical environment and workload, such as flexible working hours and workspaces that allow control over sensory input. Others demonstrate the need for education of supervisors and colleagues on how to work with and support autistic employees. There was some optimism among the group that perhaps some of the adjustments to working arrangements that were necessitated by the pandemic could lead to ongoing acceptance of more flexible working arrangements that are better suited to the sensory and social energy levels of many autistic people.

I am excited about the increased usage of virtual teaching and learning opportunities as this format removes many barriers for me such as inability to drive and perceptual and motor issues. Most barriers are more of an issue in person than on video chat or asynchronous communication. Also, with remote work I would have minimal sick time whereas sometimes minor illnesses make my sensory processing issues severe enough that I cannot be in public places but would still be capable of working from home or meeting via video chat. I hope that after COVID is under control that some of these things that have been put in place stay, including virtual options for attending non-local conferences. (Eva)

CHAPTER 6

Identity

I had only ever been exposed to the negative rhetoric around autism, so to be diagnosed with such an awful thing was devastating. But then, I reconnected with an autistic family I had known since school, and they showed me the positives around autism. Things like our honesty, sense of humour, loyalty, passion, attention to detail, and more. So, I started to feel it was okay. Then when I met new autistic people, it was weird. I went to an autism group meeting thing and it was the first time I had truly felt at home. It was amazing. I had never felt like I had belonged so much and it was an instant feeling. And with that feeling, with that belonging, I realised autism wasn't a bad thing. It was great. They were such an awesome bunch. If I belonged to a group with such awesome people than I am bloody honoured! I identify as autistic.

(Jade)

This chapter explores the experience of receiving a diagnosis (or reaching a point of self-diagnosis) and how this diagnosis impacted on the participants and their self-identity. It examines the extent to which they have developed (or are developing) a positive autistic identity, and the terminology they use to describe themselves and their diagnosis.

Diagnosis

Only four of the participants reported being diagnosed as a child, two of these in their teens. Of the four, two were male and two female; two were living in the United States, one in Canada, and one in Australia; and they ranged in age from twenty-five to fifty-eight at the time of completing the reflections.

I was a bright toddler who spoke early and was speaking in full sentences at a year old. . . . By the time I entered school motor delays, lack of eye contact, Inability to read body language, and talking at people about subjects of interest were apparent. I was labeled as Non-verbal learning disability with autistic tendencies at age 4 and Asperger's at 13. Academically, I excelled in most subjects but required some accommodations and tutoring in math-based courses. (Eva)

I was diagnosed when I was in Year 9 at school, age 14.5. Earlier in the year, I'd written a 6-page personal writing piece about my "speech problem". The English teacher had her suspicions, so spoke to mum who organised private testing during the July school holidays.... Terminology in the report (July 1997) => "mild Aspergers disorder". (Jane)

After 18 months of typical development I was struck by the regressive autism bomb: losing functional communication, meltdowns, withdrawal from the environment, and became a very autistic little kid. At age 2 and a half I was diagnosed and was recommended for institutionalization. Fortunately, my parents advocated on my behalf and convinced the school to take me in about a year.... By about age 5 and a half my speech and environmental awareness had progressed to a point where I knew I was autistic as my parents used the word around the house just like any other word.... There was no shame about being autistic. It just was. (Moon Man)

Of the remainder who had a formal diagnosis at the time of completing their reflection, seven were diagnosed in their twenties, twelve in their thirties, and nine in their forties or later. Consistent with the literature on late diagnosis, some explicitly reflected on being aware they were autistic prior to the diagnosis, whereas many instead alluded to a lifetime of feeling 'different' or 'faulty.' For many the diagnostic process was long and complex, and followed a series of misdiagnoses.

I was diagnosed at the age of 37. As the diagnostic process is male oriented and I was a young child back in the 1980s when autism was even less understood than it is now, all my autistic behaviours and challenges were completely missed. Instead I was given other labels such as bipolar, anxious, stroppy, difficult, overemotional, non-conformist, depressed, uncooperative, airy fairy, and extremist. Like most people my teenage years were messy, but unlike most people I concluded that this was because I was broken, inefficient, and completely unwanted. My early adult life was not much easier. (Psyche)

I was diagnosed at the age of 36 (2019). I had sought an autism diagnosis about 10 years earlier, but the psychologist I saw didn't have a background in ASD specifically and suggested I had social phobia (which never really made sense to me). I started to self-identify (internally) a few years ago, but last year I decided that I wanted to formally seek a diagnosis . . . so that I could be more open about my identity (the strengths and the challenges).... I realised that I felt like I wasn't being completely honest with people because I wasn't outwardly identifying myself as autistic. (Scarlett)

My diagnosis story is a bit convoluted, and my feelings about my diagnosis have changed over time. My social difficulties, sensory issues and fixated interests were all strongly present since I was a child. However, when I was professionally assessed in 1984 at the age of 12 the diagnosis I received was ADD. At the time of my assessment as a child the only autism condition was "infantile autism" which I did not meet criteria for. I was reassessed in my 20's, but my well established ADHD diagnosis technically excluded me from receiving the new DSM-IV Asperger's diagnosis as the criteria didn't allow both ADHD and Asperger's to be diagnosed at the same time.... All this masking and compensating for my difficulties had a terrible effect on my mental health and in 2019 I was admitted to a psychiatric hospital for a about a month which was a very frightening and humbling experience.... I was officially diagnosed ASD in my final week in hospital. (Trevor)

The diagnostic process was often described by AFAB participants as being a slow and convoluted process, consistent with the literature on gender differences in diagnostic experiences. Female-identifying participants often came to the realisation that they were autistic following the recognition of autism in male partners or family members, and learning more about autism in women.

I was sixteen years old when I stumbled on an online article talking about the experience of an autistic woman.... She talked about how she didn't like shopping or makeup or all of the 'typical' things that girls enjoy, and suddenly it was like my whole life finally made sense.... After that, I immersed myself in autism literature (and autism questionnaires) because I guess I thought I needed to somehow prove to myself that I was autistic. So, time passed, and finally, when I was twenty-three, I underwent a psycho-educational assessment where I was officially diagnosed as autistic (or asperger's). (Emma)

My diagnosis story is a fairly long one. I didn't know very much about autism at all before 2007; my only encounters were a couple of films about autistic people such as Rain Man. I remember the first time I read about Aspergers was in 2007. I had not long been with my now ex-husband when I started googling his behaviour, as I was finding it tricky to understand. He had this habit of looking at me when he was talking to my parents, which I didn't really understand. Aspergers came up, and that started an avalanche of research on my part. I read lots of online articles, which were very enlightening about my ex, but also raised questions about myself, and my Dad. Then I read Tony Attwood's Aspergers guidebook from cover to cover. I remember reading the part about girls and being beside myself for weeks afterward. I didn't really talk to anyone about it, I just kept reading and re-reading.... There was a book by Sarah Hendrickx and after I read that, I knew. (Louise)

The diagnosis was described by the majority of the participants as having a significant positive impact on their life. For many of those diagnosed as an adult – particularly those diagnosed during university studies or employment challenges – the motivation for seeking a diagnosis was to be able to access necessary accommodations to support them in their work or study. However, when I asked about the positive outcomes of the diagnosis, few reflected on these pragmatic outcomes, or mentioned them more than in passing.

> *The diagnosis has been positive for me because of the accommodations I've been able to receive (light filters at work, a temporary handicap parking permit to keep me from having to drive through brightly lit parking structures on campus).* (Trina)

Far more evident in the reflections was a consistent expression of the impact on identity, self-esteem, and self-worth that resulted from the diagnosis. Even amongst those diagnosed in childhood, the diagnosis was described as having a significant positive impact on self-concept. But for those diagnosed as adults, finally having a name, a reason, and a framework for understanding why they were 'different' from others brought an overwhelming sense of relief. For many this was accompanied by the realisation that – contrary to a lifetime of self-doubt and internal criticism – they were not fundamentally flawed but rather living in a world that was not designed to accommodate their needs. This is a common finding in research on adult-diagnosed autistics, that the revelation that one is a perfectly normal and adequate autistic person, not a broken neurotypical person, is life-changing (Hickey, Crabtree, and Stott 2018; Tan 2018; Arnold, Huang, et al. 2020; Lilley, Lawson, et al. 2022). While beyond the scope of this book, it would be remiss of me not to mention that this is why it is so important that we all continue to advocate for access to low-cost diagnostic services for people of all ages.

> *Receiving a diagnosis suddenly explained SO much of my entire life and my daily experience. So many seemingly random things suddenly made sense and came together as part of one bigger, common picture. It gave me a strong sense of relief about the past and the present (that certain things are not my fault; it's just the way I'm wired) and also an important sense of possibility about the future. It also gave me a better understanding of where some recurrent issues come from and how best to address them.* (Amy)

> *The diagnosis was a great relief. I could finally understand why I behave, think, and see the world and other people the way I do. This realization has helped me to learn how I can better navigate in the society and overcome my cognitive and emotional limitations. The diagnosis has helped me to revise my identity in a positive way.* (Betty)

> *The diagnosis changed my life because it helped me understand my life in a different way. It helped me realize that I don't need to be 'fixed'. I'm just different from most people, and that's totally okay. The diagnosis took away a lot*

of my self-loathing and hatred. When you think you're supposed to be a certain way, but you're unable to be that way, you start to think that it's all your fault that you can't be like that. If it's so easy for everyone else, why is it so hard for you? I'm sure you can imagine how those thoughts can spiral into self-loathing and negativity. (Emma)

Receiving a diagnosis also led to the revelation that they were not alone in their way of being in the world, and that they were in fact part of a community with similar strengths and challenges. Many reported seeking out connections with the autistic community – whether online or in person – and the sense of connection and belonging this brought to their lives.

The diagnosis was perhaps the most pivotal moment of my life. To learn that your weirdness has a name, and that other human beings struggle with the same things you do, see the world the way you do, was a profound revelation. I came to have a much deeper and nuanced understanding of myself and "normal" people, and that has helped me to better understand people and empathize with them. (Dave)

It was an intense experience and situation. I'd spent a long time building an identity and simply accepting that I was some kind of undefined "crazy," destigmatizing the frames of that term, and making peace with the idea that I'd never meet anyone else like me. And then all of a sudden POW there were not just others like me but a WHOLE COMMUNITY of others like me with culture and language and history and belongingness and, also, I wasn't broken I was exactly as I needed to be. (Sunny)

I know who my people are because my diagnosis made me know more about who I am. This is huge because I've never felt more a part of society than I have when I joined the autistic community, whether through online fora or simply being "out" to other autistics and forging relationships with people like me. (Evelyn)

For many, this change in perspective led to being kinder to themselves, more realistic in their expectations, and accepting of their limitations. For some this extended to significant life changes, such as a change in career (including being the impetus for the transition into a career in academia). Similar experiences have been reported in studies with late-diagnosed autistic adults outside the academic setting, including changes in careers, relationships, and living arrangements (Leedham, Thompson, et al. 2020).

Before I realized that I'm autistic, I put a lot of pressure on myself to understand social rules and meet every social demand. I was in awe of colleagues who could teach class, attend back-to-back meetings, and have energy to attend an event at the end of the day. I blamed myself for not working hard enough, for not being available enough to students, for not speaking up in meetings, or for misunderstanding a situation everyone else seemed to get. Realizing that I am autistic helped me develop compassion for myself, rather than blaming myself for being wrong or incompetent. Through research and continued learning, I've also found some practical tools and strategies to make life and work easier. (Marie)

I think I'm probably a lot nicer to myself now. I just cut myself a lot more slack. I don't beat myself up over not being able to do or be okay with the same things that non autistic people can do or are okay with. (Charlotte)

... having the diagnosis confirmed was a very positive thing for me, and really validated a lot of my feelings about being different. It also helped me understand why I had been feeling overwhelmed in certain environments, as I learned about sensory overload and started being able to take steps to mitigate it. Realizing that I'm autistic led to an intense reevaluation of my life history, and ultimately led me to go back to school and completely change my career path. (Dee)

I went back to grad school to get my doctoral degree researching autism and higher education. I spent the past 3 years studying autism so I was able to educate myself while immersing in Autistic social groups. (Kelly)

The group identified few negative outcomes of diagnosis (although they did reflect on negative outcomes from disclosure, which will be discussed in Chapter 7). In fact, the predominant negative emotions expressed were grief and regret that they had not being diagnosed earlier.

... it was a huge relief ... it was also a source of grief, regret and anger that I believe I am still processing. My diagnosis began a process I still participate in today, sometimes by will and other times by accident ... where I may have a random or associated memory come to mind and then have to re-write the meaning of that memory viewing it through the lens of my diagnosis. (Flora)

It made me take full stock of my life and caused me both pain and relief because now I could begin to forgive myself for areas of my life I had little or no control over. I was sad that I didn't understand myself earlier and could live a more full life knowing how my neurology affected me. I was relieved because I could move forward now with the rest of my life. (Kelly)

This initial relief was followed quite quickly by a lot of anger.... A mourning of all that I had lost, a miserable childhood, precarious and often suicidal teens and early twenties, the money and time lost on trying to fit in, the self-medicating with alcohol and self-destructive behaviour because no amount of effort on my part gave me a feeling of being connected to other people. The horrible trauma of school and work and all the confusing and dangerous social interactions that all of a sudden made perfect sense ... (Louise)

There was a period of grieving and feeling very let down by the system. Looking back, I was a textbook Autistic kid. These days, I reckon I would have been diagnosed as a toddler. It did feel like a real blow, but also was the beginning of being able to structure a more sustainable lifestyle. (Ruth)

The consistent message that receiving an autism diagnosis was a predominantly positive experience that helped this group of academics to make sense of themselves, to find their place in the world, and to accept that they are not 'flawed neurotypical' human beings is a consistent finding across studies with other cohorts of people, as summarised in a recent meta-ethnographic systematic review (Gellini and Marczak 2023).

Identity

There is a growing body of literature on the link between diagnosis, acceptance, and identity, with consistent findings that those who have a positive perception of autism and have integrated this into their self-identity tend to have higher self-esteem, along with a greater degree of self-acceptance and self-compassion (Corden, Brewer, and Cage 2021).

Many of the participants reported having developed a strong sense of autistic identity, integrating their diagnosis into their self-identity in a very positive way. For many this was associated with making connections with other autistic people, either as life partners and close friends or broader social networks. This protective value of group identity has also been noted in research with older autistic adults, with post-diagnosis connection to autistic peers serving as a buffer to feelings of isolation and loneliness (Hickey, Crabtree, and Stott 2018).

> *My autistic identity is now a huge part of who I am. Since learning I'm autistic, I've become involved in the autistic community, taken up autism research as a career, and become an autistic activist and advocate. My partner is autistic, as are most of my friends. I feel much more comfortable and confident since immersing myself in the autistic world. I'm proud to be autistic, I love my autistic community and I'm passionate about making the world a better place for the next generation of autistic people. I definitely struggle with internalised ableism at times and still deal with feeling "broken" or "not good enough", but it's much easier to deal with those feelings now compared to before my diagnosis.* (Alex)

> *All of this contributed to forming my positive autistic self. Finally thinking, I can stop trying and failing to do things I will probably never be able to do because my brain isn't wired that way, I can stop trying to fit in – I ain't gonna fit in anyway! Being autistic is not the only thing that makes me different as I'm also mixed race. I feel proud to be autistic now. I love it when autistic people in the public eye 'come out'. Finally, at 44, I have accepted myself.* (Olivia)

Those diagnosed as children also expressed a sense of positive autistic identity. Consistent with previous research (Riccio, Kapp, et al. 2021), they noted that this was underpinned by their parents' positive framing of autism and acceptance of them as they were while also supporting them with their challenges. For some, early polarizing perspectives of autism (likely developed as a form of defence mechanism) evolved to more nuanced understandings of the value of all neurotypes.

> *My parents focused on my abilities, strengths, and interests rather than what I couldn't do. Certainly the challenges and disabilities of autism at that time were recognized and addressed. However, the philosophy was that they were barriers that needed to be torn down in order to achieve success.* (Moon Man)

> *Today, my autistic identity is intertwined with my understanding of the neurodiversity approach, which I do understand to require the acceptance of people regardless of their neurotype. I'm still conscious of the various strengths my autism gives me, but I reject the idea that there should be any link between someone's ability and their worth as a person.* (Scott)

For many, a fundamental part of accepting and valuing their autistic identity was recognizing the strengths and abilities that are associated with autism, rather than just the challenges that are reflected in the diagnostic criteria.

> *If I weren't autistic, I don't think I'd do so well in academia. The intense focus and passion I have I attribute in part at least to autism. And it's a part of myself I love. And I don't think I'd choose not to be autistic if I could. I'd choose for people to have treated me better, but not to be different.* (Evelyn)

> *I have a very clear understanding of the challenges I face – and the way that autism is my disability – but I also have a strong appreciation for the way it enhances my life, and gives me strengths and skills that a lot of allistics don't have. I can now see and understand myself and the way that I relate to people as a difference in processing, rather than as something being fundamentally wrong with me.... I've now built my life around my autism, to help nourish my autistic strengths while reducing the things that disable me.* (Ella)

> *I do feel autism gives me strengths in some way. I work for [organisation] and even though I am a newbie, I can do three times as much work as a person with five years of experience. However, it brings out extremities in me as well as I tend to be exceptionally well or exceptionally bad in any work item, never mediocre. In fact, I prefer people with boons and banes compared to well-rounded people. As an example, I would prefer someone get an 'A' and an 'F' over two 'C's'.* (Proline)

Others reported being on the journey to acceptance, reflecting on their transition from seeing autism as a problem or a negative aspect of themselves, to be ashamed of and overcome, to seeing it as a core part of themselves. The challenges they describe in this process are similar to the stages Gill (1997) describes as 'coming to feel we belong' (an individual acknowledging that they have the right to be included in society as an equal) and 'coming together' (integrating the different parts of one's internal self), which he posits are two of the four stages of disability identity integration.

> *I believe I'm still in the early stages of this process, but I think I'm on my way toward a positive autistic identity. I do not see autism as a disease or a problem to be solved.* (Marie)

> *It took me quite a while to really embrace the identity – 6 years ago the DSM had only recently transitioned away from Asperger's and I had a lot of internalised ableism around the word 'autistic'. I also had literally no idea how to bring it up in conversation with people (I still don't), particularly with people who already knew me as a 'functional adult' and who I predicted would start in with the whole 'you don't look autistic' thing. I've come a long way since then but it's an ongoing process and there are still people in my life who don't know I'm autistic.... Still a long way to go on this too and a lot of ableist cultural baggage to unpack but it's made a huge impact on me this year. Also seeing how me being open and positive about my identity helps other people around me makes it a bit easier.* (Morgan)

Those who had in a sense 'completed' the journey recognised that this was a process that needed to be worked through, and would be said to have completed all four of the identity integration stages, the remaining two being 'coming home' (integrating with the disability community) and 'coming out' (integrating how we feel with how we present ourselves) (Gill 1997).

> *Now I am 42, I feel very comfortable with who I am as an autistic person and what that means to me personally in terms of my identity. It is taken five years, but now I can be confident about which autistic traits are true of me and which are not, and how to work with these to give me the best experience of life.* (Psyche)

Several participants reflected on having mixed or conflicted feelings about autism and their identity as an autistic person. For some this was due to the trade-off between the strengths and challenges associated with being autistic. However, for many it related to concerns about public misperceptions about autism, anticipated and experienced ableism, internalised ableism (Huang, Hwang, et al. 2022), and the ongoing risks of discrimination and marginalisation that they faced as an autistic person.

> *There are many positive aspects of being autistic which I like about myself and help me in my life. I like my unique way of thinking and my ability to focus intensely on something. I like my ability to accumulate and remember useful*

> *information which I am respected for. I like my honesty and loyalty and moral integrity. I can relate easily to neurodiverse people as I understand the experience of being different. I also greatly enjoy a good stim. However, there are also many aspects of being autistic that quite frankly are a pain in the arse and can be burdensome to me and to my family. Especially my anxiety, vulnerability to stress, sensory issues, executive function problems and how hard I need to work in social situations. My ability to focus has a downside and that is I find it hard to let go of things that are in my best interests to let go of.... I used to think my autistic traits were something to be ashamed of and tried to hide them. But, I'm more accepting of my differences and that has made me less miserable than I had been before I could do that.* (Trevor)

> *I would say it's mixed. I don't buy into the more extreme end of the neurodiversity movement that completely ignores impairment – either I would rather not have autism or I would rather have had a diagnosis in childhood so I could have developed a functional way of being in this world at a much earlier age.... But I'm also aware that resentment is pointless since my particular diagnosis wasn't available in childhood, and also that autism is a big part of who I am. Quite simply I'm too early in the process of adjusting and have too much else going on (for example the more recent ADHD diagnosis) to have yet come to a stable relationship with the diagnosis.* (Liam)

Previous research with autistic women has identified the importance of a culture of understanding and acceptance, as well as access to appropriate health and social care, in the relationship between autism and well-being (Harmens, Sedgewick, and Hobson 2022). This study found that, while diagnosis is initially associated with improvements in identity and well-being, the improvement is not linear without the supportive environment. A recent meta-synthesis of qualitative studies in the United Kingdom concluded that most autistic people receive limited post-diagnosis support (Wilson, Thompson, et al. 2023), a systemic problem which is not unique to that country. This was evident in a number of the reflections, particularly in relation to the lack of understanding and acceptance of autism in their workplaces and the associated stigma, which limited their capacity to acknowledge their autistic identity.

> *I have mixed feelings about my autism. I am feeling fine with it but the fact that I am hiding it makes me uncomfortable. The decision to hide it comes from understanding the fear my loved ones have that people might reject me, criticize me, make fun of me or not take me seriously anymore, especially professionally.... I try to support other autistic people, especially autistic students but I feel uncomfortable not telling them that I do not only understand what they are going through from the outside, but that I have been there myself. It feels dishonest.* (Sophia)

> *I am autistic and say it. I think it helps me and gives me some advantages. It gives me disadvantages/has its drawbacks too. I am not necessarily ashamed but I've learned to be cautious about saying it. I need to come up with a short and sweet way for people to get it without inducing bias. Is that positive? I think I feel positive about it.* (Isabella)

> *I feel like most of my strengths arise from my autistic brain. I still struggle with allistic wants and needs, especially when they won't articulate them directly. Being "out" with my identity has been a mixed bag, though. It makes me feel included among other neurodivergent people, but at my university there is still a stereotype of cognitive difference as marker of inferiority, so although I will disclose it when relevant, I don't broadcast it.* (Saskia)

> *I feel a little guilty that I haven't really embraced it yet. I always feel like an imposter, no matter what groups I'm in. I feel guilty for not being "out, loud and proud", but I honestly hate the word "Autism" because of the stigma and misinformation and misunderstandings and the way people make those limiting judgements.... When I'm with Autistic people, I'm more relaxed and feel safer about everything, but still feel guilty about not defining myself.* (Ava)

Terminology

The appropriate language for talking about autism is a constant topic of debate in the academic literature, professional practice, policy, and the autistic and autism communities (Kenny, Hattersley, et al. 2016; Bury, Jellett, et al. 2023; Keating, Hickman, et al. 2023). Just as there is no absolute consensus in any of those forums, the participants expressed a diversity of views. However, there were some common themes and predominant perspectives.

Not surprisingly, the most common theme in the reflections on terminology was the distinction between Identity-First and Person-First language. Only two participants noted a preference for PFL and five reported being comfortable with both and using the two interchangeably. Those who preferred PFL spoke of the stigma and negative attitudes associated with autism, and the use of the word 'autistic' as an insult. Those who used both spoke of the choice of term being context-specific, including what aspects of their autistic experience they are trying to describe or the grammatical structure of the sentence.

> *I would prefer to be referred to as a person on the autism spectrum. I actually don't like the word autistic. I think it has really negative connotations, and that might be because of, perhaps my age where there was a word growing up that was kind of similar, that was really quite derogatory, that was used to describe another group of people.* (Charlotte)

I vacillate between 'I am autistic' and 'I have autism' depending on the circumstances. Probably more often the latter because it comes up in the context of addressing particular sensory and cognitive issues, which isn't usually really a whole-person sort of discussion. (Liam)

I say 'I'm autistic' and I also say 'I have autism', 'my autism means that'. I'm a linguist so I use whichever fits better grammatically into what I'm saying. What makes me angry is neurotypical people telling autistic people that they should say this, shouldn't say that … it's our lived experience and we have the right to describe it any way we choose. (Olivia)

However, the overwhelming majority expressed a preference for IFL. The primary reason given for this preference relates to identity (see the 'Identity' section above), with these individuals seeing their autism as an integral part of who they are as a holistic human being. There were frequent references to PFL serving to separate the 'autism' from the 'person' and to carry the connotation that autism is something inherently bad or wrong.

Being autistic is part of my identity. "Autistic" is another category that describes my identity, much like terms that describe other people's ethnicity, race, gender, age, etc. (Betty)

I use identity-first language pretty much exclusively. I wouldn't have a principled objection to person-first language if one described neurotypicals the same way (as "people with typical development" or something), but as we don't, it seems like person-first language probably does indeed reflect stigma towards autism. (Scott)

The choice of terminology was also influenced by the complexities around the term 'Asperger's'. Many of those diagnosed after 1994 (DSM-4) would have been given this diagnosis, but it officially ceased to exist in the minds of clinicians when it was eliminated from the DSM-IV in 2013. Further, Asperger's is a controversial label in the autism community due to the revelations about Hans Asperger's role in the Nazis' eugenics program. However, consistent our with previous research in the general population (Smith and Jones 2020), those diagnosed with Asperger's are divided on whether to move away from this identification.

I exclusively identify as autistic. I find Asperger's problematic due to its Nazi-connected history; the fact it's often used within the autistic community by people who wish to somehow differentiate themselves from 'them' – some mythological idea of an 'actually' 'disabled', 'lower functioning' autistic Other (a form of ableist supremacy); and because it's not my actual diagnosis. (Ella)

I tend to use 'Aspergers' and 'Aspie', but it makes some people flare up, either because they think I'm being 'ableist', or because they think Hans Asperger was a

Nazi. My own view is that it's irrelevant what his political views are, and it's absurd to refrain from using a scientist's name because we reject his politics. That seems a dangerous rabbit hole. (Mia)

A related topic discussed in a several reflections was the use of functioning labels, with participants commenting on the harmful, separatist, and misleading nature of this terminology. The 'functioning' concept is based on a misrepresentation of the autism spectrum as a linear concept, with people being 'very autistic' (low functioning) at one end and 'not very autistic' (high functioning) at the other end. The autism spectrum is multidimensional, with people having strengths in some areas and limitations in others (Figure 6.1). Reductionist labels are harmful (Kapp 2023), particularly for those most vulnerable to marginalisation such as non-speaking autistics whose capacity is often underestimated.

I hate functioning labels and never refer to myself as "high-functioning" or anything along those lines, I think such terms are a gross oversimplification and certainly don't represent my experience. My functioning and capabilities fluctuate massively across time and context. (Alex)

I try to just keep it simple and say I am autistic. If someone tells me I must be "high-functioning", I try to explain that it's a spectrum and that neurodiversity is a part of human diversity. Occasionally, I've had people tell me that I am "too social" to be autistic and that I must have Asperger Syndrome instead. I usually just say: No, there is no more Asperger Syndrome. It is autism, and I struggle with social interaction too, but many women on the spectrum become very good at blending in socially. (Trina)

However, as Eva notes below, sometimes the focus on words rather than intentions can serve to further divide the autism community and make it difficult for autistic people to speak up.

I think sometimes there is too much focus on saying things the right way and choosing the right words in advocacy and I worry sometimes this creates more barriers where a social error may be misconstrued as a micro aggression. I am always trying to figure out what terms for autism this particular audience wants and not upsetting other autistic people or other researchers while still getting a message across. (Eva)

Some Final Thoughts

All of the participants in this study identified as autistic; thirty-four of the thirty-seven had a formal diagnosis by the time of completing the study, increasing to thirty-five by the time of writing. Many experienced significant challenges and barriers in reaching this point, not only the timely and

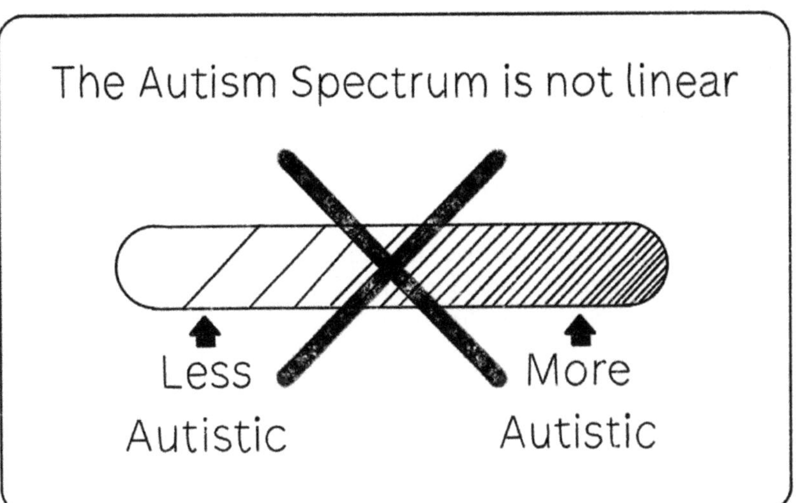

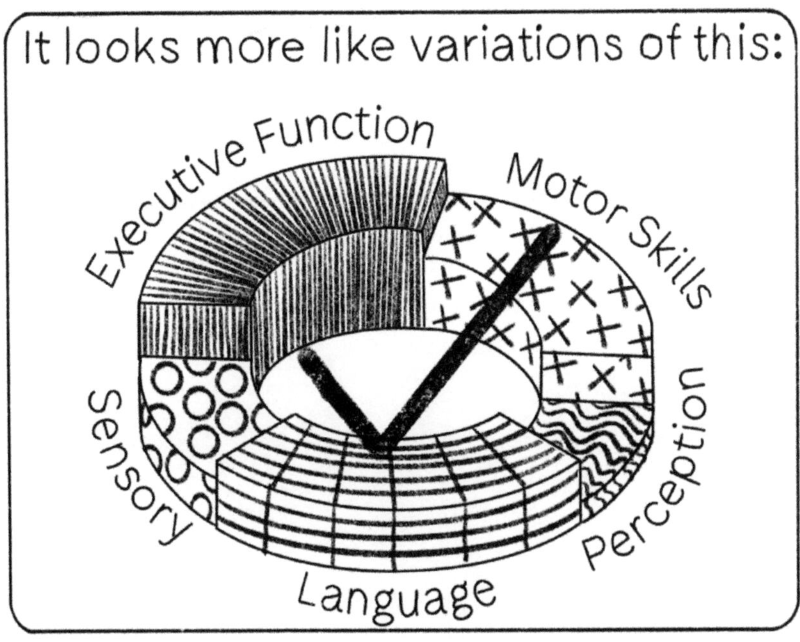

Figure 6.1 The autism spectrum. Source: Art by Chloë van der Reijden.

expensive process of a formal autism diagnosis, but for many a series of misdiagnoses along the way. However, the benefits of the diagnosis were considerable in terms of understanding and accepting themselves, being able to overcome decades of self-doubt, and being able to seek necessary accommodations to achieve their potential. This is an important finding for those who are considering whether to seek a diagnosis (particularly for parents who are considering seeking a diagnosis for their child, and wondering whether the positive outcomes will outweigh the negative). It is also an important finding for policy makers who in many countries currently only provide public diagnostic services for children, making adult diagnoses unattainable for many due to the limited availability and excessive costs of private services.

CHAPTER 7

Disclosure

> *I'm interested in the possibility of using autistic brainpower to sort of "crowd-fund" a way out of climate change.... When I spoke about my idea to the head of the [school] at [university] (sort of my "boss"), I prefaced it by telling her that I'd recently been diagnosed with autism. She told me she was very sorry, and that she has a [niece or nephew] with it, and that's really too bad."*
>
> (Lisa)

In academia, as in any profession, one of the toughest decisions facing an autistic person is whether and when to disclose their diagnosis. On the one hand, disclosure can bring awareness, understanding, and support. On the other, it can bring misunderstanding, stigma, and discrimination. In this chapter participants reflect on their decisions to disclose (or not to disclose) to employers, colleagues, staff, and students – and the impacts of these decisions. This chapter also addresses the issue of masking (hiding their autistic characteristics), including when and why participants feel the need to mask and the impacts this has on them.

Almost one-third of the group reported that they had not disclosed their autism diagnosis to their employer, including their direct supervisor and the organisation more broadly. Consistent with research with autistic adults in general employment (Romualdez, Heasman, et al. 2021), the primary reason given for not disclosing was the risk of subsequent discrimination, largely due to widespread misunderstandings of what autism is and what autistic people are able to do. Related to this was the concern that people may doubt their diagnosis as they do not fit the 'stereotype' of autistic people. Several reflected on being directly advised by mentors or others whose advice they respected that disclosure would negatively impact their career prospects in academia.

> *My sense is the sheer volume of societal misconceptions about what autism is, how it presents, who can have autism (i.e., if one only got information about autism from the mainstream media or popular culture, it would be easy to assume autistic people were only white male children), how it affects people, what accommodations might be needed, and the inherent challenges (but with little or no*

consideration of inherent strengths) would create a minefield of discomfort and challenging social situations for me – as well as facilitate misconceptions about me. I see how people change and how differently they treat people who are disabled, or queer, or people of colour, or any other marginalised group that is stigmatised. I particularly see how autistics are treated in the public space. Autistics who are read by allistics as being "really" disabled are treated with condescension, positioned as an "inspiration", and have their voices silenced because they are assumed to be incompetent. Autistics who are read by allistics as being too "high functioning" are treated with disdain, gaslit about their experiences of disability, and silenced because they are assumed to be "not autistic enough" to be disabled. I don't want to experience that treatment, so I don't disclose. (Ella)

At this point, I have been working at my organization for 15 years without [them] knowing that I am autistic. I am not sure what the response or outcome would be if I were to disclose after all this time. With this in mind, I worry that I might not find acceptance or understanding from the institution or from my colleagues. I worry that I might be passed over for leadership roles or that some colleagues might treat me with disrespect. (Marie)

I only told one colleague from another university, who is a friend of mine. She strongly recommended me not to tell anyone because of the very likely negative outcomes of disclosure. (Sophia)

She told me being autistic would likely "be seen as a red flag" and could weaken my otherwise strong application. So since then I have kept my professional life pretty separate from my autistic life, which definitely feels a little traumatic at times. I've disclosed to friends and occasional people, but for the most part I mask my heart out. In a meeting about an autistic student the other day, someone was explaining how autistic people can experience the world and said "unlike how we all do," and I cried after the meeting. (Amelia)

Cautious or partial disclosure appeared to be the norm, with most participants choosing to disclose to one or two individuals on a need-to-know basis, such as disclosing to a supervisor or colleague to resolve an issue or seek necessary supports. Some reported more 'subtle' disclosure, such as participating in closed-group activities that enabled them to connect with other autistic academics. A smaller number had made broad public disclosures, and those were predominantly individuals researching and/or teaching in autism-specific areas.

Many of those who had disclosed reflected on positive outcomes that had resulted from doing so. Primary among these were access to supports and accommodations, and acceptance of their different ways of working and communicating.

Positive outcomes included support from the organisation and supervisor, which included working from home arrangements, a separate office, and greater understanding for both myself and my supervisor of my work style and habits. (Baz)

It helped with communication with my boss tremendously and with some others. It helps me be able to ask questions and ask for help. (Isabella)

Others reflected on the role their disclosure played in increasing autism awareness and acceptance among their colleagues, with this acting as a catalyst for others to seek out more information about autism.

I have found people to be very receptive and supportive, which is nice.... I've also started to mention it in my work, when I write or present my research. I have been wanting to disclose to some people around me for some time now, and it's felt good to be able to do so, and to see not only the positive reaction of people, but also their interest in learning more about what autism is (and isn't). (Amy)

The responses I've gotten have generally been positive, at least as far as I can tell. Sometimes I can see that the person I'm talking to doesn't really know what I mean when I say that I'm autistic, but generally people have been interested in what I have to say about it.... I also think it has been helpful in terms of increasing people's understanding when I get particularly stressed or when maybe my interactions seem "off" to them. If I tell someone I'm getting overloaded from the sensory environment, or stressed out from too much uncertainty, I feel like they accept that as a valid difficulty because they've already come to understand that I may be processing things very differently than they are. At the same time, I usually feel uncomfortable admitting that I'm having any trouble, because I don't want to be seen as lesser-than or needing help. (Dee)

For some this extended to others recognising and seeking out their expertise as autistic academics, whether this was specifically in terms of 'lived experience' of autism for the purpose of research projects, or particular skill sets that they had as autistic people, such as hyperfocus.

Disclosure has led to positive things like being approached to seek my expertise as an autistic person when it comes to research, or getting work as a consultant for developing a program for autistic students. It has also helped me to connect more with other autistic people as well, and to some great autism researchers who actually value us, value our input, and conduct research that is aimed to actually benefit us. (Jade)

My first disclosure ... also led to me being asked to prepare a literature review for a grant application for research evaluating a project around access to healthcare for Autistic people. Because I already knew the literature, I was able to produce a comprehensive review in the time allocated which was well beyond the salient dot points expected. The CI for this project actually raised it at the monthly college meeting and commended me highly which was unexpected and quite lovely.... Another CI questioned the hours I claimed for thematic analysis

> *of 3,000 senate inquiry submissions as she thought I had accidentally claimed too few hours (around half of the expected time). I explained my monotropic focus as a characteristic of autism and she was quite taken aback and made a comment like, "we need more Autistic research officers!"* (Ruth)

Several commented on the positive impact of disclosure – when accompanied by acceptance – on their self-identity. This included comfort with both their identity as an autistic person and their internal need for honesty and integrity in the way they present themselves to the world.

> *I received a lot of support and encouragement from my colleagues. The disclosure in a safe environment was incredibly empowering and it helped me stabilize my identity as autistic person in a positive way.* (Betty)

> *The positive outcomes of disclosure, for me, are really personal. I committed long ago to truthfulness as a core professional value.... Who would voluntarily call themselves autistic in an institution where a lot of people still believe in meritocracy? I haven't benefited much socially from disclosure, but for me personally it's one more thing that I can be authentic about (at least one-to-one).* (Saskia)

> *The positive of disclosing . . . is that now I don't feel like I am keeping any secrets intentionally from people. There is a strong likelihood that they know and I don't feel like I'm being "fake" with anyone. It's actually more about the fact that since then I feel like I can be 'autistic' me and that's OK.* (Scarlett)

Also noted in several of the reflections was the potential for their disclosure and acceptance to flow on to positive outcomes for other autistic people and the community more broadly. Previous research has identified this altruistic view of the potential benefits of disclosure in non-academic employment, including the ability to serve as a role model for other autistic people and to demonstrate to workplaces the strengths that autistic people can bring (Romualdez, Heasman, et al. 2021).

> *I can be openly autistic in my job.... People have greater understanding for when accommodations and greater understanding are needed.... Students on the autism spectrum may be encouraged to see that autistic people can be successful (at least in academia!).* (Moon Man)

> *Positive outcomes have been numerous and varied. For one thing, autism researchers use a distressingly large amount of deficit and pathology language in a completely unselfconscious way, but it seems like knowing about my autism helps them remember to use more objective and neutral terms, or even strengths-based ones – and if they don't, I can sometimes remind them, depending on the context and whether such a reminder seems like it will be welcomed and whether it will be helpful.* (Scott)

> *I think my disclosure has been a good thing for our department at work though – people definitely think a little more carefully about how they speak about autism, knowing I will be there.... Disclosure has helped me to be kinder to myself. It can feel very exposing, and sometimes I worry that people are analysing my every move, looking for the signs etc., but I try to remind myself that every time they look at me and see a fellow human being, that is a step forward for autism ACCEPTANCE rather than autism AWARENESS.... Now, instead of trying to fit in, I tell people straight away as soon as I am struggling with facial expression or body language – I tell them, I'm sorry, I'm not good with non-verbal communication, so I will just listen to your words. I feel able to say "I need to write this down" instead of desperately trying to remember. And with the additional energy that gives me not having to mask or feel pressured to hold eye contact etc. I can find common ground with people and build relationships with them. What I've found is that being open in my autism has other effects I didn't foresee. People talk more openly about their mental health issues and physical health issues around me. They are more open about their sexuality, relationships, funny little passions and habits ... it is like my difference allows them to show their own differences without shame. I love that.* (Louise)

A minority of participants commented that the impact of their disclosure at work was neutral, or even non-existent, although I would suggest this is actually a negative outcome as it reflects a lack of awareness and/or willingness to provide a more accommodating environment.

> *There was no positive or negative outcome to the disclosure because it was never discussed again. My boss said something about how I could wear noise-cancelling earphones if I felt like it, but I work in an open concept office and everyone wears earphones when they feel like it. I wasn't referred to any resources or given any information. I believe the company has no program for autistic employees ... and therefore nothing to see when someone reaches out.* (Lisa)

> *In terms of the outcomes of disclosure, it's mostly been 'meh'. I've fortunately not had any actively negative responses, most people have just kind of said 'oh ok' and moved on with the conversation (presumably because I'm good at masking so people haven't experienced my autism particularly strongly). The downside of that though is that both my strengths and capabilities and my struggles and needs end up flying under the radar – I've only ever had one supervisor actively ask what I needed and encourage me to get formal accommodations, and maybe two or three people who acknowledge the impact being autistic has on me in terms of strengths and capabilities that others don't have.* (Morgan)

Unfortunately, many of the participants reflected on negative outcomes from disclosure. These individuals reported negative changes in their interactions with supervisors and colleagues, both subtle and overt.

> *Negative outcomes included a perceived change in my colleagues' approach to me, subtle and small changes in behaviour or their approach towards; but it is quite difficult to pin point these changes, however I do feel they are negative in nature, as it feels like a small "screen" has risen between me and some of my colleagues (not all).* (Baz)

> *After I had delivered the talk to the hundreds of disability support staff at the staff development day, I noticed immediately that some of my colleagues treated me slightly differently when we travelled back to our hometown on the bus. I had had a few "well done, you are very brave" sort of comments, but I had also noticed some frosty looks and body language.... In hindsight, I don't think it helped me at all. People did treat me differently, and shockingly (considering the nature of the work), they treated me a lot worse.... It was obvious that most of my colleagues, no matter how well meaning, viewed autistics in terms of deficits and dysfunction.* (Psyche)

Lack of autism knowledge and deeply held misperceptions were seen to be at the heart of much of the negative reaction resulting from disclosure. This included both people doubting their capabilities (even where they had been performing the role effectively prior to diagnosis) and people doubting their diagnosis because they did not fit the stereotypes represented in the media. While both of these experiences have been reported in general community studies (Leedham, Thompson, et al. 2020; Huang, Hwang, et al. 2022), it is disappointing that this still occurs in university settings, including disciplines and speciality areas that arguably ought to be well-informed about autism. This meant that, for many, disclosure was accompanied by an ongoing need to educate colleagues about their specific needs and about autism more generally.

> *In hindsight, thinking people would simply understand was a ridiculous thought. I still disclose regularly, though I'm much better at it now. The most common responses I'd get were "you don't seem autistic," and when I highlighted difficulties the most common response was "don't use autism as an excuse."* (Dave)

> *I should acknowledge I've also had a bunch of internalised ableism to navigate around disclosure, as well as weighing up whether it's worth having to blow the cognitive load on shifting people's incorrect mental models, especially since I mask fairly effectively. So it's not just as simple as saying 'I'm autistic' – after that comes the bit where you have to decide exactly how much of your invisible experience you want to make visible, and which bits are safe to talk about and which are less safe. That's something I was naïve about initially too – that it would just be a matter of saying the words and then everyone would know everything they need to know.* (Morgan)

An interesting observation from several of those working in autism research – and from a personal perspective, the reason I came to autism research later in my academic career – was the assertion by others that autistic people (and those related to autistic people) should not do autism research because we are intrinsically biased and will therefore be unable to undertake rigorous research.

> *Where I've had the most negative pushback is from people outside of my friendly little social services research bubble from other corners of autism and disability research.... Every now and then I'm reminded that there are people who still feel that being a member of the population you research is "biased" (because straight, white, men are clearly the only people with sufficient objectivity to research the experiences of black lesbians, right? LOL).* (Sunny)

> *The main negatives of disclosure are people potentially assuming I am biased because I am researching autism and am autistic (but also the constant dismissal, disbelieving looks ... having to constantly educate on autism and what it means to be autistic).* (Louise)

Twenty-six of the participants provided advice to autistic readers on whether and how to disclose. Due to the variation in the responses, and the importance of this advice, I have not summarised it but instead included verbatim advice (minus any potentially identifying information) as Appendix A.

Camouflaging

Camouflaging (or masking) refers to hiding autistic characteristics in social situations in order to appear non-autistic and 'fit in' with others. As the literature in this area has grown, with more in-depth research into these behaviours, scholars developed a typology in which 'masking' is seen as a subset of 'camouflaging' behaviour, with the former specifically referring to strategies used to hide autistic characteristics. However, many autistic people continue to use the term 'masking' to describe the full range of behaviours, and this is reflected in some of the quotes in this chapter. Camouflaging behaviour is typically measured using the Camouflaging Autistic Traits Questionnaire (CAT-Q) (Hull, Mandy, et al. 2019), which consists of three subscales: masking, compensation (strategies used to compensate for difficulties in social situations), and assimilation (strategies used to try to fit in with others in social situations).

There is considerable evidence that autistic women engage in higher rates of camouflaging than autistic men (McQuaid, Lee, and Wallace

2022), although some research suggests that this is the case for masking and assimilation but not for compensation (Hull, Lai, et al. 2020).

The specific behaviours that make up camouflaging vary between individuals and across contexts. However, a useful list of examples is provided in a recent paper by Cook, Crane, et al. (2022). In this study, seventeen autistic adults watched video recordings of themselves engaging in a social interaction and identified and described their camouflaging behaviours (see Table 7.1). In reading this list it is important to keep in mind that, while some of these behaviours may seem natural and instinctive to the reader, this is a list of actions that these autistic people report consciously engaging in to facilitate a positive social interaction. Although this list is not exhaustive, it gives some idea how effortful social interaction can be for autistic people.

The majority of participants reported feeling pressured to mask at work, but also noted that this is not exclusive to the work environment but rather a pervasive aspect of their lives, consistent with research with the broader autism population (Cage and Troxell-Whitman 2019). Masking serves as both a survival mechanism, to protect ourselves from criticism and rejection from others, and also an internalised need to adapt our behaviour to make others feel more comfortable around us.

> *I am just coming recently to the realisation that I am autistic, so I am also leading to the conclusion that I have been masking all my life in many situations without even knowing. This is a source of exhaustion, and I am very well aware than when the exhaustion is too intense, I can fail at masking and this can be upsetting to people.... I do tend to escape from situations that would put me in such conditions, provided that attendance is optional. This is something that is most of the time not perceived well by others, so I tend to force myself, but it still not satisfactory for anyone as it can be seen that you are not enjoying being there.* (Henry)

> *It's hard to say really, because I feel like I need to mask around anyone and everyone. Often, it's the judgemental, or resentful, or cold reaction from others that makes me want to mask more than I already am, or otherwise confirms that I was right to mask. I think it's not that I receive active, explicit or conscious pressure to "act less autistic", it's more that people reject you for being yourself, they mistrust, resent or dislike you, even when you're masking. Masking protects you in a way because you know they're judging and rejecting the mask rather than rejecting your true self. It feels less hurtful, because they're rejecting the neurotypical persona of you, not the actual you.* (Evelyn)

> *I still try to keep the physical stims to a minimum in front of other people. They draw attention and I don't like that. The wrist twirls aren't too bad but the stims I do when I'm stressed are rocking, flapping, foot jiggling & pacing, and*

Table 7.1 *Examples of autistic camouflaging behaviours (data from Cook, Crane, et al. 2022)*

Category[a]	Behaviour description
Masking	• Avoiding or limiting time speaking about oneself or disclosing personal information (e.g., information about one's relationship, financial status, daily activities, special interests, or hobbies) • Reducing the frequency or minimising the visibility of non-gesture hand movements, including fidgeting movements and stimming hand movements • Avoiding sharing factual, detailed, or precise information • Reducing repetitive movements involving the torso, legs, or entire body, including rocking and fidgeting • Avoiding disclosing one's autism diagnosis or discussing the topic of autism • Altering physical appearance to appear more conventional or typical
Innocuous socialising Passive encouragement	• Maintaining eye contact or maintaining the appearance of eye contact (i.e., looking at a social partner's forehead, nose or mouth) • Mirroring another person's verbal (e.g., accent) or non-verbal behaviours (hand movements, body language, smile, or facial expressions) • Smiling at others when speaking or listening • Using verbal minimal encouragers (e.g., 'oh really', 'yes', 'yeah', and 'okay') • Laughing after one's own or others' statements
Centring social partner	• Guiding discussion to or maintaining discussion on topics of conversation that are related to one's social partner or that may be of interest to one's social partner • Allowing or relying on one's social partner to guide topics of conversation
Deferential engagement	• Apologising or providing excuses for perceived social errors or poor social performance • Seeking approval, permission, or validation from one's conversational partner • Avoiding confrontation or complaints and/or being cooperative, respectful, and agreeable
Reducing social risks	• Avoiding words or remarks that could be perceived as rude, offensive, distressing, or patronising • Discussing typical 'small talk' topics such as the weather, commuting, or weekend activities • Avoiding or limiting honest or direct statements • Avoiding questions or topics of conversation related to more personal or private aspects of others' lives (e.g., relationships, social activities, or general life outside work)

Table 7.1 (*cont.*)

Category[a]	Behaviour description
	• Avoiding or limiting discussion on topics of conversation that may generate controversy or debate • Avoiding appearing [too] knowledgeable about specific topics or information • Avoiding making jokes
Modelling neurotypical communication	• Altering communicative gestures so these appear more like neurotypical gestures or increasing use of conventional gestures • Altering body language so this appears more like neurotypical body language • Rephrasing or slowing speech, purposefully wording comments or providing clarifying comments • Altering facial expressions so these appear more similar to neurotypical facial expressions • Changing the tone of one's voice or the emphasis placed on words to sound more conventional or typical
Active self-presentation Reciprocal social behaviours	• Asking one's social partner questions • Commenting, providing elaborating information, or otherwise talking in a way that builds or maintains a conversation • Establishing and discussing points of commonality with one's social partner • Keeping an even balance between talking and listening • Sharing factual information (unrelated to oneself) with others
Risky social behaviours	• Making jokes or sharing humorous anecdotes • Disclosing information about one's education, employment, daily activities, or relationship status • Discussing one's perceived weaknesses, vulnerabilities, or feelings of inadequacy
Comfortable and familiar social behaviours Comfortable topics	• Discussing topics of conversations that one is knowledgeable about or interested in, finds easy, or is comfortable discussing, or have been received well by others in the past
Scripts	• Using an established repertoire of phrases, comments, questions, or anecdotes that are pre-planned or practiced, or have previously been well received by others

[a] edited to clarify that that this reflects the risk of misinterpretation by neurotypicals that in sharing this knowledge autistic people are 'showing off'.

> *I do not feel able to do that in front of other people. I think about the bad old days when the mentally-ill were exhibited and I feel like I would be in that cage. I feel that people are frightened of expressions like that. It freaks people out.* (Olivia)

> *I have occasionally dropped the mask at work, but I've discovered that it's always a mistake. I'm too vulnerable without the mask, and NTs hate vulnerability.* (Mia)

> *... in group meetings when we're going around doing update on what we're doing etc. I'm not prepared to say in front of entire group that I'm not coping. I'm more likely to open up and say I'm actually not OK in one-on-one conversations. Also in Zoom meetings of ~ 10 people, the expectation is that camera is ON, but I feel on display and I have to concentrate a lot.* (Jane).

Several commented that the pressure to mask is particularly high in academia, where competence is judged on social skills and presentation. These academics felt concerned that being their authentic autistic selves could result in them being seen as less credible by both students and peers.

> *I have spent most of my life either consciously or subconsciously masking my autistic traits, so it is very difficult for me to completely "unmask" and be genuinely autistic in any situation. ... **There's an expectation than academics should look, speak, and behave a certain way, and I suspect that some people may perceive me as less credible if I was acting in visibly autistic ways and not conforming to those expectations**.* (Alex)

> *I often feel like I have to mask and act neurotypical: make eye contact, small talk, etc. I used to be more 'myself' (not too worried about social conventions) sometimes when I was younger (in high school), and that didn't always go over well with others. ... So to avoid social ostracism, I learned to adopt the required conventions to 'fit in'. **Unfortunately, I often find that academics are not much better than high schoolers in terms of cliques and needlessly judging people or gossiping**. Nowadays, I still often feel like I have to please and be extra polite and nice, when sometimes I just feel like not interacting, not talking, or even leaving and being alone.* (Amy)

> *I would say in front of students particularly, and this isn't the students' fault or anything like that, but in front of students, I probably mask a fair bit because I don't want them to think that I'm not capable I guess.* (Charlotte)

Some also provided concrete examples of situations – both as university students and as academics – where they had experienced ableist attitudes that had demonstrated to them the importance of masking. This ranged from subtle microaggressions to comments on their behaviours and exerted explicit pressure on them to behave in a non-autistic manner.

> *I have definitely felt pressure to mask my autism at work. I have worked at uni whilst studying and have definitely found that the culture is not conducive to disclosure of one's diagnosis. All my peers would learn about psychological conditions alongside me and they'd hint at knowing someone who had particular diagnoses, but no-one would ever admit to the "shame" of having had a*

psychological condition. It annoyed me, somewhat, that we, psychologists in training, are so fearful of stigma that we hide our own truth. It does nothing more but to further increase stigma among our cohort. (Jade)

I have felt pressured to mask during a presentation I was giving at uni. I had to stop swaying from side to side (this is one way I regulate myself when feeling nervous, anxious or under pressure). I felt embarrassed someone noticed, I felt angry I was asked to stop. (Baz)

These reflections are consistent with previous research into the experiences of autistic people, which demonstrates the extent to which our neurotype feel pressured to hide our thoughts, feeling, behaviours, and other fundamental aspects of ourselves in order to be accepted and feel safe. For example, a survey of 262 autistic adults found that the two most common reasons for masking were 'to "pass" or fit into neurotypical society' and to 'avoid bullying and retaliation' (Cage and Troxell-Whitman 2019).

A minority of the participants commented that they found less pressure to mask their autistic traits in academia than in other workplaces, although these individuals were typically in roles that involved autism research and/or working from home.

I feel less pressure in academia to mask my autism than I did in the regular workplace. But I also think that's probably because in academia, I get to work from home a lot of the time, so I don't really have to.... I can do what I like, unlike in the regular workplace ... like in the normal world outside the academic bubble. (Charlotte)

I don't feel any particularly novel pressure in my current environment to mask my autism, and in fact I've enjoyed the university culture that makes it acceptable – even expected and celebrated – to be enthusiastic about those "narrow, restricted interests" that are called research questions. Plus I am definitely not the only person in my department who has atypical social interactions, so I feel a lot more freedom to be myself than I have in other environments. (Dee)

My partner and I both work in the same team and the head of our team is really brilliant. She actively supports Autistic researchers and realises that the benefits of Autistic-led research also come with some difficulties. She's totally unfazed to walk into the office to find one of us pacing or stimming or even having a bit of a cry at our desk. She's also very supportive when an Autistic team member just needs to take some time out when things get a bit much and she actively helps seek solutions and accommodations. Of course, this is only possible because the head of our team (and the team itself) produces a lot of high impact work for the university so she has a lot of clout with senior executives because of that. (Ruth)

Fortunately, I rarely feel a need to significantly mask when at work. It's more minor self-reminders such as remembering to make a certain amount of real or fake eye contact, making sure I keep the ebb and flow of conversation going, and realizing that there's often meaning behind what people say. (Moon Man)

However, my "work" is sort of unusual in that I'm doing autism research as an autistic person. There, if anything, I almost feel the opposite pressure – to behave in a more autistic manner – because of that old problem where autistic advocates are dismissed on the grounds that we can be unrepresentative of the whole heterogeneous and diverse autistic constellation. (Scott)

It is important to note that these reflections were written during the height of the COVID-19 pandemic, when many of the participants were working partially or completely at home. This meant that the pressure to mask was less constant and less intense, with significant benefit for both productivity and well-being.

Remote working has had some affordances around being able to mask by not giving up things entirely – e.g. being able to stim/have weighted animals outside of the video frame. It's still 'masking' in terms of 'hiding', but at least I can still help myself regulate in a way that I can't when I'm physically in a room with someone and my whole body is visible. (Morgan)

Impact

Words like 'drained' and 'exhausted' were common across the reflections on the impacts of masking, with many referring to the effort of masking at work resulting in complete energy depletion, limiting their ability to interact with friends and family or to engage in any activities outside of work.

Usually, the more masking I do, the more exhausted I am at the end of the day. In situations where I don't have to mask (e.g., working alone or meeting with a student one-on-one), I usually don't need as much time to recover at the end of the day. (Emma)

I think I often feel drained by the ends of hours, meetings, or days that I work around others. I much prefer working alone because it's safer from judgement and I don't have to mask so much. I often feel depressed and burnt out, so masking really takes it out of me. It costs a lot of attention remembering to modulate my voice and intonation to sound sincere, enthusiastic, etc. when my natural state is often less animated and more tired around people who aren't close, trusted friends, family, etc. That forced attention, that feeling of hypervigilance and self-monitoring is stressful, and one more tax on my working memory that makes everything else harder, including decision making and information processing. Forcing eye contact, or the other non-verbal behaviours can consume so much of my focus to achieve and maintain that I struggle to listen to people around me because I'm trying so hard to look "normal". (Evelyn)

The long-term impacts of masking are considerable, with many describing ongoing physical and mental health issues requiring medication, hospitalisation, and breaks from work to cope with and/or recover from the cumulative impact of this daily exhaustion.

> *The impact is intense exhaustion and stress – to the extreme, enough to require medication (betablockers in order to get in to work). When I get stressed, it's an intense physical reaction (feeling sick, stomach churning, lurches of adrenaline).* (Olivia)

> *Masking my autism means that I need to work harder at everything that I do. There is a constant underlying anxiety behind all my endeavours, and I am utterly exhausted at the end of each workday. After a while, I burn out completely and my health suffers. In the last few years, I have been plagued with various stress-triggered immune system issues and other illnesses. In times of severe stress I go non-verbal. Those moments are the worst, as I cannot mask my way through it. People just assume that I am refusing to talk to them. Masking is harder work than the work itself.* (Psyche)

> *Masking is utterly exhausting – it destroys my mental health, physically drains me, and emotionally kills me. I can only keep it up for so long before I crash and have a meltdown. Over my life, masking has led to everything from crying in my room for hours or not being able to function for days to having near-constant migraines that last up to a week or losing my entire 20s to significant mental health issues. This is because masking takes an incredible amount of mental, emotional, and physical labour. And masking is labour – it's a job I have to do to make neurotypicals feel more comfortable because I seem more like them. In this sense, it's very one-sided labour. Neurotypicals do not think about how to make life, interactions, work spaces, studying environments, or anything else easier or more comfortable for autistic people, but it is expected that autistic people will do this labour just to survive and be treated with a bare minimum of respect.* (Ella)

It was also concerning to see the extent to which participants internalised the pressure to mask and the negative feedback when they allowed the mask to slip. Many of the reflections made reference to feeling isolated, rejected, or ashamed due to their differences from the neurotypical majority.

> *The impact masking has had and continues to have on me is profound – a sense of not belonging anywhere – not being understood – of feeling lonely but not wanting company. It makes mundane everyday tasks seem overwhelming.... I like social anonymity so that I don't have to mask. If I go into a coffee shop where no-one knows me or my name or my order it is a straight forward scripted interaction. I have several cafes in my local area on rotation to ensure no single staff member could remember me. These are the lengths I will go to in order to avoid a situation where I would need to mask.* (Flora)

Jeez it is so incredibly taxing and stressful – exhausting. And honestly it wears down your self-esteem. You know – much about you is shameful and all wrong. (Isabella)

Some Final Thoughts

I am often asked by early career academics whether they should disclose their diagnosis, and I wish I could confidently advise them to do so. Sadly, my experience and the experiences of the participants in this study suggest that academic institutions have a long way to go before they are truly inclusive for autistic people. However, I also see some hope in some of the reflections, from those participants who have found a place where their strengths and contributions are recognised and valued.

A qualitative study with autistic adults in the United Kingdom (employed in non-academic contexts) found that the three key variables in positive outcomes from disclosure were (1) understanding of autism for both employers and colleagues, (2) willingness to make adaptations (adjustments), and (3) an inclusive organisational culture (Romualdez, Walker, and Remington 2021). It is evident that these same variables are essential, and achievable, for autistic academics to thrive in our universities.

There is considerable anecdotal evidence, and a small but growing body of research, that the pattern of periods of career success interspersed with periods of unemployment is a result of this cumulative effort. For some, this results from reaching a point where they are too emotionally and physically depleted to continue to camouflage, and the mask slips and the change in their behaviour is misinterpreted, leading to negative interactions in the workplace. For many, this results from pushing themselves beyond the point of exhaustion, resulting in the experience of autistic burnout (Raymaker, Teo, et al. 2020; Mantzalas, Richdale, et al. 2022; Tomczak and Kulikowski 2024). These outcomes could be avoided by providing environments in which autistic people felt comfortable to be themselves, were valued for their strengths, and were not stigmatised for their differences.

CHAPTER 8

Adjustments

> *... one of the reasons I have wanted to be open about being autistic – besides an interest in raising awareness that we are in academia, and hoping that that awareness will reduce some of the stigma around disclosure – is that most of the time the only accommodation I need is basic understanding that my thought processes or communication style might be different from what is expected. Even if people don't fully understand how autism might affect those things, they usually at least know that it is a social-communication disability, and so if I miss some social cue or don't express something in a typical way, they at least have a chance of deciding to cut me some slack about it rather than taking it as some kind of character flaw.*
>
> (Dee)

While the concept of reasonable adjustments is well-established in academia, and it is enshrined in university policy that we must support the provision of these adjustments for our students, autistic employees may not always feel empowered to ask for necessary adjustments to thrive in an academic workplace. In this chapter, participants reflect on the process of requesting and receiving adjustments, including those that have been denied and those that they wish they could ask for.

Some of the group have reasonable workplace accommodations, some limited accommodations, and some have none. Those with accommodations have often had to overcome significant barriers to obtain them.

Over one-third of the participants noted in their reflections that they had not asked for any adjustments at work. However, only two said that this was because their organisation was sufficiently supportive or that they could not currently think of anything specific that they needed. Several explained that they had not asked for much-needed adjustments because the process of doing so was too intimidating or complex.

> *I have been remiss in turning in my accommodation request. I cannot write it like they asked. I wrote one and they asked me to change it – they (the diversity/HR office) aren't accommodating me. In fact the other diversity and inclusion office caused major meltdowns. The whole list was denied and I need to redo it.*

What's stopping me is reformatting it in a way that makes no sense to me. And I am beyond burned out currently. (Isabella)

I honestly haven't been sure what kinds of things might be helpful, and the university office of disability services seems mostly geared toward undergraduate needs when it comes to the kinds of accommodations they are used to providing.... And employment accommodations for graduate student employees are harder to get, from what I have heard from others. It seems like it is mostly a bureaucratic issue, in that there are separate offices to approach for accommodations as a student versus an employee. But there is also the issue that graduate employees (at least in the social sciences, where I am) are typically working for an individual faculty member either alone or as one of a small number of teaching or research assistants. So asking for any kind of adjustment usually comes down to working something out with that specific faculty member with regard to the specific work that is being done, on a case-by-case basis. (Dee)

Some, particularly those in part-time or casual employment, had not asked for adjustments – even where these were important to maintaining their mental and physical health – due to concerns that doing so would negatively impact on their current and future employment prospects.

I work on casual contracts as a research assistant, casual marker, and in similar short-term roles. It's all done very informally. I will be informally approached by an academic and asked if I could accept a contract doing X for so many hours per week. If I don't say yes, then it'll go to someone else. There are SO many people who can accept these roles. I'm sure if I were to say I needed adjustments, they'd be taken aback because they can easily get someone else to do it with no need for adjustments. I wouldn't be offered more work from other academics or from them. Why would an academic offer me a short-term casual RA job knowing I need adjustments when they know they can pick from any number of other candidates to give the work to? It's obviously easier to get literally anyone else to do the work. So I work to hide my disabilities and health issues to reduce the impact on my career. It's sad. I wish I could just be sick, disabled, autistic, AND considered for work, but that's not reality. (Jade)

I have been denied multiple adjustments while studying.... I therefore don't ask for adjustments at work, because I can tell many academics would rather hire and work with people they deem 'easy' to work with, rather than 'difficult' because they have questions, need help, or ask for specific accommodations. (Ella)

The remainder had not asked for adjustments because they felt unable to do so, having not disclosed their diagnosis to their workplace. As discussed in Chapter 7, the risks of disclosure outweigh the benefits for many autistic people in the current environment of academia.

I haven't asked because I haven't disclosed for fear of stigma, judgment, or discrimination. I don't trust HR or other services in terms of confidentiality, and there are no accountability mechanisms as far as I know, so it's not exactly a trust-inducing environment, especially when people (even people who work in diversity or disability-related positions and who really should know better) are so blatantly ignorant about autism. (Amy)

What's stopping me from asking is that I haven't disclosed.... Also because I mask constantly and present well (not that I intend to! but people often create an idea of me that I find completely misrepresentational. E.g. 'you're so relaxed!' – er no, that's exhaustion masquerading as calmness). (Olivia)

I don't have any adjustments since my employer doesn't know about my autism. I try to participate to the meeting online because driving to work adds a lot of stress and fatigue for me. But this is not always allowed, even in the time of pandemic. (Sophia)

Workplace Accommodations (Not) Received

Among those who had been provided with workplace accommodations, these were typically limited to working locations and patterns or (limited) environmental adjustments to address sensory sensitivities. Several participants discussed adjustments in their work to enable them to *work from home* part or all of the time. For some participants this was formally negotiated as part of a disability accommodation; for some it was an informal arrangement with a direct supervisor; and for others it was a matter of specifically seeking out roles that allowed for off-campus working. In all cases, the flexibility to work away from the office – in a familiar environment with the capacity to control sensory input and minimise both travel and social contact – was described as highly beneficial to both personal well-being and work productivity.

Working from home adjustments: I can work from home as often and as much as I need to. It's awesome and has made a significant difference to the quality of my life! It is also not a requirement that I sign into Microsoft Teams all of the time. I can attend meetings online and do not have to attend in person. I have the flexibility of working my hours across the week when it best suits my mental health. I take as many breaks as I need to, and if working from the office I can come and go as I need. (Baz)

As I have not disclosed that I am autistic, I've never directly requested nor been granted adjustments in the workplace. I've organised adjustments without disclosing. For example, I work exclusively from home, which is a perfect set up for me. This naturally occurred with my first research assistant contract, and then with my second teaching assistant contract. Once I experienced it, and realised how much more suitable it was for me (it was transformative!), I started communicating that I worked externally before finalising future contracts. This coming semester, for example, I was offered two teaching assistant positions, and I communicated that I would prefer to be marking only as this allowed me to work from home.... Most of my work and communication is conducted via email at times that suit me. (Ella)

Most adjustments I have had in my program and practicum work have been related to transportation or requesting remote meetings. With my sensory processing issues and inability to drive, sometimes it is easier for me to meet with an advisor via video chat or phone or with a program for collaborating on documents virtually versus meeting in person. Often, this is done anyway as I collaborate with internet-based educational websites which operate out of province or even out of country. The pandemic has made this option available as the default versus sometimes having to push for it or going to a public place on a day when I am not feeling good and appearing visibly distressed. Even minor illness or being tired can interfere with my ability to be in groups in person or handle a public place. (Eva)

An important element of the increased comfort and capacity associated with working away from the office for many participants was the ability to control the number and duration of online meetings, and particularly to be able to attend with their camera off in order to be able to participate fully.

This is the first job where I have asked for any adjustments, but I don't have many because the main adjustment is that I work from home wherever possible! My supervisor has never put any pressure on me to come in more often and has made it clear that as long as I am getting work done, she doesn't care where it is done. I have always had some difficulty managing online meetings because some people at my organisation insist on having cameras on, which causes so much anxiety that I cannot access those meetings at all. (Louise)

Several reflected on *sensory adjustments* in their work environment that had been made in response to their requests. However, these adjustments are typically minor and narrow in scope – often being limited to those that require no or minimal financial outlay, are initiated by an individual or workgroup rather than the organisation itself, and are in the context of other (often minor) requests that are not addressed.

My employer in [location] provided light filters in the shared teacher's room where I worked and assigned me a single classroom to teach in where they used light filters in the front of the room. (Trina)

Adjustments have been arranged within my team without involving HR. They have allowed me to use a different room away from offending noises and changed the lighting in one of the rooms for me. They have also allowed me to arrange half days when supervising onsite in the training clinic due to the excessive social demands of a full day. (Trevor)

The only adjustments that my employer made for me to accommodate me being autistic was to allow me to wear a hat or sunglasses inside the building. The sound of people slamming the gates onto the [location] was even more distressing than the terrible fluorescent strip lights, but no accommodations or adjustments were made there. Sometimes, my boss would remember to write down work instructions instead of just giving them to me verbally. (Psyche)

Institutional policies around status-based 'entitlements' come into play in many organisations. Consider the difference in experiences of Jane and Morgan, who both work in universities in the same country; Morgan's university is clearly less rigid in following arbitrary rules when addressing the welfare of staff.

> *Wear cap when lights too bright (or sunnies when I forget my cap) . . . Light immediately above my desk off . . . Noise cancelling headphones . . . Open plan area not ideal. But I'm a lecturer . . . (Senior Lecturer / Associate Professor / Professor => office).* (Jane)

> *My own office (back before I had a management role and wasn't entitled to one) . . . Space/furniture to lie down in my office . . . High end noise cancelling headphones instead of the standard issue cheap headsets that hurt my ears and don't block noise . . . Microwave in my office so I don't have to go in the communal kitchen (they did also supply a bar fridge but it stopped working so I just bought my own) . . . Depending on attendees, some meetings conducted with lights off (not really a formal accommodation per se).* (Morgan)

Even among those who had disclosed their diagnosis to their employer and had sought some adjustments to their work environment or arrangements, there were some accommodations that they did not feel they were able to ask for. The most common of these related to issues mentioned above – that is, issues related to the rigidity of institutional policies in relation to working location and physical/sensory environment.

> *I would like to be able to work from home more than the 1 day/week part-timers are allowed. I haven't yet had the conversation, cos I've been on extended leave. . . . If I ever travel for conferences again – I'd like to have a travel day, and recovery day before attending conferences. As well as a recovery day at home after I've returned home before returning to work. But domestic conferences it's expected that you'll fly just before the conference, and return to work straight away afterwards.* (Jane)

> *I hadn't asked to swap the fluorescent strip lights to a lower wattage. I actually saw the maintenance guy replace the lower wattage bulbs with really powerfully bright ones, so I naturally assumed that it would be totally futile to ask. I did mention that I found it made me incredibly anxious just working on a casual basis, as my work hours could not be guaranteed from one week to the next and I never received my hours until the day before. This gave me little to no time to prepare and I felt like I was on call and not allowed a life of my own. The fact*

> *that my working hours were also dependent on how much the boss liked me also fuelled my anxiety twentyfold. Being on a casual contract felt like being in a popularity contest.... A nightmare for an autistic person!* (Psyche)

Another theme evident in several of the reflections is related to social interaction and communication. As discussed in Chapter 5, academia presents a considerable challenge for many autistic people due to the heavy reliance on the hidden curriculum, the frequency of (and value placed on) social interactions, and the diversity of the academic roles. Several of the participants commented that they could be more effective, and less exhausted, in the workplace if they could be freed from the expectation of engaging in an exhausting degree of social contact, if they could delegate some of the 'people' tasks, and if they could have access to an appropriate support service to assist with translating non-autistic communication.

> *I would dearly love a person who could do some of the people labour for me, but I'm not high ranking enough to "qualify" for my own EA [executive assistant], and our whole paradigm of admin assistance is predicated on administrative tasks – if I say I want someone to manage my calendar for me, nobody bats an eye, but there's just no model in place for us to be able to conceptualise things beyond that. I'd also love to be able to not engage in the social norms and rituals that are expected without facing social punishment but I just don't think people are willing to change their paradigms.* (Morgan)

> *However, it would be good to have a dedicated interlocutor for working out structured arguments for lectures and publications. A lot of people want this especially for the latter though, but whether there's someone compatible in terms of interests who actually can be an interlocutor is up to chance.* (Liam)

Another important communication issue, as Louise notes below, is the way that people talk about autism, which is typically very deficit-focused and (as I commented in a previous editorial piece) it is confronting for an autistic person to work in an environment where your colleagues continue to use the word 'autism' as an insult (Jones 2019).

> *The biggest adjustment I would like, but haven't asked for, is for people I work with to change their language around autism, which can be very ableist and stigmatising e.g. lots of talk about deficits. That bothers me.* (Louise)

What Makes It (Un)Workable?

By far the most common theme in the reflections as to how necessary accommodations were obtained related to the decisions and actions of individuals and small groups. That is, workplace and work-style adjustments were agreed to and implemented by direct supervisors and/or immediate colleagues, rather than as a result of institutional policies.

> *Most adjustments have been small and made personally by my colleagues rather than a larger effort by the university – which has worked well. Examples include willingness to explain Hidden Curriculum and lowering the lights in colleagues' offices.* (Moon Man)

> *My current employer is fantastic at accommodating Autistic staff, though I suspect that this may be isolated to our department/team. The head of our team does a lot for the university rankings and is very highly regarded. She understands that having Autistic academics on her team is highly beneficial, but accommodations also must be made. She basically handles everything with senior exec which provides a buffer for us and we don't have to deal with the politics. We tell her what we need and she makes it happen. She's pretty amazing like that.* (Ruth)

> *It was relatively easy, mainly because I have a great working relationship with my current supervisor. She's very flexible and doesn't mind how I do my work, because I submit it before deadline and always submit very high-quality work. The latest teaching contracts were a bit more difficult to organise, because there was a chance I could miss out on work completely by saying 'no' to the teaching jobs and asking for only marking jobs. This would have been challenging from a financial perspective, and may have forced me to consider other work options.* (Ella)

> *Even here in [place], I have had administrators and officials turn off lights for me when I have an appointment with them. They don't ask for documentation; they just turn off the lights if they can.* (Trina)

> *One thing I've come across recently though that I didn't ask for because I never thought I would be 'allowed' to request that other people change their behaviour is people being very explicit and direct with me, and translating/explaining the tacit stuff behind behaviours. My incoming boss has done this completely of her own volition to try and accommodate me (she told me it was a deliberate accommodation strategy on her behalf), and she is very direct with me and will explain/meta-narrate everything that she does. She also helps translate other people's actions for me and makes the time to unpack the political stuff behind behaviours for me. It makes such a difference but I don't think I'd be able to ask someone else to do it.* (Morgan)

Other participants discussed ways that they themselves had made adjustments to their workplace or working conditions in order to address their needs. Not surprisingly, the extent to which this was possible was associated with the level of seniority and the specific job role of the individual, with those in research-only, leadership, and consultant roles having significantly more control over their working arrangements than those in junior positions or standard academic roles.

However, even before I knew I was autistic, I made several adjustments for myself, without realizing it. Here is a brief summary: I disabled the fluorescent lights in my office and brought several lamps, for softer lighting. . . . I added a sound machine, to make white noise and soften some of the sounds outside my office. . . . I kept various timers and clocks at my desk, to avoid missing a meeting. (Marie)

I'm a PI so it's more about adjustments I make for myself. . . . Some things that I do are 1) work from home (even before the pandemic) in an environment where I control the sensory input and everything is set up for me; 2) build in breaks where I can run around and move and process, especially when I get trapped in long meetings; 3) the work itself is set up so that I can work more hours/more intensely when my brain is working and take time off if it gets foggy/ I get overwhelmed and can't think; 4) I set aside money in my grants to pay for a helper at conferences and with travel; 5) I hire RAs and work with my university staff to help with my learning disability related to numbers (this matters a lot with things like budget management); 6) I have strong relationships with colleagues and mentors who I trust to talk to about social protocols and get help with things like tactful phrasing on emails and how to approach people about things I need/academic etiquette; 7) I work with my office manager to make sure that my office is as sensory-friendly as possible – this isn't just for me for the scant time I spend there, but also I work with a lot of folks from the community and students who are also neurodivergent and it's helpful to them as well to have a sensory friendly place they can go to. On one hand, easy – I just did them all for myself. On the other hand, hard – I had to figure out that this was a career where I could do that, and then get a PhD and work my way up into it, and find mentors and colleagues, and find a university where I felt like I could do it, and get funding to get the position, basically build it all from the ground up. Unlike a more typical job with a boss, an office, etc. it's not a matter of asking human resources for specific things – this is a situation where my job and my adjustments were linked from the very start. (Sunny)

In the early years, I did not accommodate/innovate for myself. I trained in-person and coached in-person. In the last 5 years I clearly stated in contracts that it would save my clients a lot of money if they didn't have to fly me in to speak at conferences or trainings so we moved to online training prior to the pandemic and I haven't looked back since. I also moved to phone coaching and insisted on no-video and none of my clients pushed back on it. (Kelly)

Participants identified a number of barriers to requesting, and receiving, workplace accommodations even when they did have (and were willing to disclose) a diagnosis. The need to provide detailed personal information to 'justify' accommodations is confronting and acts as a deterrent to many. This is consistent with research into the experiences of ableism among academics with disabilities, which has identified that access to reasonable adjustments relies on self-advocacy and that the burden of proof is placed on the individual, with no consideration by academy for the significant time and effort required for this process and how it can negatively impact the well-being and productivity of academics (Brown and Ramlackhan 2022; Lindsay and Fuentes 2022). Not only is this requirement to 'prove' our disability and our limitations invasive of our privacy, but it poses an additional challenge when we are aware that discrimination is rife and that this information is being provided to the same people who will determine our future career advancement (Morrison 2019).

> *In order to register with equity and diversity I needed to provide formal documentation relating to my autism diagnosis. My initial diagnosis report was completed by an educational psychologist and contained personal information that I was not comfortable sharing. I later obtained an assessment from a neuropsychologist in relation to my PhD and provided equity and diversity with this report, [and] although it still contained information I was not comfortable with sharing, it was in less detail.* (Flora)

Lack of understanding was a significant barrier, particularly given that in many cases these accommodations relate to things that are not visible or easily explained to someone who has limited knowledge of autism. As noted in the study of ableism in academia by Brown and Ramlackhan, those with invisible disabilities (such as autism) can feel further marginalised even within the already marginalised category of "disabled academics" (Brown and Ramlackhan 2022) as they are seen by others as – and may internalise this themselves to feel – 'not disabled enough' to be provided with the adjustments that they actually require. In relation to autism specifically, a review of employment-related posts in an online autism community revealed that many who struggling with aspects of their work environment were undecided whether to seek accommodations, due to the risk of people either assuming they were incompetent or dismissing them as not really having a problem (Nagib and Wilton 2021).

> *I think the hardest part about requesting accommodations is having to justify them to those in authority. Another issue is that if you're able to mask pretty well, people may not understand why you're requesting accommodations, since everything looks fine from the outside (thus making it harder for you to justify them).* (Emma)

> *These adjustments, although minimal, were very difficult for me to attain in the workplace. For the majority of the time, the responsibility for my sensory distress in the workplace was placed on me. For instance, I was questioned about whether the lights and the slamming gates were really so awful, or whether I could just put up with it. My boss would relate to her own neurotypical experience of being able to ignore annoying sensory input with apparently little*

understanding of how autistic people are unable to do this, despite her having worked with autistic people for nearly 20 years. (Psyche)

For some there was a sense that asking for accommodations was pointless, based on previous experience that non-autistic colleagues would dismiss the requests as unnecessary. For others, there was a reluctance to ask for accommodations that might cost the organisation money or inconvenience their colleagues. A recent Australian study into the experiences of disabled academics found that, like my group, many of these individuals felt they should 'push through' rather than apply for workplace accommodations that they needed and were entitled to due to the internalised ableism associated with workplace norms (Humphrys, Rodgers, et al. 2022).

> *The overwhelming and noisy brown bag seminar … which usually has something like 40 people packed into a room more suitable for 20 – standing room only, generally – probably a fire hazard – should never have been offered to an autistic person. It was utterly pointless, since I could hardly focus on the actual seminar due to my coping strategy for the sensory distress beforehand … it was completely ridiculous for me to be attending the thing at all. Wholly useless. Now that I think of it, I guess I did make a few noises about not attending it or getting it recorded regularly, but I didn't get the sense that anyone was interested in responding to my requests, so I dropped the matter. No sense pouring energy into advocating for something when it was clear that nobody in the department was interested in my concerns.* (Scott)

> *I think I am lucky. Many of the adjustments were arranged without my specifically asking for them when I commented on the difficulty with some of the sensory issues. They asked what lighting changes I needed and arranged for them. As long as I give a logical reason for changes and they don't cause much disruption or cost too much they were easily won. There are some I haven't asked for. But they couldn't be accommodated without unreasonable expense. What stops me asking is the fear of being too [much] trouble to others or inconveniencing others to meet my needs.* (Trevor)

It was concerning to note the use of words like 'lucky' and 'fortunate' in many of the reflections when these individuals were discussing reasonable and necessary accommodations that had been provided to them. This reflects an academic culture where not only are their own requests often denied, but they see others denied accommodations that are basic human rights.

> *I have a colleague who needs CART [computer-aided real-time transcription] due to an auditory processing delay, and their experience has been a nightmare. My institution does not have a centralized ADA [Americans with Disabilities Act] coordination office. Departments are expected to determine and pay for*

individual workers' accommodations. So individuals have to out themselves to their chair, and then hope their chair thinks it's worth taking money from the budget to accommodate them. CART is expensive, so my colleague's department chair keeps not having it for meetings (including faculty meetings, so my colleague literally cannot do their job), and then telling my colleague that they need to be patient because accommodating them has been so hard on the department. It is outrageous. (Saskia)

I know many people at the same institution who have been denied things. I heard from another disabled person that some of the disability management people in my institution's HR apparently didn't know what captioning was. How is it possible for someone to have a job providing disability accommodations yet not be familiar with captioning? Granted, this is a second-hand example, but there's simply too many similar examples for me not to assume that it would take far, far more energy to advocate for formal supports – with less certainty of success – than to simply focus on coping. (Scott)

What Accommodations Should be Provided?

On first reading Dave's reflection (below), the thought that crossed my mind (and will probably cross the minds of most autistic academics who read it) was "Where does Dave work, and do they want to hire me too?"

Flexible schedule – I'm not hourly, no time card, so long as I get the work done (40+ hrs/week worth of work) I'm largely left to my own devices. This is critical for my sensory issues, as some hours/days I perform poorly while others I'm hyper-productive, this allows me to work at my best and give them the most bang for the buck.

Stimming – as they understand autism and how it expresses, I am free to stim when needed – this can include fidgeting, rocking, standing up during a meeting and pacing, etc. The freedom to stim, ironically, reduces my need to stim – the environment feels inclusive and accommodating and that lowers my stress level, allowing me to better focus on the work itself.

Coaching – as human interaction can be baffling, complex, or confusing for me, and my employers understand this, they are always willing/looking for ways to coach me on my language and interactions and provide valuable feedback on how to be a better leader/communicator. For those of us on the spectrum, this is a clear pathway to better relations with colleagues.

Patience – when I do mess up (and any difficult, complex task does not always end with success), my employers recognize that this is something I wish to be good at, but occasionally make mistakes, so they are careful not to jump to conclusions and have frank, honest discussions with me to help me uncover what went wrong, how it could be perceived, and some strategies for better ways to communicate. Now, most such instances are avoided as I'm free to ask for advice or run a statement by them to receive some pre-emptive coaching/advice on how to best broach/cover a particular topic/discussion.

Sensory-friendly environment – in particular, I have severe sensory issues. Having some control over the lighting and noise levels of my workplace is vital. On particularly rough days, I often have the freedom to work from home, allowing me to get the work done in a sensory-safe environment. (Dave)

As you will have seen from this chapter, Dave's experience is an exception rather than the rule. When I asked participants for their recommendations as to accommodations and adjustments that should be provided to autistic academics, there were many common suggestions. However, they were also keen to point out that every autistic person will have different needs and that what would work best for them may not be ideal for someone else. Table 8.1, which presents their collated suggestions, is provided not as a checklist per se but rather as a starting point for thought and discussion – for autistic academics, their supervisors, and their institutions.

For ease of reference, I have categorised these into four broad groupings, based on the consistent findings of the literature into reasonable adjustments for autistic people in workplaces more generally conducted with diverse groups including autistic employees (Lindsay, Osten, et al. 2021; Waisman-Nitzan, Gal, and Schreuer 2021), employers of autistic people (Waisman-Nitzan, Gal, and Schreuer 2019), 'experts' (Tomczak 2022), and non-autistic employees (Petty, Tunstall, et al. 2023). While there were some nuances in the specific aspects discussed or the terminology used, each of these recommended accommodations fell within the broad categories of environment, flexibility, communication, and attitudes.

Another accommodation that was reflected on, somewhat wistfully, in many of the reflections was access to a mentor. Participants were divided on whether this should be an autistic mentor who has worked out how to survive in the academic environment, or a non-autistic mentor who has a thorough understanding of autism and genuine empathy for autistic people. However, there was a consistent belief that access to someone who could assist them in navigating the social and political contexts and interpreting the hidden rules would be of significant benefit.

It could also be helpful to have an autistic mentor or peer who may be able to translate important information from neurotypical into autistic. (Psyche)

A system of academic tutor (with a comprehensive and experienced colleague willing to help an autistic colleague) could maybe be a good idea. I would love to have someone I could ask all the questions I have about how to act in meeting

Table 8.1 *Workplace accommodations suggested by participants*

Environment	• Facilitate environmental adjustments to address their individual sensory needs (e.g., lights, heating and cooling, sound-dampening modifications). • Where possible provide an individual office or a quiet, private (solitary) place to work, with capacity to control light and other sensory input. • Provide quiet and consistent working space (no hot-desking [flexible workspaces that aren't assigned to a specific employee]). • Provide access to a dedicated quiet space (if they don't have an individual office). • Allow and normalise use of headphones, sunglasses/caps, and other sensory aids. • Provide maps and visual guides to campus facilities . • Don't require attendance at lunch meetings (the noise and smells are distracting, and we need downtime in the day). • If attendance at social events is required, organise them during the working day and in sensory-friendly environments.
Flexibility	• Offer the option to work from home (part or full-time) if feasible. • Provide flexibility in working days/hours to accommodate fluctuating energy/well-being levels. • Develop flexible work roles/structures (e.g., meaningful part-time roles and/or ability to limit engagement in specific activities). • Enable them to control the amount of time spent in environments they find overwhelming (for sensory and/or social reasons). • Allow for breaks between meetings. • Offer alternative arrangements for meetings such as option to attend via telephone rather than in person, or to attend fewer meetings. • Provide the option to not attend social events that may be seen as desirable to attend by senior staff, without explicit or implicit penalty. • Enable access to periods of uninterrupted work. • Provide (as much as possible) a reasonably regular schedule for teaching, meetings, etc. to reduce uncertainty .
Communication	• Provide specific, clearly communicated task expectations. • Provide specific, clearly communicated deadlines. • Provide access to a communication bridge/translator. • Allow them to take notes, and provide written instructions instead of expecting them to follow verbal instructions. • Interpret/clarify the hidden curriculum, and offer support in navigating formal institutions and structures. • Ensure that agendas and minutes for meetings are supplied in a timely fashion, and write down important information, notes, and instructions. • Be prepared to provide details on how to do something more than once, and understand the need to know *why* it is done that way. • Allow participation in online meetings without camera, and participation using chat instead of speaking.

Table 8.1 (*cont.*)

	• At the beginning of a meeting, provide an agenda and/or say a few words about its structure (what to expect). • As much as possible, allow them to communicate in a way that is comfortable (e.g., email rather than phone call).
Attitudes	• Provide training for staff so they understand how autism actually presents and can move past stigma and stereotypes. • Provide autism education and human rights education for all faculty, professional staff, and leaders. • Allow additional time to process complicated information and for tasks that require conscious thinking-through that neurotypicals usually can do more intuitively and quickly. • Empower them to move, especially in meetings that tend to continue for hours and require a lot of self-regulation, normalising the use of fidget toys and other sensory aids, but also giving autistic people the control over their own time to be able to escape and decompress if necessary.

and who could help me understand the reaction of my colleagues. It would be maybe interesting to have colleagues playing that role that are familiar with autism, for example some who have autistic kids. Maybe some kind of network identifying people in academia able and willing to help. But a deep knowledge of autism and a personal experience with autism would in my opinion be the key for it to work. Those colleagues should also be trained to be able to give autistic people the help they need. An identical system with maybe a student tutor and a professor tutor could be available for autistic students. (Sophia)

As Mellifont (2023) notes, and as noted by this group in previous chapters, not all autistic academics will want to disclose in order to access reasonable adjustments given the costs of doing so, but all staff should be aware of the adjustments that are potentially available.

Some Final Thoughts

It is important to note that these reflections were completed during the COVID-19 pandemic when lockdowns were commonplace, and remote working became common practice worldwide. Many of the adjustments that facilitated productivity and well-being for the group – and thousands of other autistic academics – were implemented by organisations in response to this catastrophic event. There is increasing evidence that working from home is particularly beneficial to autistic employees and can increase both their access to employment and their contribution to the workplace (Kalmanovich-Cohen and Stanton 2023).

I can't resist making the statement that it has taken a global pandemic for me to find a work environment that feels comfortable for me. Since March 2020, we have been working remotely, which has radically improved my working life. Working remotely has drastically reduced the number of unplanned and spontaneous meetings. The ability to have a space to work without the potential of students or colleagues "just dropping by" has given me the time and space to recover from demanding meetings, classes, or events during the workday. It has also given me more space for work that requires concentration, like grading papers or planning for classes. This last point is a significant one. Before shifting to remote work, I saved all class planning and paper grading, when I could think without so many interruptions. This left very little time for family and friends. With the energy regained from the above improvements, I have been able to engage in scholarship. (Marie)

Universities are getting better at providing accommodations for autistic students, although they still have a long way to go. However, it appears they have much further to go in relation to autistic staff, starting with shifting attitudes (not seeing autism as a deficit) and providing explicit practical supports in identifying and accessing appropriate adjustments.

As a student, I felt protected to seek all the accommodations I needed. I advocated for myself and I advocated for change for all students with disabilities. Now, as someone trying to carve out a career for myself in a competitive field, I just suffer through it.... What I've learnt about accommodations is that people don't like to change. People think the way they do things is okay as it is. So I wouldn't be asking for any accommodations that requires people to change their behaviour. For example, while I'd benefit from the lunch room being a bit quieter just for 10 minutes a day, there is no way I'd ask for that accommodation. That's just a means to get everyone angry and annoyed because they don't have empathy and they don't like change. (Jade)

A minority of this group of autistic academics have been able to obtain all or most of the accommodations they require to work productively and safely. Others have been able to access many of those they have requested. While there is a positive aspect to this finding, in that it demonstrates that it is possible for autistic academics to find supportive colleagues and workplaces, it is also concerning to think that our ability to access safe and supportive working environments remains contingent on the goodwill of individuals. As Martin (2020) has articulated, supportive colleagues are a force for good, but are not the solution to addressing institutional obstacles to inclusion. Without an institution-wide approach that ensures access to reasonable adjustments for all autistic employees, tenable working conditions will be available only to those who are fortunate enough to have informed and empathetic supervisors and colleagues. Further, there is evidence that without accompanying education and policy to address misunderstanding and stigma, the provision of reasonable accommodations can lead to resentment from co-workers (Patton 2019) who feel that their autistic colleague doesn't 'deserve' the adjustments made.

The barriers for autistic people in accessing reasonable accommodations are significant in all fields of employment, in terms of both processes for requesting them and processes for actually having them consistently implemented once they are approved (Davies, Heasman, et al. 2022). The stigma associated with autism alongside the 'hidden' nature of many of our challenges make disclosure risky and the need for accommodations difficult to communicate. However, not being provided with these accommodations has a significant negative impact on their physical and mental well-being (Davies, Heasman, et al. 2022), leading to autistic burnout (Raymaker, Teo, et al. 2020; Mantzalas, Richdale, et al. 2022), job termination, and the loss of a valuable resource for our institutions, colleagues, and students.

CHAPTER 9
Conferences

> *At conferences, I often find the sensory overload to be one of the biggest challenges. There are usually huge crowds of delegates in attendance, in venues with terrible acoustics, harsh lighting, awful carpet, and freezing air-conditioning. Combine that with the fact that I'm usually unfamiliar with the venue, and the venues are often huge, and by the time I find the location for the first keynote presentation I'm often already on edge. I then have to sit in a room full of people, remain relatively still and quiet, and attempt to pay attention to the presentations, often for quite a few hours with minimal or no respite. That's a huge drain on my executive functioning, sensory processing, and energy.*
>
> (Alex)

The field of autism research is moving from its troubled history of research *on* autistic people to research *with* autistic people. This recognition of the need for research *both with and by* autistic people means there is also a need to understand the extent to which autism conferences include or exclude the voices of autistic people. In this chapter, participants reflect on their experiences in attending conferences as recipients of knowledge, active participants in the conversation, and conveyors of information. Topics discussed include sensory issues, conference organisation, social interaction and networking, in-session interaction, in-session information, inclusion, and online conferences.

Attendance at academic conferences is an important aspect of an academic role, providing an opportunity to participate with a community of scholars in your area of expertise. Conference attendance is seen as both a 'perk' and a requirement of academia, providing the researcher with a range of benefits, for example, constructing our identity as an academic, expanding the depth and breadth of our knowledge, and building connections and networks (Edelheim, Thomas, et al. 2018). There is also some evidence that journal articles previously presented at conferences are more likely to be cited (de Leon and McQuillin 2018).

There is a dearth of literature on the extent to which conferences – including autism conferences – are accessible to autistic academics. There is a small body of research on the need to make conferences in all disciplines accessible to people with disabilities (Callus 2017), some of which touches on issues of neurodiversity (Irish 2020). There is a parallel body of literature on the extent to which the ableist nature of academia limits opportunities for autistic researchers, which includes aspects of important 'profile-raising' activities such as conferences (Mellifont 2023).

A number of advocacy organisations provide guidelines and recommendations for making conferences autism-friendly, and we increasingly see conference websites including accessibility information. For example, in 2019 the National Autistic Society Conference, Cork Autism Conference, Asia Pacific Autism Conference, and Autism Society Conference all provided details of strategies implemented to make their conferences more inclusive and accessible for autistic participants.

Pre-conference supports included full program information and venue maps, pre-conference tours of the venue, and pre-registration for autistic delegates. Environmental supports typically included seats reserved for autistic delegates (to allow for easy access to exits), reserved seating outside the main conference room for anyone who requires a break during the sessions, a dedicated quiet room for autistic attendees and speakers, and/or a quiet dining room space for attendees who wish to eat in silence.

Commonly noted sensory adjustments included minimising the use of bright and flashing lights (including requests not to take photographs using a flash); fragrance-free policies, including asking attendees not to wear strong perfumes or colognes and ensuring the lunch menu is free of any strong aromas; provision of ear plugs; and turning off hand dryers in the bathrooms and providing paper towels. Strategies to address social demands included colour-coded badges to allow participants to indicate how they would like to interact with other delegates, the option to provide written questions in advance of the session for those who prefer not to ask questions aloud, respectful language for communications guidelines, and an audio/video recording of the conference for all attendees to review in their own time.

However, we still see calls for papers for autism conferences that utilise terminology and perspectives that are discouraging and potentially harmful to autistic people, and instructions for preparing and presenting papers and posters that do not reflect accessibility and inclusion. These reminders include 'maintain eye contact', 'keep your hands still', and 'vary your tone of voice' while presenting (or recording a presentation).

Further, much of what is written about autistic people as conference attendees assumes that we are there either as 'beneficiaries' of information (members of the community attending to learn about advances in autism research) or as passive recipients (graduate students or early career researchers developing our knowledge of the field), rather than as active participants in the conversation (discussants, collaborators, fellow researchers) or conveyors of information (presenters of papers and panel sessions).

Sensory Issues

Sensory issues were a significant challenge for the majority of the group. This was the case for both conferences and training courses, with numerous references to training rooms within and outside organisations not being conducive to learning. While the issues most commonly mentioned were sight and sound, all six senses (i.e., taste, small, vision, hearing, touch, and proprioception) were raised as causing unique and synergistic challenges.

> *Environmental mindfulness goes a long way. Reducing background noise, lowering lights and avoiding direct lighting, as well as temperature goes a long way.* (Moon Man)

Several practical suggestions were made in relation to each of the senses. Visual sensitivity could be addressed by reducing the brightness of lights, avoiding direct lighting, following accessibility guidelines for presentation, and allowing people to wear sunglasses or caps. Suggestions to address auditory sensitivity included selecting training rooms with good acoustics, reducing background noise, silent clapping, paper towels rather than hand dryers, scheduled quiet sessions, and availability and acceptance of headphones and earplugs. Smell and taste issues were predominantly raised in the context of food, including the range of food options and the ability to access separate eating areas.

> *Some understanding that people have different tolerances for loud, bright rooms and/or long, grueling schedules would be really helpful.* (Dee)

> *Have breaks that are quiet! (Normally meal breaks are the noisiest part of face-to-face conferences, when everyone is finding food and there are LOTS of conversations happening rather than listening to ONE person present.)* (Jane)

Tactile aspects that were found to be challenging included air-conditioning/ temperature extremes, uncomfortable chairs, and crowding, although there was recognition that conferences and training programs are inherently crowded. Proprioception – awareness of the position and movement of the body– is an issue that may not occur to non-autistic people but can make conferences and training sessions very uncomfortable for autistic people, for example, bumping into people or objects in tightly packed spaces.

> *Also, the expectation that I sit in a chair and listen for a whole day without being allowed to get up and move my body builds up anxiety and I'm unable to concentrate. Being allowed to stand up the back and subtly stim (jigging my legs, pacing, rocking and swaying my head). I've never been to a conference that worked for me. But those that allow me to get up and move around are much easier and allow better concentration.* (Trevor)

A commonly suggested strategy for addressing the synergistic sensory overload (and social overload) was providing a quiet room, or low-sensory space, where people could take a break and reset. However, it is important that this is not seen as a replacement for addressing the sensory and other issues across all aspects of the conference/training course venue and activities. One person also commented that there are downsides to such a space as it can lead to further stigmatisation and exclusion.

> *Efforts were made at all of them to cater to autistic needs, and they had quiet rooms, some had social badges, that type of thing. However, most venues are just not built to accommodate sensory sensitivities, with terrible acoustics and poorly designed spaces that encourage crowding; that can make conferences and workshops hard despite the best efforts of the organisers.* (Louise)

> *The autism conferences often include accommodations like quiet spaces but I find these make me more aware of the difficult aspects. With separate spaces for break times etc., it often feels like an us and them situation. Often, the dedicated quiet space is quite far from the main common area and it feels quite segregated. At the last autism conference I attended, I felt very excluded from the academic side of things as the majority of Autistic participants were representing community groups so I didn't get the chance to properly engage with other researchers or network.* (Ruth)

Organisation

The theme of organisation encompassed three sub-themes: information, scheduling, and logistics. Having access to *comprehensive detailed information* prior to the conference was consistently mentioned as important, which is not surprising given the anxiety many autistic people feel when contemplating new experiences and uncertainty about what they will encounter. A common reflection was that conferences could be made considerably less stressful by providing attendees with detailed agendas/schedules, talk synopses, and notes; maps, location information, and directions; and information about accessibility, including dietary and accommodation needs. The value of having access to a human being – a name and a phone number – to answer questions was also emphasised. For conference presenters, clear information about the technology available, the room layout, and the session structure is also critical.

> *I feel that all workshops and conferences should have the following as a minimum: a conference pack, sent out beforehand, with details of the location, photos, programme or agenda, maps, travel details, and as much detail as possible about what will happen and in what order.* (Louise)

> *Further accommodations include plenty of notice of schedules, a good description of the venue with plenty of photos of access points, and accommodating to dietary and disability-related needs.* (Jade)

> *Providing an agenda is always helpful regarding parking, food options and directions with visual cues as opposed to an address and room number. Having the mobile number of a facilitator is always helpful in the event I get lost when I am already at a venue and need explicit instructions from someone to help me get to where I need to go.* (Flora)

> *My anxiety over technology is a bit excessive in these situations, and I feel that sometimes those who work with tech support in conferences don't understand the level of stress this can cause some people. Mostly – I just need to know exactly what kind of room I will be in, what kind of technology is available and/or what I must bring for myself, and who exactly I can contact for help. And I want this information well in advance.* (Trina)

Scheduling was problematic for many, with concerns about the duration of sessions, the infrequency and brevity of session breaks, and the impact this has on both the ability to process information and the extent of social and sensory overload. This results in attendees missing sessions they would have liked to attend due to the need to create a break time. The scheduling of poster sessions was another aspect that is typically done in a way that excludes autistic participants. These sessions are often scheduled for late in the day, in small spaces and with a concurrent expectation of social interaction. Suggestions included outdoor poster sessions, scheduled 'quiet time' poster sessions, and the use of QR codes.

> *Have longer breaks. Sometimes morning tea is 15 minutes – that's not enough time to find something to eat and go to the toilet (plus queue) – let alone talk with others about session (if you want) or have quiet time (if needed).* (Jane)

> *If there are poster sessions, please allow quiet times with QR codes on the posters so people can go through and collect QR codes of the posters they'd like to know more about. From there participants can get in touch with the presenters with their questions.* (Kelly)

My worst ever experience at a conference . . . was this awful hotel where they jammed a bunch of posters into narrow, overcrowded hallways – absolutely terrible. That was ironic because the very same conference was, the year before, the most accessible I ever attended, because the posters were outdoors in a giant tent that allowed sound to dissipate easily. (Scott)

Logistics can also be challenging, with the stress associated with travel and being in unfamiliar surroundings meaning that autistic attendees can be exhausted and overwhelmed before the conference even starts. The group reflected on things that are within control of conference organisers, such as session start and end times, accommodation options for autistic attendees, and remote attendance options. They also suggested changes that employers could make to enable autistic researchers to participate more fully in conferences, such as preparation and recovery time built into conference travel arrangements.

I have never attended an in-person conference that worked well for me. Between travel, time zone changes, unfamiliar food, and sleeping in an unfamiliar place, I am usually exhausted by the first day of the conference. Once the event begins, the socializing is even more difficult than it might otherwise be. (Marie)

More travel flexibility rather than "fly in, conference, fly out" to reduce number of nights = hotel stay cost. Need travel and recovery time built into travel time. (Jane)

I more dislike the process of travelling than I dislike conferences themselves. Intercontinental travel is particularly stressful because I simply can't sleep on airplanes, and I've only recently gradually become able to eat some airplane food, which means that I'm arriving hungry and tired and stressed in an unfamiliar foreign country. Highly suboptimal for my general functioning. The last time I had a proper meltdown – still a long time ago – was an intercontinental trip, albeit not one related to a conference. For intercontinental travel, it would be great to have financial support that would allow a decent chunk of time to recover from the trip before the conference. (Scott)

Social Interaction and Networking

A common theme in the reflections was the draining nature of the constant social interaction that is a feature of conferences and training sessions. This included scheduled networking sessions, unstructured interaction between sessions and on breaks, and after-hours social gatherings. Many autistic people find social interaction emotionally and physically draining, and do not see this as the 'fun' and 'relaxing' aspect of these events, as many neurotypical people do. Adding this constant social input to the sensory overload and executive functioning challenges faced by autistic people leads to overload and exhaustion. Many commented that these events could be made far less stressful if the number and duration of social activities were reduced, or if these aspects were made optional and non-participation wasn't frowned on.

> *What I find difficult about conferences is the networking, which I'm absolutely rubbish at. I tend to gravitate toward people I already know, or go to my hotel room if I have one to rest.* (Liam)

> *Not judging people for not observing certain pointless social conventions like making eye contact or small talk (if people could be less judgmental about harmless differences in general, that would be great).* (Amy)

> *Networking is clearly important in a lot of these situations, but very often that's expected to happen in loud environments with lots of other people talking, which makes it hard to focus or even just hear what the other person's saying.* (Dee)

Participants also commented that, where social interaction/networking is needed, there are a range of steps that could be taken to make this more feasible for autistic attendees. Suggestions included facilitated networking sessions with specified conversation topics to avoid the awkwardness of making small talk; having mentors, buddies, or colleagues support the autistic attendee by buffering them from excessive social interaction; and, ideally, increasing acceptance of autistic people and not judging them on their social skills or ability to mimic non-autistic communication.

> *I once attended a conference that had an event pairing newcomers to the conference with buddies. We were given time for structured conversation with our buddy and were encouraged to connect throughout the conference. This was helpful for me, since it's often hard to network without support.* (Marie)

> *Limit the amount of social time and where networking is required ensure this is structured to a time-frame or similar to speed dating set up where questions are pre-planned.* (Flora)

> *Less noisy, putting people with a mentor and a small cohort to help people network.* (Isabella)

The group identified a number of strategies that could be implemented to reduce the impact of social overload from constant interaction, in addition to the suggestions presented earlier (and the recommendations about the scheduling of sessions and breaks). Providing an autistic social space where people feel able to relax and be themselves would be a welcome relief from the exhaustion of constant masking, and also present opportunities to connect with people with similar interests and communication styles. For autism-focused conferences, it was suggested this could be extended into facilitated social interaction sessions that are structured in a way that supports autistic communication preferences.

> *Being able to meet fellow autistics could be nice for mutual understanding, support and networking.* (Amy)

> *I suppose if we wore our sunflower lanyards discreetly, and there was a room set aside for the autistic/anxious/otherwise struggling people, then that could be a great comfort – just to meet one other person with whom I can relax makes all the difference, and if this could be fostered in some way, that would be fab.* (Mia)

As seen at some autism conferences, the use of conversation badges would be a welcome addition to conferences, workshops, and training sessions and would be of value to many autistic and non-autistic people alike. These badges/stickers allow people to visually communicate whether they are open to interaction or need to have some time out from social interaction. However, it was acknowledged that for these to be effective, there was a need to normalise the choice not to interact – rather than have the 'red' badge interpreted as being unfriendly or unlikeable.

> *I've also heard of some autism conferences using "interaction badges" to indicate whether you don't want to be approached at all, only want to interact with people you know, etc. I haven't been to one that did that, but the idea definitely appeals.* (Amelia)

> *I have been to conferences where they have had colour coding systems for participants to indicate their communication preferences (please leave me alone – to I'm happy to chat). At one such conference I desperately wanted to pick the "please don't talk to me colour" but I felt like people would judge me for doing so, so I didn't. Each day getting back to my hotel room I would end up in tears because I was just utterly exhausted. Not just from the actual conversations and interactions but from the constant threat of potential interactions.* (Scarlett)

In-Session Interaction

The theme of in-session interaction consisted of two sub-themes, one related to the format of sessions and the other to the rules of engagement. Consistent with research on university studies, the issues of groupwork and being called on to speak impromptu were raised as problematic in the *format* of sessions. Conferences and workshops, like university classes, present attendees with the challenge of working in groups with people they do not know and being expected to confidently articulate their views in front of a room full of strangers. These sessions could be made far less confrontational for autistic attendees by normalising the choice to observe and listen rather than actively participate, allowing people to move in and out of groups to accommodate different communication modalities.

> *One thing I have noticed is that training and workshops have quite an emphasis lately on group work and group activities. I understand this from a teaching perspective, but it can be very draining for some of us to have to do this all day. It is also difficult for me sometimes as I need time to process the information being delivered. Sometimes in workshops etc. it would be nice to have the option to just sit, listen, absorb and then apply later.* (Scarlett)

> *I also find it frustrating how workshops constantly force attendees to participate in small groups or require attendance 'grades' (by speaking up/asking questions throughout the workshop). It would be helpful if more introverted methods (e.g., writing thoughts out on paper instead of having to speak them) were utilized for these purposes.* (Emma)

> *I feel that organisers should be flexible and make it clear to people that they can leave if they need.* (Louise)

> *I get very impatient at training sessions/workshops. In a 2 hour session, the presenter sometimes spends 20 minutes (honestly – I time it) on icebreakers! I consider this a complete waste of time. I just want them to get to point. I find more icebreakers extremely awkward so they don't 'break the ice' at all, if anything, they create more ice! Actually I'm terrible at these things – I'd just prefer to read the paper on it. I find that events tend to lack depth and detail and I find this frustrating.* (Olivia)

Academia is uniquely competitive and combative, making many conferences and workshops a hostile environment for autistic attendees. These interactions could be made more comfortable and beneficial by setting basic ground rules around interactions. Useful parameters for respectful communication could include how and when to ask questions, normalising 'questions on notice', and session chairs stepping in to deflect hostility.

> *No requirements for speakers to speak to others before their talk (nerves can make it hard to speak or to mask effectively).* (Evelyn)

> *We must have guidelines set in place especially for the audience as to when they can ask questions, not to interrupt the speaker and so on. While these things might seem unnecessary at first glance, but I have seen that most university administrators especially like to use the rules, which were made to protect minorities, against us and justifying reverse discrimination that way. We must make sure to put such unruly people in check and for this reason, the guidelines for the conference will be helpful which should mention the*

consequences of not following them. I generally had more trouble as a speaker than as an attendee. (Proline)

Setting up rules for inclusive, respectful, and meaningful communication throughout the proceedings, trainings, workshops, etc. For example, a list of statements could be made, informing how we would like to talk to each other, what values do we want to promote when we discuss something together, how a respectful disagreement could look like. Such list could be read out loud at the beginning of an event. (Betty)

Otherwise conferences and workshops are ok for me, except when I'm caught out by a question that requires fact recall, which is often difficult for me at the best of times. In my area of scholarship, most discussion is conceptual, which I'm good at. But a common means of aggressive territory marking is to demand the recall of facts or authors and such, and I've been caught out more than once and put in a very embarrassing situation of looking like I don't know what I'm talking about. (Liam)

In-Session Information

The reflections raised several issues around the format and content of information in conference sessions and workshops. Recommendations about the transmission of information focused on the need to consider different information-processing styles and speeds, the structure of information, and the length of presentations. Some noted the importance of minimum accessible design standards and catering to the range of communication needs as standard good practice rather than as something that is available only if specifically requested. This included closed captioning/subtitles for all presentations, the availability of written notes before rather than after the session, and other tools needed for accessible communication.

Keep training short and accessible (visual with written description and/or subtitles); record and share speeches and/or allow access afterwards. (Kelly)

Having multiple modes of delivering content is also helpful. What I find best is when Powerpoint is used as an outline or memory guide in which to talk or discuss a subject rather than reading from the visual aid. (Moon Man)

The academic talks could be more accessible, with printouts (large-type) of the talks themselves, in case there is no CART service. I don't require CART myself but I know autistic people who have auditory processing issues and can't follow verbal presentations in real time. They literally cannot participate in the talks that cover their own scholarship. This is a travesty. (Saskia)

Participants also commented on the two-way nature of communication in conferences and training sessions, noting that approaches that facilitate audience communication with the presenter also need to be considered. The issue of information content was also raised, with some commenting on attending conference sessions that were triggering due to the inclusion of ableist and offensive language or perspectives.

> *For presentations/conferences about autism, compulsory requirement for non-autistic presenters to submit their presentation to autistic sensitivity readers prior to the event to ensure ableist language is removed and ableist conclusions are critically interrogated.* (Ella)

> *Depending on the conference, sometimes the content of the presentations is a challenge in itself – I have walked out of a number of conference presentations in tears because the content was so blatantly offensive (e.g., genetic research discussing options for preventing autism) and/or because the presenter went into graphic detail about triggering topics like self-harm and suicide without giving any kind of content warning.* (Alex)

Inclusion

Awareness, acceptance, and inclusion were seen as key aspects of conferences that are often missing, resulting in autistic academics feeling isolated, excluded, and stigmatised. The group reflected on the importance of academia as a whole becoming more aware of the challenges and strengths of autistic people, breaking down stereotypes, and providing a more inclusive and welcoming environment. This includes being aware of the impact of assumptions about social interaction, information processing, and sensory needs. It also includes eliminating harmful misperceptions – often associated with functioning labels – such as that as highly intelligent, educated people we should be able to 'handle' these challenges, and that adjustments and accessibility provisions are an optional added extra rather than essential for equal participation.

> *A lot of the above suggestions, however, would only help if widespread ignorance about autism was eliminated first. For example, accessing a sensory room at an academic conference could be difficult because of assumptions about what autistic people look like, how we behave, or who we are. It could also 'out' us as autistics in environments where that might not be safe because of stigma, and there could be concerns about possibly losing our jobs because we 'out' ourselves. As long as people continue to look down on us, make judgments about us, or think of accessibility in design or delivery as an optional bonus that most people don't really need because we're academics and can 'function normally', then the*

above list won't help. We need widespread education about what autism is, what it actually means for autistic people, and what it means in the academic environment. (Ella)

I think the most useful accommodation is for the conference organisers to actively model acceptance and to make it clear that everyone is welcome at the conference. (Alex)

It would also be beneficial to have some kind of contact for accessibility matters at conferences who knows what they are doing. (Scott)

Particularly in the context of autism conferences, there is a need for more proactive steps to include autistic voices, encourage and support autistic presenters, recognise the importance of intersectionality, and actively seek out and celebrate varied autistic experiences. This does not mean seeing autistic people as the 'end-users' or 'targets' of (autism) research, invited to participate as token laypeople, but identifying and recognising the strengths of autistic academics as equals in the task of scientific enquiry.

Consider accommodations as advancements to the way we develop accessible conferences and training programs that inevitably benefit everyone. (Kelly)

Proactive inclusion of autistic presenters, especially autistics of colour. (Ella)

Online Conferences

The last two years have seen an unprecedented rise in online conferences and training sessions, with very few face-to-face events since the commencement of the COVID-19 pandemic. Some of the participants reflected on the advantages of online conferences, particularly the removal of anxiety associated with travel and the sensory and social overload of constant interaction. They expressed a wish that the option of virtual attendance would become an ongoing option post-pandemic.

I'm an extreme case, but my sensory issues make any large gathering problematic. Thanks to the pandemic, I have discovered a solid strategy – give audiences the option to attend virtually. If I can participate via Zoom, I can adjust volume and brightness as needed and any stimming behaviors can easily be masked by simply turning off my camera. (Dave)

As far as conferences and workshops go, it's actually been great to start off my academic conference-going career during a pandemic, because online conferences are much less exhausting. I attended the American Sociological Association's annual meeting online last summer, and really enjoyed all of the sessions I listened to; I even felt confident enough to speak up and ask questions in a few of them. I learned that some of those sessions would have been held in a large, very loud hotel banquet hall with multiple panels going on simultaneously, which sounds like a) a recipe for sensory overload, and b) a guarantee I would not have gotten anything out of them. So having a remote-attendance option is something I hope conferences maintain in the future, even when they are held in person again. (Dee)

I think some of the modifications made to conferences and large seminars for the pandemic have removed many barriers to me for conferences. As a non-driver with sensory processing issues, attending a conference on Zoom and being able to switch groups and enter breakout rooms without figuring out how to move tables and chairs around the room and where to sit and to travel to the conference, without having to navigate public transportation (or even unfamiliar airports) without getting lost or disoriented.... When the pandemic ends, I hope that there is some continuation of remote and hybrid delivery especially for large seminars.... I think more quality remote instruction sticking around post-Covid would open many doors and would put me on the same level playing field as my non-disabled colleagues. I want the world to open up a little more ... but not too much. (Eva)

However, others commented that online conferences can be as much, or even more, challenging than face-to-face events. Concerns included the sensory overload from the online interface, difficulties in processing information without some of the usual visual cues, and the challenge of knowing when to speak.

I don't really know what the best practical form would be. I thought for a long time that Zoom conferences would make things easier for me. But since I took part in a lot of them since last year, I find it actually very difficult to follow (hard to concentrate) and it is even harder to know when to talk and when to listen. (Sophia)

I suspect that the uptake of more virtual conferences might assist in this area? Although I don't really enjoy hours of online sessions all in one day. (Scarlett)

The group made a number of recommendations for how online conferences could be made more autism-friendly, including allowing (and normalising) the option of having your camera off, scheduling sessions with adequate breaks, allowing for asynchronous viewing of sessions, and 'flipped learning' to enable participants to formulate ideas for discussion before the session.

To make them more accommodating for autistic academics they could be held online; cameras and microphones can be off if wanted and needed. (Baz)

I have not attended many online conferences, but I believe they could work well for me – especially if there were either recordings available or a schedule that is spaced out evenly. (Marie)

> *A conference that worked for me was one that I helped organize recently, which was a flipped webinar. Participants wrote blog posts which had to be read ahead of time by the other participants, who sent questions in advance so everyone would have time to think in advance about them.* (Liam)

Some Final Thoughts

It is clear that there is a lot we can do – and a lot that needs to be done – to make conferences more inclusive for autistic people, as audiences, participants, and presenters. It is particularly noteworthy that many of the issues raised by the group were in the context of autism conferences (the context where the meaningful inclusion of autistic people should be the highest priority). It is also clear that this *is* possible:

> *I did attend two conferences in the States in 2018 and 2019 that "worked" well for me, probably because they were conferences designed for autism inclusion. This was the College Autism Summit (formerly College Inclusion Summit). Lighting and food choices were a significant part of the reason I felt comfortable in this venue. As a vegan, I had worried significantly about what I would eat during the conference, but they were prepared for this. The lighting all over the venue was also excellent. They did not use bright, fluorescent lighting in any part of the conference space, and this made the entire experience much easier for me. I am sure it made most of the attendees more comfortable too.* (Trina)

The recommendations in the literature, and the accessibility provisions of an increasing number of conferences, are a step in the right direction in providing a more inclusive environment for attendees (passive recipients of information) but do not fully address the needs of autistic *participants*. A review of the literature within the theoretical framework of universal design provided a range of recommendations across areas such as online booking, communication (e.g., wayfinding and mobile applications), conference accommodation (e.g., seating and quiet room), catering, and policies and procedures (Irish 2020).

The sensory issues raised by the group were reflected in the adjustments made in the conferences noted at the beginning of this chapter and should be standard at all autism conferences (reducing, or enabling participants to control, levels of sensory input).

Within the theme of organisation, it is encouraging to see conferences moving to address the need for detailed information to be available to participants before and during events. In this regard, increasingly innovative technological solutions to assist with this (such as conference apps and virtual tours) could be made available to attendees. However, other aspects remain problematic, such as scheduling sessions to allow for reasonable breaks and to avoid information and sensory overload. It is important to acknowledge that conference organisers face competing challenges – scheduling multiple sessions within limited time frames is one such challenge – so creative solutions are needed. For example, rather than having long breaks between sessions or late starts and early finishes (which would address the needs of many autistic participants), perhaps sessions could be recorded for watching at a later time or autistic people could be involved in the scheduling of sessions to avoid clustering of presentations that will be of interest to the same audience.

Social interaction and networking – posited by the academy to be one of the primary benefits of academic conferences – was raised as a significant challenge by many. While the use of 'social interaction badges' at some conferences was seen by many as a step in the right direction, it is important to note that the lack of social acceptance of the need to have a break from interaction inhibits many autistic attendees from availing themselves of this option. Further, it is important to ensure that giving us the option not to interact is not seen as the sole solution. Autistic academics come to autism conferences for the same reason as non-autistic academics: to increase our knowledge and our networks. A truly inclusive conference would include providing social and networking opportunities that address the communication needs and styles of autistic people.

The move to online conferences – forced upon academia by the pandemic – has not been without its problems for academics of all neurotypes. Challenges of online conferences that have been identified include information overload, lack of social connection, tribalism, and increasing the digital divide (Etzion, Gehman, and Davis 2021). While not specific to autistic participants, a recent paper in *GigaScience* provides comprehensive recommendations for more inclusive online conferences to facilitate the participation of traditionally underrepresented groups (Levitis, Gould van Praag, Gau, et al. 2021).

Largely missing from the literature and from conference guidelines, but very evident in the reflections of the group, were the barriers to autistic people as active participants in and contributors to academic conferences – as presenters, panellists, discussants, and collaborators.

For real inclusion to be possible, conference organisers need to reimagine aspects of the nature, content, and structure of conference sessions and interactions to better include and empower autistic academics. If we are to make autistic researchers feel welcome and able to participate, we need to review the guidelines we provide for preparation of papers (using inclusive language, avoiding ableism), presentation of papers (not including 'requirements' around eye contact or body language), asking questions in sessions, and other aspects of the two-way communication of information.

> *That said, there is also a scientific culture that is part of what makes these conferences interesting to us as academics. So I'm less keen on advocating for making them into community spaces for lay people – if you're an autistic researcher you're probably going to be able to keep up with the scientific jargon for example. So I advocate for re-examining these spaces for ways they promote systems of oppression – for example assumptions about people's capacity to pay or to travel – and implementing structural changes in collaboration with communities to become less oppressive while ALSO attending fully to the excitement and advancement of scientific inquiry and knowledge dissemination. I think it is possible to do both, it will just take some breaking down of assumptions and shifts in the power dynamics of whose perspectives and decisions are coming to the table.* (Sunny)

> *A lot of people don't seem to realise that autistic adults are generally chronically ill people. We have all sorts of issues. One of the more obvious is that of digestive issues and intolerances that require dietary considerations. But, then there are the chronic pain conditions and the conditions that cause severe fatigue. These are very common among autistic people, and I think conferences that are trying to be accessible to autistic people should be considering these issues. You know? Add extra rest times between presentations. Add numerous seating options so those with pain can change posture regularly.* (Jade)

> *Rethink the whole thing from the ground up. Everyone just seems to have accepted that there is a standard recipe for a conference or workshop and that's just how it is and nobody questions it. If we started from identifying what we actually wanted to achieve and then only created activities that served to achieve those goals things would be rather different.* (Morgan)

Most importantly, as autistic researchers (especially at an autism conference), we should be respected and valued for our expertise. We come to the table as equals: we are academics with research skills and qualifications, just like our non-autistic colleagues. Being autistic means that we may have some challenges that you do not have – and we may need some adjustments made to enable us to function at our best – but being autistic means that we also have some strengths and unique perspectives that non-autistic researchers do not have.

CHAPTER 10

Aspirations

> *What matters most to me . . . is that I have a cognitively challenging job that has a positive impact on my species. If I had been asked to create my own dream job, it would not have been as good as this.*
>
> (Dave)

What next for autistics in the academy? In this chapter participants reflect on their career aspirations: the roles they aspire to and their expectations as to whether they will achieve their career goals. For those goals that seem out of reach, are the barriers intrinsic to being autistic or are they systemic and structural?

Is This Our Forever Job?

Approximately one-third of the participants expressed the view that they are in their 'forever job'. For some this meant literally the exact role they were in at the time of writing their reflection, whereas for others it meant more broadly a career in academia.

> *Absolutely [this is my forever job]. I love the work, the way it's structured, the accommodations and supports I receive, the people I work with, etc. We are now funded with an endowment, and it was explained to me I had a job for the rest of my life. I think I'll keep it =)* (Dave)

> *I . . . would like to continue my work in academia because it gives me a clear structure, allows me to pursue my interests, allows me to contribute to society, creates conditions for bringing out my skills and abilities, especially concerning my ability to "immerse" into a particular problem and dig into it very deeply and methodically, and because it allows me to challenge myself and overcome my limitations, for example in social situations, presenting myself in front of a public.* (Betty)

For some this forever role represented successfully finding the perfect fit: a role where they felt they belonged and were valued, and in which they could use their skills to do something meaningful. These participants commented on the synergy between the skills and characteristics that are required for success in the role and their strengths as an autistic person. Equally important was having a role in which they were able to make a contribution to their community, whether this was the autistic community specifically or the broader community.

> *I believe that my current job is my "forever job". The main reason for this is that it is perfectly suited for an autistic person like me. I can look into small details including one case where a regular person would have missed the mistake but I was very careful and my supervisor congratulated me for pointing that mistake. I would like to work on the same thing for long term, however, I would also love to get promoted as well since having more disposable income always helps.* (Proline)

> *I like the University job at the moment as it is flexible, and my employer is supportive of my needs in regards to sensory and social needs and has a good attitude towards my autism. They value my work enough that they are willing to modify the job to suit me so long as I get the work done. I need above all things a workplace that is flexible and doesn't require me to work all day in a traditional office setting where the sensory fatigue from fluorescent lights, abrasive sounds and the constant demands of social performance would exhaust me. I do most my work at home and then come into the university to supervise students and do some teaching and then I go home.* (Trevor)

> *The position I am in currently is a 'layperson' position in that I have started the Autism Training Academy which offers online asynchronous micro-training about autism and neurodiversity for the education, healthcare, and government sector. It is a direct result of my first research and I am committed to it for the foreseeable future. I am committed to it because it makes a difference to my community (educating professionals about autism).* (Kelly)

Sadly, for others, it represented a reluctant acceptance that this was 'as good as it gets' and that the barriers they faced as an autistic person would prevent them from advancing further towards their career goals. These barriers included social exhaustion, communication challenges, and the need for stability and certainty due to difficulty coping with change and uncertainty.

> *Unfortunately yes [this is my forever job]. I cannot go elsewhere in academia as fully promoted and low pubs. I mean maybe some sort of teaching admin. But I am so fried. I would like to go back to my old career – I even tried. But I don't think that is possible. Or I would like to do something with diversity maybe. Not sure. But I would definitely like creative projects.* (Isabella)

> *I don't think my position specifically is my forever job, but I think the broader category of 'mid level leadership on a professional classification in the same*

university' is kind of my forever fate. I can't move to another institution, I can't move into academic roles because PhD programs aren't accessible to me . . . and while COVID has potentially opened up possibilities in other industries that allow remote working, I'm really risk averse about moving.... That said, I do derive satisfaction from my role and what I do. (Morgan)

Since I really like to feel safe, I am probably going to keep that job forever, even if I thought about quitting several times because it is very exhausting for me to pretend being someone else on a daily basis. But I am not sure it would be any different in another job. (Sophia)

Approximately one-third of the participants described their current role as not being their 'forever job', but for most that was in the context of it being part of their journey within academia. For those who were early in their academic careers, and particularly those completing doctorates or in junior roles, their current positions were seen as a step on the way to their career goals. Similarly, for those in fixed-term contract roles, this was part of the process of seeking an ongoing academic position.

No, it is not my "forever job" but more of a "stepping stone" job to an academic position with more opportunities and challenges and intellectual stimulation. (Baz)

At the moment, my main focus is my PhD, so I hope that's not my forever job! I would very much like to stay on my current team, though. [Current supervisor] is incredibly supportive and understanding when it comes to the Autistic researchers on the team. Her vision seems to be focused on building a research team where Autistic researchers feature prominently, and she understands that there needs to be support that goes along with that. (Ruth)

I'm not in my "forever job" just yet. Right now I have a series of short sporadic contracts to help with various projects. (Jade)

For some who had been in academia for longer, there was a recognition that the barriers and challenges they had faced over time had taken a toll on them. While they were keen to remain in academia, they reflected on the need to look for a role with different task demands (e.g., less teaching) or in different environments (e.g., away from bullying and discrimination).

I don't think I can lecture forever. I used to think so but it is just so tiring. I'd like to stay with the university though. There are enough oddballs that I fit in fairly well! (Olivia)

I would love to leave the job I have because my harasser is still in the department, yet it's hard to beat my university in terms of quality, funding, and the quality of life available in the city we live in.... I feel like I'm at a crossroads; either I move up in administration and actually push for transparency and anti-racism, anti-ableism, anti-sexism initiatives in academia . . . or

> *I pull back, find a lower-level teaching job near the mountains, and spend as much time as I can involved in things that make me happy (climbing mountain trails, being outside, maybe starting gardening).* (Saskia)

For a minority there was the reluctant acceptance that they needed to leave their current role and that academia was not, or may not be, the right career for them. Reasons for this included struggling with the social and capacity expectations of inflexible workloads, dealing with burnout and mental health issues, bullying and discrimination, and untenable working conditions. For the protection of the participants, I have not provided direct quotes in this instance.

The remainder were unsure whether they were in their forever job, or forever career. Some were struggling with aspects of their current role and exploring the possibility of leaving academia, whereas others were pleasantly surprised by the work they were doing and were exploring the possibility of staying in academia. However, among those keen to remain in academia there was a consciousness that this may not be possible, either due to the impact of the job demands on their health and well-being, specific aspects of the role, or the tumultuous and uncertain nature of the academic environment.

> *Now I have left the research administration role in the autism specific early learning and care centre, my main role is a PhD candidate and I am absolutely loving it. I am now seriously considering a long term career in academia as I feel best suited to the field and the most valued that I have ever been. I love the flexibility of working at my own pace on my own research project, and being able to organise my own workload.* (Psyche)

> *It's hard to say whether I'll want to stay in this job for the long term. I relocated to be near it, and I like it for the most part now that I'm familiar with it. I have seventy students on my caseload, though, and that is a lot to manage. When I'm doing well, I can manage it alright. But sometimes coping with mental health factors and just the "time tax" of being disabled makes work/life balance harder to maintain, so I'm not sure yet if it will be sustainable in the long term. I sure would like to never have to interview ever again, though! So that gives me some incentive to stay as long as I can manage.* (Amelia)

> *I think academia is a more precarious career path today than it might have been a decade ago. Especially since the pandemic, many institutions are suffering financially, and even tenured academics have lost jobs. I would love to keep working in academia and at my current institution long-term, but because of these changes, I don't count on my current position as a forever job.* (Marie)

Interestingly, two commented that they do not believe in the concept of a 'forever job', as they see their lives and careers as forever evolving as opportunities arise.

I don't believe in a "forever job" for myself. I would like to continue evolving professionally, and this will involve moving from one campus to another. I may like to stay in [country] long-term (possibly indefinitely) and work on multiple campuses. (Trina)

Theoretically however I don't believe in the notion of a forever job as life and opportunities are constantly changing and evolving. I am aware this is very likely my literal interpretation of forever!! (Flora)

What Roles Do We Aspire To?

Among those who were committed to building an enduring career in academia, aspirations not surprisingly included a pragmatic focus on aspects such as tenure and job security, as well as promotion to the next step on the academic career ladder.

My eventual goal (at least right now) is to get a tenure-track faculty position once I am done with my degree. I'm open to the possibility of a non-academic job as a researcher somewhere, though, because it's the research aspect that really appeals to me. I am nervous about the application and interviewing process once that time comes, but I hope I have built up some solid experience and credentials by then. (Dee)

I'm currently near the top of Level B (Lecturer). I'd like to be promoted in the next few years to Level C (Senior Lecturer). I do not have a PhD, so whether I get promoted depends on whether having a PhD affects this. (Jane)

I would love to get promoted in my current position. Even though it comes with a higher responsibility of having to supervise some workers … there are many coworkers who call me an angel and wish I were their mentor. So, I believe I would enjoy the added responsibility in order to get a higher income. However, I do not want to rush for that and I want to take my time instead. (Proline)

I would like to have the opportunity to become a manager of the team I am moving back to (and worked with for 7+ years previously). I know my current manager is supportive of me learning the ropes to potentially do this but my past experience in acting manager has been a huge challenge for me.… The difficulty working full time has been a barrier to this type of position in the past, I feel like people often don't take me seriously, and I have noticed that I find auditory processing in meetings more challenging than I probably realised, which means in strategic planning meetings I am often caught off guard and struggle to keep up although I have excellent critical and analytical thinking skills but I just don't get to contribute effectively and become overwhelmed and tune out. On the positive side a lot of this insight has come since my diagnosis so I believe that this will definitely allow me to work on strategies and gives me more confidence to actually consider a management role in the future. (Scarlett)

Some reflected on their longer-term career aspirations, typically a full professor or the equivalent. Note that while the terminology is different, the following three quotes are effectively referring to the same role; in the Australian academic system the term 'professor' is used only for this highest level (the US 'full professor'). However, these autistic academics also reflected on the barriers that would potentially make attaining this level difficult or unachievable.

> *I aspire to one day become a professor. I think I will achieve that role, but that is dependent on projects I can be a part of and then publications that I get published. Without being able to conduct research, be a part of project and then write up manuscripts for publication, then I will not achieve that role.* (Baz)

> *Is there another role I aspire to? I don't know. If you asked me maybe a few years ago, I would have said, "I'd like to be a level E professor."... I don't know whether that's feasible, because of the work-life balance thing. I don't see a lot of people at that level [who] have a very good work-life balance, and I have so many spoons to dedicate for each day. I just don't know whether I can, to be honest.... Ideally, in an ideal world, it's not gonna happen, but I'd like to just work three or four days a week, and that's it. And get paid for three or four days a week, like not get paid for three days, but work five.* (Charlotte)

> *Mostly I just want to keep growing my research and making an increasing impact on the community I care about. I got a late start since I had a first career so there's probably a cap to how much I can accomplish, but I'm doing my best to speed the curve. My long-term goal is to improve employment outcomes for autistic people with skilled training in a wide variety of fields.... At the university I'm on a research faculty track, which promotes Assistant Professor, Associate Professor, Full Professor, Professor Emeritus. Assuming the world doesn't implode more, and the NIH keeps funding me, completing these pathways [is] not out of reach. Mostly I can't really dawdle.* (Sunny)

Others were very clear that they did not aspire to be promoted, as they felt that the demands of more senior roles would be inconsistent with their ways of working and interacting, but instead had aspirations around the types of tasks they would like to focus on and the environment in which they would like to work.

> *I don't aspire to the next highest position on the official achievement ladder: becoming a department chair, provost, or another kind of administrator. I believe these roles would bring added social stress and difficulty for me. However, I do have specific aspirations. I would like to write more and pursue further education (either formally or informally). I also aspire to working 100% remotely on a long-term basis, teaching online rather than in-person. I think I will achieve the goal of more writing and learning. However, I'm unsure about whether I will be able to work 100% remotely long-term.* (Marie)

> *My professional aspirations are rather prosaic. I am not particularly interested in climbing the social hierarchy of a University. My aspirations are to stay in the bubble of work that interests me and not get too stressed by extra responsibilities.* (Trevor)

Not surprisingly, given that so many of us are attracted to academia as it seems the ideal career for us to focus on and utilise our special interests and ability to hyperfocus, a common theme in the reflections was the aspiration to work more directly and fully in research roles. The concept of being able to immerse oneself in data and information gathering, combined with the joy of writing and sharing knowledge, is a strong attraction. However, participants also reflected on the accompanying challenges from the 'distractions' such as conferences, networking, and office politics that can limit our ability to demonstrate our skills as researchers.

> *I would love to work in research in a more direct way (i.e., not editing research manuscripts but actually being involved in the work itself). I love statistics and getting to know the data, but unless you've been to school for data science (and not behavioral research, in my case) people won't look twice at your credentials. And the worst part is, the longer that I'm out of the research scene, the harder it will be to get back into it. Another issue is that with research, you're typically expected to be involved in Symposiums and whatnot, and that's just not something that I can do, so it's another roadblock.... Honestly, if I could just run analyses in the corner of an office and not have to worry about playing the social politics game – or traveling for various conferences – I'd be a happy camper.* (Emma)

> *My ideal job would be to be a writer and/or researcher, for a science magazine or BBC information programmes or something like that. Something where I get to read and write all day but I don't have someone picking holes in everything I do. I love writing and researching, and I enjoy presenting complex subjects in simple ways. I really struggle with deadlines, managing competing priorities, and anything "peoply" such as social interactions, open plan offices, office politics, etc.* (Louise)

Another common theme in the reflections was participants' desire to use the combination of their discipline expertise and their lived experience to undertake high-quality research that would benefit autistic people. This altruistic drive was a consistent theme in earlier chapters, such as reasons for entering academia and positives aspects of academia as a career for autistic people. It is likely that this reflects both the underlying empathetic nature of autistic people and their specific desire to save other autistic people from their own lived experience of discrimination and victimisation. While the literature is slowly starting to acknowledge that autistic people do not 'lack' empathy, as suggested by the stereotypical representation, but rather differ from non-autistic people in their ways of expressing empathy (Milton, Gurbuz, and López 2022; Ekdahl 2023), it is concerning to note that autistic prosocial behaviour is often still interpreted as a deficit or an unexpected outcome (Hase, Haynes, and Hasler 2023).

> *My forever job would be as a full-time psychology/medical researcher focusing on autism and the medical conditions that often come along with it. My biggest barrier to getting to my "forever job" would be health issues, not autism. But, this is the thing about autism. The health issues I have, that impact on my achieving my aspirations, are very common in autism. So, it's not autism impacting on my aspirations, but, it kinda is the autistic life. So many of us have chronic health issues that have a great impact on our lives. I'm happy to say I'm one of many autistic people fighting for more research on our health issues.* (Jade)

> *My ultimate goal is to obtain a faculty position that would allow me to do research. Because the research would be specifically around autism, I do probably feel a deeper investment in this path than most people would – I feel some level of duty towards the autistic community to be successful as an autism researcher. I feel an obligation to increase the meaningful representation of autistic people in this field.... I hate thinking about the actual application processes and doing work like thinking about potential postdoc placements and such. I avoid that. So while I have been intensely producing research output and while I have been connecting with people and networking in order to set up research collaborations (which I enjoy), I have not really been doing any networking or preparation for the upcoming postdoc stage – I will put that off as long as possible.* (Scott)

> *I could happily work my way up to research via a lecturing/researching role, but the goal is to be mostly a researcher. I want to use my experience of being autistic and my academic qualifications/experience to make a difference via books, initiatives, consultancy, informing practice and I think research is a great way to get into that. I'll get there eventually, I'm confident of that because I'm very good at research and I have a lot of passion.* (Evelyn)

This altruistic desire to help others was reflected not only in the types of research the participants wanted to undertake but also in the other roles they aspired to. There were numerous references to wanting to take on roles that involved mentoring, supporting, and/or advocating for autistic people and other marginalised groups.

> *What I really would like to do is to advocate for autism, to spread awareness of what autism is and more so what it is not. In my country there still are a lot of clichés about autism, like the idea that autistic people are violent, unable to have social contacts, unable to feel empathy.... I feel that it is my duty to try to fight those misrepresentations. I also need to feel useful and to have the feeling that my life and my experience can help others.* (Sophia)

> *Mentoring, making people feel like they belong and have something to contribute. I think I'm fairly well positioned to do this in my current role, though you can always do more.* (Amy)

Similarly, those who were considering, or aspiring to, careers in teaching, administration, or other aspects of academia were attracted by the opportunity to help and support others, rather than by material or status benefits for themselves.

> *I never thought I would like administration but it turns out I love being on a steep learning curve and understanding how systems work. One of my favorite TV programs is How It's Made, the one that shows factories producing stuff. Admin experience has been like the How It's Made of academia, and I have really loved what I've learned. . . . I rarely aspire to specific roles, but I would like to facilitate expanding educational access.* (Saskia)

> *I would like to utilize aspects of the skills I have learned to take on a community role in education or disability advocacy. I think my future role will include many components of what I do now, but likely not in the same format.* (Eva)

Some Final Thoughts

A common thread throughout the participants' reflections, in the context of both their current roles and those they aspire to, was the desire to find a role that 'fits', that is, a role where they can be themselves and use their skills in a meaningful way. Similarly, qualitative research with autistic adults across different employment contexts in Australia identified three key themes: wanting a fulfilling career that matches their interests and skills in a suitable environment, wanting stable employment, and having low hope for finding meaningful work (Hayward, McVilly, and Stokes 2019). Sadly, this third theme was evident among my participants, with many commenting that they had taken, or would likely have to take, a job that was unfulfilling due to the lack of acceptance of and accommodation for their needs as an autistic person.

It is perhaps not surprising that few of the participants believed that a leadership position was within reach for them in academia. This does not reflect a lack of academic skills, knowledge, or expertise, but rather our struggles with hidden curriculum, social expectations, and the emotional and physical energy demands of constant masking. The risks associated with disclosing an autism diagnosis were discussed in Chapter 7. Not only does this make it difficult for junior and mid-career academics to disclose; it means there are few visible role models of autistic people in senior management and leadership roles. A search of library databases for articles or other resources on autistic leadership returns very few articles on autistic people as leaders (Roberson, Quigley, et al. 2021), other than a handful of case studies on small autism advocacy organisations (van den Bosch, Krzeminska, et al. 2019). There is a body of literature on the types of management and leadership styles best suited to supervising autistic employees (Martin, Flanagan, et al. 2023); for example, a book chapter entitled 'Leadership and Autism' concludes with 'a discussion of how employees with ASD [*sic*] may position themselves to be effective followers and members of teams in the workplace' (Hurley-Hanson, Giannantonio, and Griffiths 2020a).

If we are to support autistic people to thrive in academia, we need to raise and support their aspirations. This includes reducing barriers to disclosure and increasing access to supports so that those already in academia can remain and progress in their careers (Raymaker, Sharer, et al. 2022), and in turn inspire and support the next generation. It also includes not seeing autistics as only suited to 'niche' and narrowly defined roles (Ezerins, Vogus, et al. 2023), but recognising their diverse strengths and creating truly inclusive work environments that enable them to bring this range of contributions to the academic workplace.

CHAPTER 11

Advice (for Academia)

> *I participated recently in an event, which brought together neurotypical people and autistic people from different fields to try to find solutions to make studies at the university more inclusive. That was very exciting and everybody was very nice. I felt a little sad as the event was ending because it really was a nice parenthesis of understanding and tolerance.*
>
> (Sophia)

In this chapter participants reflect on the steps that senior academics and academic institutions could take to better support early career autistic academics. They also reflect candidly on the things that non-autistic colleagues and friends could do to make them feel more comfortable in both work and social settings.

Advice for Peers and Colleagues

> *The most important thing neurotypical people need to do, in work, social, or any settings is, #1 be accepting. There's a difference between saying you're accepting and actually having that attitude. Practically, I think the most important things are to listen to us, and to address sensory issues.... But, if a neurotypical can't understand our experience, it does not then give them the right to water it down to a point that they CAN relate to it and understand. They need to stop and accept that when we're describing our experience, it might seem exaggerated to them, but it's true for us. It is exactly how we say it is. And, if they have the power to address sensory issues, they should absolutely do that, as an access issue and an issue of humanity.* (Jade)

I asked the participants how their peers and colleagues could make them feel more comfortable in a social setting and also in a workplace setting. As there was so much overlap in their responses across the two settings, which is probably not surprising given the social nature of the academic work environment, I combined these for analysis. I have grouped the common themes in the reflections into three categories, using as a framework the three stages reflected in the iterative renaming of Autism Appreciation Month: autism awareness (knowing what autism is), autism acceptance (accepting autistic people in the workplace/community), and autism appreciation (recognising and valuing the contributions that autistic people make to the workplace/community). See Figure 11.1.

Awareness

At its most basic this stemmed from the desire that non-autistic peers and colleagues would *learn about autism*. This included taking steps to learn about autism generally, and share that knowledge with others, as well as to engage in open communication with autistic colleagues about their own experiences and needs.

> *If I had to choose the most important thing that neurotypical people could do to make me more comfortable, I think it would be to take the responsibility to educate themselves about neurodiversity and to share what they learn with others.* (Marie)

> *I would benefit greatly from allistic people educating themselves about autism, the diversity of autistic presentations and experiences, and ableism – and then acting from this place of knowledge in social settings, rather than one of ignorance based on unfounded stereotypes. My sense is that if allistic people understood what it meant to be actually autistic, then many of the social issues they perpetrate – such as excluding people who do not perform in allistic ways, bullying people for breaking social norms, and infantilising autistic people – would decrease.... We are currently too often a terrifying and strange 'other' based on a caricature of stereotypes, and it is this ignorance about who we are as people that drives allistic people's social discrimination against us.* (Ella)

> *If you are aware of my diagnosis then talk to me about it – ask questions – be engaged. Don't act like you don't know or that I am so fragile (or stupid) that I won't be able to handle a conversation about my own condition.* (Flora)

It also included being open to truly understanding the meaning of the autism spectrum. Autism is not linear, from 'not at all autistic' to 'extremely autistic'; we each have a unique combination of strengths and challenges (see Chapter 6). Truly understanding this means understanding that the *way we experience the world* is fundamentally different to the way that non-autistic people experience the world. It also means understanding that there will be tasks we struggle with that seem 'easy' to you, or days we struggle with things we found easy yesterday; but there are also things we find easy that you might struggle with.[1]

[1] A thorough explanation of what it feels like to be autistic, and how that differs from the ways that non-autistic people experience the world, is beyond the scope of this book. I have written extensively about this in my previous book, *Growing in to Autism*, and have also included a list of recommended readings in Appendix C.

AWARENESS

We recognise the importance of understanding autism as an intrinsic part of an individual's identity, and this includes our autistic staff members

ACCEPTANCE

We embrace the opportunity to renew existing processes, procedures and policies though the lens of autistic lived experience. Improving accessibility and inclusivity benefits everyone.

APPRECIATION

We experience the organisation-wide benefits of supporting autistic staff members who are thriving and excelling as teachers and researchers in their fields of interest. It has influenced the way we approach recruitment to ensure we attract autistic job applicants.

Figure 11.1 Awareness, acceptance, and appreciation. Source: Art by Chloë van der Reijden.

> *Listen, learn about autism, assume competency, be aware that needs and abilities change sometimes moment-to-moment, believe us when we say we need help or cannot do it today (we're not trying to be difficult), ask questions and get to know us.* (Kelly)

> *It would be useful for people to understand what it's like to really have no fuel left in the tank. Working in academia is demanding and exhausting. I don't think there are too many people out there who are committed and innovative teachers, and also producing good research with frequent publications who get up feeling as fresh as a daisy. So, when you say, "I'm exhausted", the common response (whether said aloud or not) seems to be, "we're all exhausted". What people don't seem to understand is just what "exhausted" looks like for Autistics. I think, for most people, it might mean an early night or a lazy weekend at home. For me, it means not having the energy to take the few extra steps to check the mail on my way up the driveway; it's not having the energy to even decide what to have for dinner, let alone make it; it's dishes left unwashed, Mum's phone call not returned, the cupboards being bare when the grocery shopping is put off once again.* (Ruth)

Not surprisingly, a number of participants referred to the *stereotypes* around autism (Hurley-Hanson, Giannantonio, and Griffiths 2020b; Fontes and Pino-Juste 2022; Wodziński, Rządeczka, and Moskalewicz 2023) and the need for people in the workplace to look beyond these overwhelming negative stereotypes of 'what autism looks like'. Many of us have had the experience of issues in the workplace being attributed to faults or limitations that are assumed to be inherent in all autistic people due to limited understanding of the diversity and strengths of autistic people.

> *Talk about autism in a more positive way, or at least one less laden with subjective negative value judgements and disorder and deficit language. Can be very irritating.* (Scott)

> *The most important thing that neurotypical people could do to make me feel more comfortable in the workplace is to drop their negative stereotypes and misconceptions about autism and autistic people. By far, social ostracism and exclusion by neurotypical people is the most disabling aspect of being autistic.* (Psyche)

Several participants mentioned *sensory issues*, although in the main sensory challenges in the workplace were seen to be things that supervisors and institutions were more likely to have the capacity to control. Considerations that would be appreciated from colleagues and peers included things such as organizing meetings and catch-ups in quieter locations and considering the sensory needs of the autistic person in choosing tables or seating locations. For others, the fact that physical contact can be very uncomfortable for some autistic people (Christopher 2019; Taylor, Holt, et al. 2020) and that being touched by others in the workplace can be distressing (Penton, Bowling, et al. 2023) was a challenge in the workplace that required understanding from others.

> *... non-autistic people make me more comfortable on a regular basis by dimming lights or moving so that I can sit in a dimmer part of the room ... Something that non-autistics could also do to make me more comfortable at work is to not expect hugs or any other kind of physical contact. One silver lining of this pandemic is that people are (hopefully) less eager to touch one another at work.* (Trina)

> *From a sensory perspective – catch up where the only noise will be you having a conversation and enjoying each other's company. No music or TV, or coffee machine in the background.* (Jane)

It is important to remember that these sensory issues are not minor inconveniences, but can cause autistic people considerable stress, discomfort, and even pain (Taels, Feyaerts, et al. 2023). As Mia notes, "sensitivity to noise seems to be regarded as laughable and contemptible among NTs," making it difficult for autistic people to communicate these needs to non-autistic colleagues.

Acceptance

Accept Me for Who I Am

A common topic in the reflections was the desire to be accepted for ourselves as we are, not to be judged and found lacking because of our differences. This included recognizing that if we speak, act, or react in a way that is unexpected, this is in most cases not because of a character flaw or a deliberate attempt to offend or annoy you, but rather a reflection of our different way of experiencing the world.

> *Not be judgmental, be welcoming, be kind, be helpful, give us the benefit of the doubt.* (Amy)

> *In terms of what NT people could do to make me feel more comfortable in a social setting, my first reaction is to say: have some flexibility and give me the benefit of the doubt if I respond to something in an atypical way. Don't assume I'm being evasive if I don't make eye contact, and don't assume I'm being rude if I'm not enthusiastic about small talk. But I think a bigger change would be to just realize how much effort social interaction costs me, so a) take it as a compliment if I seek it out with you, and b) don't expect me to do it 24/7.* (Dee)

> *The most important thing that neurotypical people could do to make me feel more comfortable in a social setting is also to drop their negative stereotypes and*

misconceptions about autism and autistic people. If people could just learn to think about autism as a naturally occurring product of neurodiversity, it would be awesome. Maybe then they would stop treating autistic people as lesser beings. (Psyche)

The constant need to mask in social situations, and the resulting exhaustion (discussed in detail in Chapter 7), could be significantly reduced if our peers and colleagues could remember that our verbal and non-verbal communication may be different to theirs, and not interpret our comments and expressions from a neurotypical frame of reference.

I need people to please not comment on my appearance. . . . I particularly dislike it when people tell me that I don't look happy. In social settings I try to adjust my face so it is doing what is expected of it, but when people tell me that I don't look right, it makes it harder than ever to look happy and cheerful. It isn't just women who are told our faces look wrong; my husband also gets told to 'Smile!' and it makes him furious. We are doing our best. (Mia)

Include Me (Gently)

As mentioned in earlier chapters, a prevailing stereotype of autism is that we are unfriendly people who do not desire human interaction. The reality is much more nuanced; it varies between individuals, between contexts, and between specific instances. There is clear and consistent evidence that autistic people, in all walks of life, are consistently isolated and excluded (Mazumder and Thompson-Hodgetts 2019; Jones, Gordon, et al. 2022). This may be because we don't 'fit in', because we don't know how to pick up on the social cues and join into conversations and activities, or because our previous non-attendance at social events is interpreted as rudeness or lack of interest. Many of the participants commented that they would like colleagues to invite them, but also to accept that if they decline invitations – even repeatedly – this is not a rejection but the reality of their limited social energy.

Reach out, don't ostracize, include. (Isabella)

Something a neurotypical person can do that would make me more comfortable in a work/social setting: invite me. But don't be offended if I end up not coming, or I only pop in for a short while. Even though at least half the time I will probably not attend a work-related social function (e.g. drinks with colleagues) I still want to be invited. I know they probably assume that I don't want to go, but if I have the energy/ capacity available I do still want to be included, but don't be upset with me or treat me differently if, when the time comes, I don't manage to get there. If you still invite me and you accept the fact I may not come, then I don't feel as awkward when I do actually manage to get there. (Scarlett)

> *Please accept that I am exhausted at the end of the working week. I don't decline socialising invitations because I don't like the people, I just have nothing left and the best part is going home on Friday and putting my pyjamas on.* (Olivia)

Some participants expressed that they would prefer not to attend social events with colleagues, or to be expected to participate in small talk at work, because they saw work and socialising as very separate things. Again, this could be addressed by making it clear that they are welcome but that you understand that they may prefer not to and will not take offence.

> *In terms of neurotypicals, I think I'd be happy if they just left me alone (in work settings). I'm there to do a job, not to make friends or 'hang out'. I think social settings are a bit more relaxed, such that neurotypical people could probably get me involved in a conversation.* (Emma)

> *I guess not encouraging me to go to restaurants for any professional reason? I'm not very motivated to camouflage for purely social reasons, I should say, so I just won't bother with a social interaction for purely social reasons if it makes me notably uncomfortable, but if there's a professional reason then you're putting pressure on me to make choices to pursue social interactions I would find stressful.* (Scott)

When your autistic friend or colleague does attend a social or work-related function, if this is not something they regularly do and are clearly not at ease with, your support can make this so much less intimidating for them. Many of us struggle with initiating conversations, particularly with people we don't know well, so if you have encouraged an autistic colleague to attend, try to introduce them to others and help them join in the conversation. I would also recommend offering them an exit strategy in case they feel overwhelmed and wish to leave early or step out for some quiet time.

> *This depends a lot on the social setting. In an unstructured social setting with neurotypical strangers, the best thing is to be there with a trusted friend or colleague who can introduce me to people, help me parse the room, translate [for] me, and be available for me to hide behind if it gets overwhelming. In a social setting with neurotypical friends I'm already comfortable.* (Sunny)

> *Follow my lead . . . if I am quiet, sit with me; if we are standing, stand beside me looking out rather than standing in front of me forcing me to make full eye-contact. I would be so grateful to have allies in the room.* (Kelly)

> *Not assume that they know why I'm leaving. I have to ghost social settings [leave without telling others] when the sensory overload overwhelms me, and sometimes I don't know exactly when that's going to happen. I'm a grownup and I can monitor my own responses to a social setting, so I know when the end is*

*approaching, but I don't know what *moment* it is going to come, and when it comes, I have to get out of the place NOW. It's rarely because I'm trying to make a rude statement about the people there.* (Saskia)

Communicate with Me

As mentioned in previous chapters, differences between autistic and non-autistic communication styles are a significant challenge in the workplace. Direct communication was a common topic in the reflections, both the need for you to communicate directly and clearly with us and the need for you to understand and accept the intent behind our direct communication style.

> *I take everything very literally and prefer only direct communication. There should be awareness that being direct is not rude, but it helps in processing better. The other thing would be to not have any assumptions. As an autistic person, nothing is implied. There should be awareness of the fact that being explicit should be encouraged instead of having everything implied.* (Proline)

> *Neurotypical people could make my life easier by SAYING WHAT THEY MEAN, and by being more forgiving of my directness and social mistakes.* (Mia)

> *The most important thing neurotypical people could do to make me feel more comfortable in a work setting or a social setting is making their expectations clear and being flexible with how those expectations are met.* (Amelia)

There were a number of references to challenges with information-processing speed, such as not being given enough time to respond to questions, to fully articulate our answers, or to ask questions for clarification.

> *Giving me more time to express myself in direct speech communication.* (Betty)

> *To make me comfortable in a social setting, I would need people to let me [have] more time to think about what I want to say and to be able to ask questions when I am not sure of what they are trying to say.* (Sophia)

> *All work settings = Give us time to respond and don't "butt in" and start talking again, as we are taking a very brief break from talking (answering your question, or explaining something) to take a breath and/or think!* (Jane)

Related to the above was the issue of not putting autistic people on the spot and expecting them to 'perform' at their best without notice. This included both spontaneous requests, such as unplanned invitations to speak, and last-minute changes to work schedules or activities.

> *To not pull me directly into a conversation where I end up having to talk about something in front of everyone with no prior warning e.g. "Oh [Baz] is currently doing/working on x,y,z" (social cue/attention directed towards [Baz] to then talk about x,y,z).* (Baz)

> *In my work setting, I would really appreciate people understanding that I need to have information in advance so that I can be prepared. I hate last minute changes in the schedules, in the expectations.... It drives me crazy, makes me anxious and I can't be productive when I am like that.* (Sophia)

Appreciation

It was disheartening to see how few of the participants reflected on how colleagues have made them feel, or could make them feel, appreciated in the workplace. Consistent with reflections elsewhere in this book – and with the experiences of autistic people reported in the literature more generally – it seems that just having others accept our right to be in the workplace is still the goal for many of us. However, as Louise describes below, there are colleagues and workplaces that do appreciate the strengths that autistic academics bring to the table.

> *In a work setting, the best way that I have been accommodated and made to feel comfortable is for people to openly notice and enjoy my little "quirks" and accommodate them. I can't stand it when people pretend not to notice, or roll their eyes about it, and I don't like it when a big deal is made either. The best colleagues I've had have been the ones where we spent social time together as well, built up relationships, learned each other's stories, strengths and difficulties, and adjusted our workloads accordingly. So I'm great at spreadsheets and detail, a colleague is great at coming up with ideas but not necessarily following through, another one is an amazing networker and social butterfly – the best workplaces will always recognise these things and adjust roles to make the most of strengths and minimise weaknesses.* (Louise)

Advice for Supervisors and Senior Academics

> *Please offer services as a bridge communicator. That has helped me enormously. Please tell us what is expected. Please try not to offer ambiguity as answers. Please read a bit or listen so you aren't operating in stereotypes about autism. Autism isn't a mental illness and a meltdown isn't an emotional or psychotic break, it's overwhelm bursting out is all. Help us not get to that stage – provide answers and help. PUT US ON TEAMS! We have strengths and are good team mates. We will likely think of things you didn't. Don't be judgmental. We are not dumb weirdos. Learn to live without eye-contact or sport talk to have a meaningful conversation. Please don't denigrate us and tell us not to be ourselves. Please support us to be the best we can be. Which is what we all should be doing for everyone.* (Isabella)

While many of the same aspects of awareness, acceptance, and appreciation were evident in the participants' reflections when I asked them what supervisors and other senior academic staff could do to support autistic academics, there were four themes that predominated.

The first related to the *hidden curriculum* (see Chapter 3) and the significant challenges this poses for autistic people, who by nature have difficulty interpreting unwritten social rules and subtle nuances of social interaction. Participants commented on how challenging they found this aspect of their role, and also gave examples of caring and supportive supervisors and senior colleagues who had provided this support to them in their roles.

> *Explain the codes of communication, behaviour and overall expectations in academia more generally, and the discipline and institution more specifically. They need to understand that it takes far more labour for us to figure that out than neurotypical people, and so there needs to be an adjustment there.* (Liam)

> *As for what senior faculty can do: as an early-career, first-generation autistic academic, I was deeply grateful for the senior people (and even peers) who would take me aside and explain social expectations and dynamics in academia. In many domains of life, you can survive by watching and mimicking the person in charge. Not sure how to eat this meal with these utensils? Watch your host. Not sure how to greet people in this country? Watch the locals. In academia, this does not always apply. Hierarchy is in the bones of academia, and you risk modeling the wrong person's behavior. I have been thought arrogant for making the same kinds of jokes and discussing research in the same way my senior advisors did. There is this idea that certain illustrious folks can get away with reckless behavior, but junior faculty certainly cannot. So when someone was kind enough to say, "You probably shouldn't do that," I was embarrassed but grateful. Senior faculty can make life much easier for early-career autistic faculty by explaining how the hierarchy works. As the saying goes, When in Rome, do as the Romans do – but I have learned that you need to know WHICH Romans you need to role-model.* (Saskia)

> *When an early career academic starts their role, they could really benefit from some clarification about the unwritten politics of academia. I am still struggling to work out the "hidden curriculum" of being an academic. Also, I would have found it useful to have some sort of map of the different people in the university and their role especially those that I need to be working with, networking with etc.... It's one thing to have this information available, it is another to provide the information directly to me and highlighting what information is important to take in and what is just important to be aware of.* (Scarlett)

> *The boss that I have now .... She's given me some good advice in terms of, for example, when I'm having trouble trying to fit everything in. And she just ... In a single word, she's just like, "Prioritise. Not everything needs to be done. Yeah, you can say no."... And that's, I feel been quite liberating for me as*

well.... So yeah, maybe just listening to some of the challenges that we have and then maybe offering some advice and strategies, like on what works would be kind of helpful, I think. (Charlotte)

The second was *clear and supportive communication.* This included providing detailed and specific instructions on tasks, being explicit with expectations. It also included being open to questions, and not making the autistic staff member feel that their questions were annoying or reflected poorly on them.

I think clear expectations and flexibility as needed are probably the most helpful steps senior academics could take in supporting early career autistic academics. A major aspect of those clear expectations would ideally include clear instructions on where to go for questions, the best medium to ask questions, etc. I tend to feel trapped in not understanding or knowing the next step sometimes, and people have generally been very kind and responsive when I finally work up the courage to ask. But it's always so helpful when people give a clear instruction like "email ______ if you have questions." (Amelia)

Provide clear instructions and feedback – comments such as 'this is interesting' or 'we could expand on this more' don't help me, if you want me to expand on something say so and tell me what it is that I am expanding on. Have the understanding that those with autism better respond to feedback when it is directive in nature. Starting feedback comments with 'you could' or 'you might' does not help when the project is not yours. (Flora)

Beyond task-related questions, this also included being willing to listen to the autistic person's concerns, being open to hearing their ideas, and accepting that they may not be comfortable raising these in group formats.

Help support challenges. Autistics may be reluctant to ask for help or indicate they are struggling – especially in front of others. Request for help [is] more likely to come from one-on-one discussions. (Jane)

Listen to them.... Answer their questions but above all, listen to their concerns and be interested in their observations. (Lisa)

Just having a basic understanding of the struggles of autism can go so far – we tend to think literally, use language literally, so vague language can lead to confusion. Try to be blunt, direct, and think carefully on your language, and please don't jump to conclusions if we come across as abrasive or insulting – chances are good we don't realize others could be insulted by our language. Never assume, always ask clarifying questions. Those of us who are successful integrating into society can do so largely because people in the past took the time to get to know us and give thought and honest answers to our questions, even though many believe "everyone knows the answer to that," – we wouldn't be asking if we knew the answer =) (Dave)

The third theme was to understand and respect the *challenges and strengths* of the autistic individual. This went beyond having a general awareness and understanding of autism (although many noted that this was still a basic need in academia), to taking the time to understand their needs as an individual. As Stephen Shore famously said, "If you've met one autistic person, you've met one autistic person."

> *Learn at least minimally about autism as a difference, not a disorder.* (Amy)

> *Fundamentally, I feel there needs to be an institution-wide cultural shift in academia about how autism is understood . . . 'coming out' as autistic when in a peer position with other academics is quite daunting. It's difficult to trust that there will be understanding, compassion, and the openness to break down misconceptions and learn from me about what I bring to the table and the hurdles I have to overcome.* (Ella)

> *Regarding senior academics, I think it would be helpful if they asked autistic academics what they need. In other words, personalized support. Don't assume every autistic person will need the exact same support because we're all different people with different struggles.* (Emma)

> *Senior academics could support younger autistics by helping to pin down and conceptualise all of the different jobs that need to be managed in an academic career, and putting that into some sort of structure. . . . My supervisor also helps me by being flexible in her approach, by listening to my needs and adapting to those (e.g. if I'm having a couple of weeks where I need more regular input) and she advocates for me to third parties as well. I think it is important for senior academics to also recognise the disparities they might see between particular skills in autistic researchers, and not to judge or demean people on that. So for example, I can conceptualise complex theories, do in depth statistical methods, and write nuanced papers but I cannot write legibly, remember something I said yesterday if I haven't written it down, and sometimes I struggle to understand really simple sentences if I'm overloaded or if I am taking it literally. I am grateful that most of my colleagues see those things and don't use it as an excuse to undermine or patronise me.* (Louise)

The fourth was the need for *flexibility in work processes*. This included openness to different ways of doing specific tasks (e.g., different teaching styles), different ways of working (e.g., working from home), and different ways of communicating.

> *Senior academics could better support early career autistic academics by allowing flexibility in achieving KPIs [key performance indicators] and allow early academics to manage their own work in a way that works for them.* (Trevor)

> *Be flexible with work style and arrangements, such as environment, social tasks such as presenting, public speaking, etc. be mindful of what causes anxieties and*

static or fried brain.... Do not "force" them to deliver a presentation or something that causes extreme levels of anxiety – the repercussions for the individual may have long lasting and far-reaching effects on them and others around them, such as partners or family members. (Baz)

Be open to using different teaching methods that suit the communication style of the instructor. Although it's a lot of prep work, I am actually looking forward to blended learning this year because I don't have to lecture, and I'll be able to use this material past the pandemic and focus on small group teaching instead. (Liam)

I also find it helpful when there is someone senior on a team who understands the situation and won't be dismissive when I come back with something like, "yes, I can do that, but I can't do it now and can we talk about it later?" Or someone who I can approach and ask to do something a different way. (Ruth)

Advice for Institutions

When I worked at [Institution] which is an autism research center, they actually, knowing all my sensory sensitivities and stuff, put me in an office shared office with two other people.... In an office by the door and by the filing cabinet, which people would have to get up all the time to access the filing cabinet, 'cause they were actually doing all clinical work ... and I'm quite sensitive to movement. Super distracting, and they thought that, "Oh, we'll just take out a light bulb above your desk, and it will be fine." No, it wasn't fine. Yeah, and this is at an Autism Research Center.... So what I would say is, apart from having my own office, if they could just listen. Like listen to the accommodations that you need. Instead of just saying, like they didn't actually ask me. Okay, so they put me in this open plan office and said, "Oh, here you go, here's the space for you to work in. Would it help for us to take out a light bulb?" Not, "Is this okay, or would it help." Or they didn't ask me before the fact, and I get it. Space is at a premium. They can't just give me my own office or anything. And that's why I ended up working from home most of the time, because I didn't have my own office, so yeah. But they could have put me in an office with someone who worked part-time, and then I just came in on the days that that other person wasn't there, 'cause there were offices that just had two people in them. I could have gotten an office like that, so that's maybe something that they could have done, which would have helped. And do you know what? It's funny, because initially they did do that. They put me in an office which just had one other person. That person worked part-time, but for some reason they thought, "Oh, no, you need to be more with the rest of the team, and put me in an office."... If people, or workplaces could just listen and then act on what they have heard, or make sure they've understood accurately and then act on what they've heard. That would be super helpful. (Charlotte)

The advice participants provided for institutions included many of the same themes and concepts as the advice provided for supervisors and senior academics, but also covered broader aspects of institutional politics, processes, and environments. To make these suggestions actionable for institutions I have presented them as a list of considerations under category headings.

Culture Change

The need for culture change at an organisation/sector level was a major theme across the reflections. This included recommendations that those in leadership positions provide training for staff, address bullying, confront ableism, and increase inclusion, issues that have been found to be problematic in other employment contexts (Whelpley, Bochantin, et al. 2019; Cooper and Kennady 2021).

Training

One of the most common reflections was the need for training of all staff on autism, and neurodiversity more generally. Such training should:

- Be comprehensive and ongoing, and provided to all staff.
- Address stereotypes and misperceptions.
- Go beyond general 'awareness' to address understanding and acceptance, including how to support autistic people in the workplace.
- Be developed and delivered by autistic trainers who can speak from a position of both academic knowledge and lived experience ('nothing about us without us').

Bullying

It was not surprising that explicit and consistent anti-bullying policies were suggested by many of the participants, given the number who had reflected on situations in which they had experienced bullying, from microaggressions through to systematic, targeted attacks that resulted in ongoing damage to their careers and mental health. Academia as a profession has been described as 'rife' with bullying (Keashly 2021), and autistic people in all walks of life are known to be particularly susceptible to becoming bullying targets (Pfeffer 2016; Ferrigno, Cicinelli, and Keller 2022). For autistic people, many of whom have difficulty reading between the lines and understanding the nuances of social interactions, strategies to address bullying in academia should include:

- Clearly worded and clearly stated policies defining bullying and sexual harassment

- Zero tolerance for bullying based on neurotypes, communication, or behavioural differences
- Clear processes for seeking and receiving support (from people who have adequate understanding of autism and how to support autistic people)
- Effective and actionable consequences for bullying and discrimination
- Whole-of-institution policies and initiatives to address stigma and misunderstanding.

Ableism

Participants commented on both explicit and subtle ableism in academic settings, including policies and processes that discriminated against autistic people, which could be addressed by:

- Implementing anti-ableism initiatives that educate allistic people about actual autistic presentations, ways of processing information, and ways of communicating
- Instituting hiring and promotion criteria that are flexible enough to accommodate neurodivergence (such as the list of examples of things that can be included as evidence of 'engagement' or 'professional standing')
- Acknowledging, utilising, promoting, and celebrating the skills and expertise that autistic academics bring to the institution.

Inclusion

There were frequent references in the reflections to the need for greater inclusion of autistic people – and other minorities and marginalised groups – in all aspects of academic life. This included:

- Not framing interactions around the assumption that all experiences and ways of being are the same
- Not discriminating against people because their autism (or other disability or characteristic) limits their capacity to participate in certain activities
- Not perceiving/describing disability adjustments for students and staff as concessions or lowering of standards
- Having a clear, simple, and consistent process for applying for accommodations with a central contact point for information and support
- Including autistic people in decision making that affects them (including policies, accommodations, autism education content).

Environmental Change

Environmental aspects of academic institutions that posed challenges for autistic academics that could easily be ameliorated by planners and policy makers, included sensory aspects, wayfinding, and working spaces.

Sensory Aspects

Make modifications to physical spaces to address the sensory hypersensitivity and hyposensitivity issues that are common among autistic people. For example:

- Reduce the use of fluorescent lighting.
- Install dimmer switches on lights.
- Reduce/eliminate the use of strongly scented air fresheners and soaps.
- Reduce the use of large, noisy, open-plan workspaces (or provide options for people who can't function in these spaces).
- Provide quiet, sensory calming spaces on campus for staff.

Wayfinding

Provide supports to assist in navigating the environment for those who may have difficulty with finding their way around the campus. For example:

- Provide campus sensory maps to help autistic people map their path or trajectory around stimulus triggers.
- Install clear signage.
- Provide clear information online, including photos of buildings (not just names or numerical identifiers).

Working Spaces

Given the known characteristics and working styles of many autistic people, open-plan, shared, noisy working spaces are not conducive to productivity and well-being. This is particularly difficult for junior academics who do not meet the 'criteria' to be allocated an office. If it is not feasible to provide the autistic academic with an office (or even a shared office space), then:

- Provide a desk in a quiet, low-traffic area.
- Provide a workspace for the individual that is as sensory-friendly/appropriate as possible.

- If open plan/shared spaces are genuinely the only option, at least allocate the autistic academic a specific desk to provide a sense of consistency – do not expect them to 'hot desk'.

Flexibility

The need for flexibility was raised across many of the reflections, including flexibility in employment types and conditions, in ways of working, and ways of being.

Employment Structure

The standard full-time academic role, with its allocation of teaching, research, and administration, poses challenges for many working in the profession, but some of these challenges can be particularly difficult for autistic people. Considerations that participants believed would contribute to their longevity in academic careers, and maximise their value to the sector, included:

- The option of working part-time, in meaningful tenure-track roles (rather than choosing between a full-time role that will burn them out or a part-time role with minimal potential for advancement)
- The ability to vary the balance of research/teaching/administration, based on recognised individual strengths and challenges
- Openness to unconventional job positions for people who struggle with a particular skill but excel in other areas.

Ways of Working

A number of the participants noted that the extended lockdowns experienced in many countries – and across most universities – during the COVID-19 pandemic had demonstrated that allowing more flexibility in working conditions actually increased productivity. They expressed cautious optimism that academic institutions may thus be more open to negotiating working conditions that would enable autistic academics both to be more productive and to maintain their well-being, such as:

- Working from home, either predominantly or at least a portion of the time (depending on the actual needs of the role), rather than expecting them to be in the office every day, as historically done
- Being able to work the hours that they were most productive, as long as they met the requirements of the role

- Having control over the ways in which they do tasks, as long as they meet their KPIs
- Having this right to flexibility recognised in official HR documents, so it is not at the whim of individual supervisors.

Ways of Being

There are many aspects of our autistic selves that we are called on to camouflage in order to fit in and succeed in academia, but that do not (or should not be considered to) impact on our ability to do the work that we are hired to do. Academia would be a lot more comfortable for autistic people if:

- Not making eye contact wasn't automatically seen as a sign of rudeness
- Stimming was destigmatised
- Autistic burnout was understood and recognized
- We were evaluated and rewarded for our work performance rather than our social skills
- Workplaces asked us about our individual needs and listened to the answers.

Communication

Communication-related issues were the most common items on the wish list for things that academic institutions could address to be more inclusive of autistic people. This included clearly communicating expectations, cross-cultural communication, and mentoring.

Expectations

Many autistic people are rule followers and many of us are drawn to academia by the expectation of clearly defined procedures, processes, and policies. However, we find ourselves confused by the lack of clarity in both the day-to-day and the long-term expectations of our supervisors and leaders. Participants expressed a desire for:

- Clearly defined systems for specifying workload
- Clearly defined systems for evaluating performance
- Clear metrics for the various aspects of job roles/descriptions
- Specific goals and objectives
- Clarity around rules (which ones are actually rules, and which are suggestions?).

Cross-Cultural Communication

The communication issues raised by participants were bi-directional, as predicted by the double empathy problem (Milton, Gurbuz, and López 2022; Ekdahl 2023). Suggestions for creating more inclusive academic institutions included changes to both expressive communication (talking to us) and receptive communication (listening to us), such as:

- Communicating clearly and directly (saying what you mean)
- Accommodating and valuing different communication styles
- Providing alternative formats for disseminating information (other than verbal, in-person, group sessions)
- Allowing for and valuing alternative research dissemination outputs such as e-posters or recorded presentations (to avoid the anxiety of in-person 'social performance')
- Communicating institutional changes as early as possible, with adequate time for adjustment and orientation.

Mentoring

I have included mentoring under the 'communication' theme as many of the participants commented that having access to a mentor would be a significant source of support in navigating the communication challenges that they faced in the predominantly neurotypical environment of academia. Such programs could include:

- Evidence-based training for mentors (including both training in mentoring and training in autism)
- Capacity for long-term mentoring relationships, to enable building of trust and rapport
- Where possible, the option of an autistic mentor who is a more senior academic.

Some Final Thoughts

Many of the suggestions that the group made could be implemented by their colleagues, supervisors, and institutions at no or minimal cost and with minimal effort. Making adjustments to the physical environment, such as installing dimmer switches, providing quiet spaces, and providing appropriate work spaces, needs to be seen as reasonable and necessary to enable autistic academics to work safely and comfortably. At the same time, behavioural and attitudinal adjustments – normalising the wearing of caps, sunglasses, ear defenders, and other sensory aids; arranging meetings in low-sensory spaces; accepting stimming and lack of eye contact as normal functional behaviours – would go a long way to making autistic people feel welcome and accepted in academia. Imagine for a moment how tiring it would be for non-autistic people if you had to hide your normal ways of moving and being for the entire workday just to be accepted as an equal.

Autistic ways of thinking and communicating aren't wrong, or inferior – they are just different to non-autistic ways. Just as you would not dismiss a colleague who speaks another language for their lack of fluency in your native tongue, don't assume your autistic colleague is less intelligent or intentionally difficult because they do not pick up on the hidden curriculum or subtle social cues.

> *Sensory friendly environments are beneficial, and we need to be more tolerant of stimming activities in professional settings – stimming helps us to calm an overworked mind and helps us to focus[;] frowning and demanding that we stop flapping our hands (or whatever the stim is) because it's distracting may make you feel better, but you've put us in a far worse position (and I promise your discomfort doesn't even approach what we're going through, and stimming is an effective strategy for calming the brain and staying on task).* (Dave)

> *I guess that in my case, I wish I could get my superiors to understand that I am capable of far more than they give me credit for. They assume that because I am blunt and not charming, that I pose a threat to them. Which I might if I'm not guided properly, in the sense that I need to be told whom we're trying to impress and what the plan is, so I don't make a misstep.* (Lisa)

> *Don't just talk to us, give us power to influence. Bring a large intersectional community to the table. Be willing to reconsider how existing structures contribute to systems of oppression and be able to make potentially radical changes to decolonize the profession.* (Sunny)

CHAPTER 12

Advice (for Autistics)

The academic stereotype of the absent-minded professor who is valued for their in-depth subject knowledge and whose quirks and eccentricities are accepted by their peers is as faulty as the stereotype of the autistic as a white, adolescent, male maths wizard. Today's academics are expected to teach, research, and engage in administrative and other activities.

In this chapter, thirty-two of the participants provide advice to autistic people considering a career in academia. They emphasise the importance of knowing what the role entails, both its strengths and its challenges; finding the right people to work with and to seek counsel from; knowing (and valuing) yourself; developing resilience; maintaining your well-being; and following your passion. I have previously published an article on this topic in the journal *Autism* (open access), which provides a thematic analysis of the responses within the context of the extant literature (Jones 2023).

However, for this final chapter I did not want to constrain the voices of the participants to brief quotes, but rather to provide the full depth of their reflections on the advice they would like to offer to autistic people embarking on, or considering, a career in academia. These candid responses reflect their thoughts at a specific point in time, for some following only a brief exposure to academia and for others looking back on a lengthy career. They range from extremely positive to acutely negative, and I encourage the (autistic) reader to reflect on them in the context of the extent to which these individuals are supported to thrive by their colleagues and institutions.

Amy

- *Know yourself: identify your values, your strengths, your weaknesses, what you can change, what you can't change, what works and doesn't work for you, how you can grow, how you can feel good (go to therapy or read self-help books if you need).*

- *Make time for breaks, fun, and relaxation, have things to look forward to.*
- *Sleep well, eat well, exercise, practice mindfulness.*
- *Make sure you have a comfortable work environment that makes you feel safe and inspired (know your sensory likes/dislikes).*
- *Focus, block out the noise (literally and figuratively).*
- *Failure, rejection, and setbacks are a normal part of life and academia: they are worth learning from but not dwelling on.*
- *Criticism is either warranted, in which case you can learn from it and improve; or it is unwarranted, in which case you can ignore it and move on.*

Ava

I'm not sure. I think that you need to have a passion for education and learning, or there's no point in being involved. I guess to look after yourself, because the teaching aspect of academia, if it is a calling for you, is much like other "giving" professions, and it can wear you out.

For the research side of it, some advice would be to also not be involved unless you're passionate, but that passion isn't enough. Don't rush into a project. If possible, join an existing project to get through the PhD. Independent research might be more satisfying, but it's much, much harder. Align yourself with researchers who actually ARE active in your research field, and who are definitely doing the same TYPE of research as your planned research. It is far too hard being the odd one out in a department or faculty. You will quickly run out of steam if your research is so different to your supervisors that you need to explain many things constantly. Don't quickly accept supervisors just because they're excited about your research plans, or excited about what you've already done; make sure they have a lot to give you, and are able to guide you to a big extent in your field, not in their different field. Never, ever accept "yes man" supervisors. They're utterly pointless. When you've completed a project, or a stage of a project, take some time off to publish it. It's academic currency, plus it's where the actual impact of your research begins.

Baz

Find a mentor, and FAST. Find someone you can actually have conversations with and communicate effectively with. If you find someone who matches or complements your thinking style and perspective this will propel you forward faster.

Read, read, read, and then read some more. Read about research methodology – I am surprised just how many senior academics lack an understanding of research methods and processes.

When you have an idea and share it, be prepared to be told it is not feasible or appropriate, and then sometime later, the person you shared it with may bestow upon you, "their" great amazing idea and approach. This can be an example of the A-F thinking. So, practice communicating effectively and articulately as this is what people want and expect. Remember it is not their fault that their brain doesn't share the amazing qualities that yours does – switch the perspective – try not to see that there is something "wrong" with you – alternatively, and with some tongue in cheek, shake your head to yourself, sigh and say, "ohh it is such a pity that these brains are stuck in this typical, predictable way. I better help them out there. What a shame they won't experience some of the things I do, If only they could experience … thinking in bursts of confetti, the feeling of being into something so intently that you forget to eat for 10 hours, word associations and where your investigations may lead your thinking, such as reading about qualitative research approaches, coming across phenomenology – that makes me think of phenols (an aromatic organic compound with the molecular formula C_6H_5OH. It is a white crystalline solid that is volatile. The molecule consists of a phenyl group ($-C_6H_5$) bonded to a hydroxy group ($-OH$). Mildly acidic, it requires careful handling because it can cause chemical burns) – chemical burns – burns – wouldn't it be fascinating to explore the lived experience of chemical burn victims, during the burn and after, what are the social and psychological impacts, I wonder if there is anything in the literature about …

Betty

- *Find hobbies that are not related to academia.*
- *Do societal work, voluntary work that can bring meaning to your life outside academia.*
- *Create networks with people outside academia to develop your values.*
- *If you want to stay in academia, look at qualifications for jobs, do committee work, learn how academia works on the institutional level, network with academics from various fields.*
- *Choose a subject of your PhD that continues work of someone else, or revises what has been already said on a particular topic.*
- *Do not start your PhD by proposing innovative research. You will never get an external grant at this stage of your career.*

Charlotte

I think the biggest piece of advice I could give you is network. Make sure you network and do it your way. Because I think in academia, it really seems to be about who you know rather than sometimes what you know. But mostly who you know, and what you know comes second when it comes to opportunities and things like that. So that would be my piece of advice for a young person considering a career in academia.

Dave

What I love most about academia is that most in this group care more about your strengths than your weaknesses. If you are really good at one thing, that is the metric by which they judge your value – there's so much weirdness and flaws in the people of academia that they are a rather open-minded and forgiving group compared to many in society.

Dee

Overall, I'm still pretty new to working in academia, but so far I think academia can be a great environment for autistics, especially compared with other jobs I've had. I like being able to work mostly independently, even when I'm part of a team, and overall I have even found the social environment to be pretty good. I like that info-dumping about my research interests is not only tolerated, it's practically required. And listening to other people do the same is often fascinating, and way better than suffering through small talk or social gossip. People in my department seem genuinely supportive of each other; I don't think I would do as well in an environment that was more cutthroat.

Ella

I would advise them that it's a challenging, stimulating, and diverse role, but that it's also not as glamourous as it seems. Most roles in contemporary academia are casual, and the hours worked (especially in teaching and marking) are not the hours that are paid for – i.e., casual workers are significantly overworked but also underpaid. I work almost full-time but am paid less than a part-time wage over the course of each year, which can be frustrating. I would also advise them that it's a very competitive industry, and that this may be a struggle for them – especially if they're autistic. A lot of success in academia seems to be based on who you know, which can be a challenge when 'networking' doesn't come naturally and 'people skills' lead to burnout. Finally, I would advise them to seek work in areas they are passionate about. I wish I were working in something that more closely aligned to my passions, but I didn't know this when I was starting out. I'm still relatively new to the industry so will seek to follow this advice in the coming years!

Emma

In terms of advice, I think it's important not to label yourself as a failure if there are certain things you can't do. Although I received many prestigious federal/provincial scholarships (equalling about $50k), I still thought of myself as a failure because I struggled with public speaking. It's important not to use such black and white thinking all of the time, but I still struggle with it. Also, I think it's important not to compare yourself so much to other people. Competition is rampant in academia, but it rarely leads to anything good. Instead, do your best with the skillset that you have. Also, be on the lookout for managers/advisors who will take advantage of your work ethic. Learn to say no so that you don't burn out.

Eva

As for what I would tell a young person beginning in academia is that it is an uncertain world right now but you have a chance to build your own career in a niche area and you might have to piece together several things unlike the made to order faculty jobs that were easier to achieve a decade ago. It is a risk but sometimes the only chance at all at gainful employment and also a chance to change small aspects of the world for the better.

Flora

(as a PhD Candidate) Be prepared that the PhD process may be the most challenging but also most rewarding process. Also, to be open minded about the fact that things won't always go to plan and very often it isn't until you have read enough literature or done enough data collection that the core contribution of your research is crystallised. Do your homework about supervisors and ensure you are well-matched in terms of fundamental value systems. I would also consider having an assessment done by an educational psychologist prior to determine strengths and weaknesses, so they don't come as a surprise or slow you down during the PhD timeline.

(as a Research Assistant) Say yes to as many opportunities as you can provided your own PhD comes first if you are also studying concurrently.

(as a Workshop Facilitator) Again, say yes to the opportunities[;] it's great to expand your teaching experience but not at the expense of your own research quality and timelines.

Isabella

Don't do it. Don't do it unless you absolutely love working on your own and are impervious to disrespect. This matters more if female. And now more than ever, don't do it if you want a job.

Jane

Follow your nose, and do what you find interesting.

Try and find your niche. Mine is biostatistics data analysis & making teaching videos (pre 2020 COVID !!)

Find the best way to communicate with your colleagues, and in what circumstances, i.e. email/teams (written), Zoom/phone, in person, etc.

Kelly

My advice for any individual considering academia is as follows:

- *Go for it. Remember that what brought you to academia won't sustain you successfully so seek out mentors who can help you gain the skills you require to navigate the many changes you'll encounter.*
- *If academia isn't something that gives you joy after trying it for an amount of time you deem is enough, then leave it. Don't get so attached to the thought of being an academic/what you think it gives you. Happiness is an important factor.*

My advice for Autistic individuals (which includes the above) is as follows:

- *Reach out to other Autistic individuals in academia and build a community that can support your growth and champion your learning.*
- *The ability to self-advocate will need to be firmly in place in order for you not to be taken advantage of during your academic career. It's okay to be working on your ability to self-advocate but you need to practice saying 'no' and setting clear boundaries all along the way with little and big things.*

- *Be prepared for spending a significant amount of time teaching others about what it means to be Autistic and in particular, your personal constellation of autism.*
- *Practice self-care otherwise burnout from overwork can be an issue.*
- *Once you are comfortable in your progress in academia, mentor an upcoming Autistic individual.*

Liam

It isn't the fantasy job it's still portrayed as in the media. They really would need to want to be an academic, and they need to find a very supportive PhD supervisor so that they can develop the coping mechanisms during grad school that they will need to survive in an academic post from day 1.

Lisa

Think twice. It will take just as much political savvy to get ahead in academia as it does in the outside world, but you'll make way less money, you'll be disconnected from a living laboratory (if you're a social science type), and you'll be just as much the brunt of jokes as you would be in an office. On the other hand, individuals are what makes the difference: if you have an opportunity to work with people that you click with, seize it by all means.

Louise

My advice to a young person considering academia would be to be fully aware of all of the facets of this type of career. So many people think it is just about learning and studying and reading and writing – do not underestimate the amount of administration you will need to do, and you can't escape the social interaction either although I do think it's better than most jobs for that! Make sure you work on your organisational skills early on, because the autonomy you have in academia can be a positive or a negative, depending on how able you are to put a structure in place for yourself and then stick to it.

Marie

I'm not usually comfortable giving advice (I'm not sure I have any wisdom), but if my past self were to ask, here's what I'd suggest:

- *Be aware that there are lots of politics, stories, and dramas going on, even if you can't see them.*
- *Find someone you trust that you can go to with questions. It's not always clear who can be that someone, but once you find them, you'll be so happy you did.*
- *You can say no to a committee or a new project.*
- *When you get an office, get a noise machine to mute outside sounds. Also, it's possible to use a lamp instead of the overhead fluorescent lights.*
- *Schedule time to recover from meetings and from class.*
- *Don't assume that you're always wrong.*
- *It's going to be impossible to know what's really expected of you.*
- *Charisma means a lot to people, but you don't need to have it to do a good job.*
- *There are many ways to be a good teacher, committee member, writer, director, etc.*

Mia

I have no advice for young people entering into Academia. Everything has changed, and what I know is probably outdated.

BUT a word on being an autistic academic, while not knowing one is autistic

I had so wanted to be an academic. I thought this was what I was born to do. I thought that all my 'differences' were because I was very academic, not realising that my idiosyncrasies were actually related to autism.

I wish I'd known just how different I am from others. For instance, I assumed that apart from a few psychopaths, most academics are driven by interest in their field, and the joy of learning and research, and the rewards of teaching. I didn't understand just how much neurotypical people care about status, and how competitive they are, and how much tribal loyalty is required; I didn't understand that you can't avoid the cliques, and I didn't understand that leaders require you to treat them with not just respect, but with a degree of adulation. I wish I'd known that small talk actually has a purpose, and I wish I'd known that my face isn't doing what neurotypical people's faces do naturally, and I wish I'd known that I alienate people simply by being.

Also, if I'd known I was autistic, perhaps something could have been done to make me more comfortable. There were plans, just before I left, to force the lecturing staff to be present in the office all day, every day. This seems to go against the spirit of academia, and one of the things I really valued about my job was the freedom to work from home for a few days a week, or for a few hours in the day. It kept me calm.

Another difficulty is that a lot of people seem to know intuitively that some rules are made to be broken. I have only recently come to understand this; I tend to follow rules, and increasingly I am discovering that nobody else bothers – or at least, they can distinguish between rules that are real and rules that are only for show. This created a big problem when I was doing my PhD, because we were required (according to the student handbook) to meet with our supervisors each week. I set up these meetings, but my supervisors thought I was setting them up because I needed help. This led to a number of misunderstandings. Once I understood that meetings weren't actually required, I found that I was free to plan my research and arrange my work schedule unimpeded. I work so much better unsupervised, and I loved doing a PhD because I had help when I needed it, but was otherwise left alone to work in my own way, at my own pace.

Moon Man

Make sure that teacher, research, and service is something you can get interested in doing. One can practice skills for teaching by giving workshops and seminars at conferences and teaching courses in community adult education organizations. Another idea is to inquire whether you might be able to observe and shadow a professor for a day to see what they do.

Morgan

I'd spend a while really getting them to unpack why they want to work in academia/higher education, what their goals are and what assumptions they are operating under regarding what they think it will be like. Then have an honest conversation about the realities so they can do an informed cost-benefit analysis, rather than just operating on all the available narratives that don't tell the whole story. But I do think overall there are a lot of affordances available in academia for autistic people that aren't available in other industries so it's worth considering, I'd just want their decisions to be informed by academia as it is actually played, rather than the way we tell people it's played.

Olivia

I don't feel that I have much advice. I wish I had known I was autistic from the beginning. Then I would have been able to recognise and manage my energy levels better. It would also have been good for me to connect with other autistic academics.

Proline

If a young person wants to have a career in academia, I will give a few suggestions. First of all, as far as possible, avoid choosing hard sciences especially for Masters or PhD. Second of all, if possible, do not choose to pursue your higher studies in the U.S., instead, choose Europe.

Psyche

The best advice I could offer to a young person considering a career in academia, whether autistic or not, is to find the subject that they are most passionate about and pursue that. Academia requires commitment, dedication, and a willingness to work really hard and for long hours, sometimes on very boring tasks, so a passion for the topic being studied or taught is utterly essential. Also, passion for the subject you are working with can help to override some of the more unpleasant aspects, such as social exclusion and feeling undervalued.

Ruth

Quite simply; don't. Don't do it unless it's something you feel extremely driven to do. My brother-in-law is a painter who works in some mine on a FIFO ['fly in, fly out'] contract. He works fewer hours and earns more than I ever will, even if I make it to Level E. It's only worth working in academia if you truly love what you do. At times, I find it hard to love my work, but I honestly don't know what else I would do. I can't imagine any other kind of job that I could sustain.

Saskia

My advice for a young person considering a career in academia is to choose a topic that they can imagine wanting to read about for the rest of their lives. Teaching something you don't find interesting enough to read about in your leisure time is the dullest, most tedious job imaginable. Researching it is even worse. We have to invest uncounted hours into our fields of interest and know the recent developments in them to have any value in academia. It won't happen if they choose a topic that doesn't have "special interest" status. I would also advise them to stay humble enough to know that there's always more to learn.

Scarlett

To be honest, if I was talking to a young autistic person who wanted to get into academia I would probably say – don't. I don't feel like the environment or the work/lifestyle that goes with academia is suited to autistic people. I hope that one day I am proven wrong.

Scott

I would strongly advise them to get undergraduate research experience in one of the fields they are considering entering. The necessity of such experience is part of the "hidden curriculum," so many of us may not realize that good grades are not enough to succeed in academia – we need other experience on a CV before we apply to graduate school. Research experience can help someone decide if the research aspects of academia are something they could succeed in or not.

I would also advise them to think carefully about questions of disability disclosure. Disclosure could hurt somebody's academic career, but then again, if one discloses, one can at least be somewhat confident that any program that hires them will be fairly accepting and supportive. . . .

I would encourage people to think carefully about all the different responsibilities they would have in a high-level academic position, and whether they would be comfortable with all those diverse roles or whether they might get stuck at a lower level in their academic career. If the latter, would they be comfortable staying at that lower level for their whole life or would they rather pursue a career outside academia?

Sophia

I am very sorry to say that I would at this point probably not encourage a young autistic person to consider a career in academia because it has been at some point very difficult for me. But if the person would really want this job, I would advise him/her to make sure he/she has enough support (from their family, partner or friends). I would also advice autistic young colleagues to focus on the students and on their research and to stay away from academic politics. Networking is very powerful in academia and this was for me one of the main obstacles. Maybe creating a network of trustworthy colleagues might be interesting, although I didn't achieve that myself.

Sunny

Generally? It depends first on where they are at in their career path. For an undergraduate, I give them a lot of advice related to exploration and letting them know that this is a good time to experiment and they don't have to make the big decisions right away because graduate school is really where the career path begins (says me with my BFA in painting and a first career in software engineering and information science!). For someone contemplating that next step into graduate work, I encourage people to think really hard about what programs, mentors, and schools are doing that align with their work, and to really start honing in on what they want to do when they are done; sometimes people worry about getting into a "good school" but that doesn't really matter if that school isn't doing the kind of research you're interested in. It's important to select a graduate program that is maximally aligned both with the kind of work you want to do and with the kind of culture and values you want to work within. In other words, I would encourage anyone who wants to do autism research that is strengths-based, neurodiversity-framed, and authentically inclusive not to apply to programs focused on curing autism that consider autistic people incapable of contributing meaningfully to science. For a graduate student contemplating their thesis or dissertation, I pass on the best advice one of my mentors gave me – "Consider what do you want to do when you're all done and craft your dissertation to teach you the skills to do it." I tend to give a lot of advice around mentors and what they can provide because they are exceedingly important both to successful completion of a graduate program and to a future in academics. It's not stated explicitly like in some trades, but I feel like the academic model remains an apprentice-journeyman-master type of system. Beyond those general things, I tailor advice a lot to the specific person and their situation. I especially enjoy mentoring people who are neurodivergent and/or who have experienced trauma and marginalization, because I can give them some pieces of what I've learned that they can't get from other mentors. I also like to pay forward what my mentors gave me.

Trevor

The advice I would give to a young person considering a career in academia is "Do what you love and you never work another day in your life". Be kind and compassionate to yourself and know that the solutions that work for most people may not work for you off the shelf. You will have some failures during the process to find what works until you establish your career and that's okay.

Trina

I think it would have to depend on the career destination. I find academia in this country (the US) to be needlessly political and would honestly advise other Americans to seek their degree outside the States if at all possible.

If the person has a disability and/or learning difference, I would advise them that higher education (in any country) was not designed with them in mind but that they can still be very successful if they are prepared to advocate for themselves and education others about ableism.

Afterword

This book reflects the lived experiences of thirty-eight autistic academics (including the author). While the reflections were collected at a specific point in time – July 2020 to June 2021 – our adventures in academia have continued. Some of us have gone on to achieve career success beyond anything we imagined was possible; some of us have remained in the roles we were in at the time of writing; and some of us have left academia due to the toll of working in an environment that can be very hostile to autistic ways of thinking and being.

The common thread in those three diverse outcomes was the impact of the people above us and the people around us. Those working in institutions that were genuinely inclusive, with supervisors and colleagues who truly accept and value neurodiversity, have thrived. Those working in institutions, roles, or teams that were unwilling to support our challenges and did not value our strengths have struggled.

I hope that reading this book has given those working in and/or running academic institutions a better understanding of the strengths of autistic academics and the value we bring to academia. I also hope it has increased their motivation, and given them some practical suggestions, to create more inclusive universities that will enable autistic academics to thrive.

APPENDIX A:

Whether, When, and How to Disclose

Amy

In terms of advice on whether or how to disclose, I'll relay the advice I found when I was looking for some advice myself:

- *First, be very sure you do want to disclose, because you can't undo it once it's done.*
- *Also, you can ask for accommodations without having to explicitly state your diagnosis – e.g., say something like: I work better in a quiet space; or: could you let me know ahead of time what to expect in terms of x, y, z; or anything else you might feel anxious about and that might be addressed in a fairly simple way by making a straightforward request that does not require explicitly disclosing anything.*
- *If it's not necessarily about getting accommodations but more about letting people know more informally, you can just say it in passing, if relevant or if the discussion somehow allows it (e.g. if it's about neurodiversity, or disability, EDI [equality, diversity, and inclusion] in academia, or having an academic career, etc.), you can preface your point with 'As an autistic person' then go on to make your point. That way you're letting people know, but it's not really the main point right then.*
- *Perhaps most importantly, ask yourself: What are my reasons for disclosing? What is my goal in doing so? This will help to see whether you even need or want to disclose.*

Baz

My advice is to disclose with someone (if possible) who you trust and who you have a close working relationship with – regardless I feel of their knowledge of autism – but the person must be open to learn about autism and how and what being autistic means to you.

My advice would be to disclose when you are comfortable, as well as when the timing is appropriate – the second should not be a definite, but I mean well timed in a way that when you disclose you are able to have ample or sufficient time to discuss anything that you need to. Disclose if it is important to you, do not feel obligated or that there is a need to.

Disclosure might result in you changing your behaviour, and this is reported as a common experience and phenomenon of other autistic people who have disclosed. I feel it is important that those who need to know of this do, and to expect some more autistic characteristics to come out, but that they will manifest individually, and are not to be taken as stereotyped behaviour.

Betty

When disclosing your diagnosis, I would focus on explaining how autistics experience the world by giving examples that will be understood by neurotypical people. Try to appeal to their everyday experience and use metaphors, e.g. you can say "autistic people reconstruct the bigger picture of the world from details. Imagine walking with binoculars all the time. Our perception of the world can be more complex but it takes us time to put all the information into a comprehensive model. This has advantages and disadvantages."

Charlotte

I kinda have a little rule now. Because I've had some really shocking experiences. In, just both academia and the outside world, in the real world, both places . . . And mainly if I can avoid it, I . . . will not work with anyone I don't know anymore. . . . So, based on my personal experience, I would say, don't disclose unless you know the people, who you're disclosing to. That would be my advice, don't disclose to people you don't know, get to know them first. And then disclose. But, yeah, I guess, what's right for other people, might differ a bit, yeah, that's what I would do, well, that's what I am doing going forward.

Dave

If you are going to have sustained/repeated interactions with others, I think at some point it is useful to disclose – sooner or later they'll detect something anyway, it may be best to be proactive about it. Invite them to be blunt and direct with you, and if they offer criticism, be quick to thank them for it and seriously consider their words, not as who/what you really are, but as how they see you – others in the neuromajority may see something similar, and if you want to change perceptions of you, you need this information. Ask them for tips or advice, explain how your own thought process works, people get more comfortable with being blunt/direct if they have a sense that you'll receive it in a positive manner. If you get defensive and argumentative, don't be surprised if they never tell you how they really think – at that stage, that's on you. I think the most important thing to remember is the neuromajority uses language differently, and they do not say what they mean – you have to translate in your head, and answer the translation, not the words they use. For example:

"You don't seem autistic" really means "I don't understand autism."

If you respond to the translation, you can have a much better dialog. When someone says "You don't seem autistic" I respond with, "yeah, there are a lot of misconceptions out there about autism. When I first found out I could be autistic, I pushed back hard because I didn't understand it."

Such exchanges invite them to be honest, you've signalled it's okay for them to be wrong by highlighting your own flaws, and people in general tend to open up in response. At a minimum, it may cause them to pause and reflect.

Emma

I think it really boils down to the individual situation. So, for me, I think it's worth disclosing if you need something. I could do my academic research jobs without disclosing, so that's what I did (in other words, I didn't need any accommodations). But if I needed something, I would have disclosed a lot sooner. However, there's always that slight chance that disclosing won't bring positive results, so that's another thing you have to consider.

Eva

I think the choice whether to or not to disclose depends on the circumstances. For instance, in some STEM fields, people with autistic traits can be simply perceived as "quirky" and "super focused in the lab" and it can be a personality type with more extreme manifestations of stereotypes expected in those fields. In other situations, it creates more barriers. For instance some autistic people in certain fields might be a "brilliant engineer who sometimes forgets to wash his hair" or "our company's best programmer who keeps to himself a lot" or "she's a brilliant author who is a little eccentric and has a lot of cats, but what writers aren't?"... I think in many cases it is situation dependent and it depends on what field the person is in within academia, how many situations create barriers, and what counts as a universal design issue versus an accommodation. If someone does disclose, certain environments (especially social sciences and humanities research fields) seek out diversity representation if researching a particular subject matter . . . especially if action or community research. One final thing to consider is individual preferences. Does one want to be part of the "Autistic Community" or do they simply want to have a "unique personality"?

Flora

As a PhD student I think it's really important for people to share their diagnosis with their supervisory team at the very least. I have come to understand that all academics regardless of whether they have an autism diagnosis generally have specific preferences and methods of working that may or may not suit the student. I used to think this meant there was something wrong with me, but I now understand supervisors are also constrained by their own experiences both personally and professionally. . . . I question whether upfront disclosure in a job application is a good idea? I was filling out a job application earlier today for a part-time research fellow position and the question asked, 'Do you have a medical condition that will prevent you from fulfilling this role?' and technically, the answer to that question is no, because autism makes me the academic that I am . . . but morally, should I have disclosed? If I get the job will I feel the need to mask and attend social events that are so tedious that I would rather poke my eyes out? I don't know what the answer is, but I feel as though if I am lucky enough to be shortlisted it is probably something I would bring up in the interview. . . . I also think there is a difference in the way that disclosure is communicated as to how the other person responds.

Isabella

This is very personal. It also depends on if it would impact tenure. I'm not tenure track so it could impact my contract renewal. But hopefully it is a bit of a safeguard. But in an ideal world without any job retribution fears, I would say disclose my neurodiverse tribe! Sing it from the rooftops and educate people. Educate them that difference is wonderful and leads to innovation and variety. Sameness is boring and overrated.

Jane

I'd had my diagnosis for ~13 years before I started full time work. This meant I had the confidence within myself of what autism meant for me. . . . Disclosure has only been positive for me.... Regardless of whether you choose to disclose or not, or use the "autism/autistic" word or not – focus on what autism means for you, cos everyone is different. This is particularly important because of autism stereotypes and judgements. If you explain what autism means for you, or what characteristics you've got, this means you're less likely to be judged by stereotypes – but what YOU are.

Kelly

Follow your comfort level when it comes to disclosing. You may need to educate people so pace yourself in relationships with others where you decide to share your diagnosis. Be prepared for negative reactions and don't take it personally. If you decide to disclose, try to disclose to someone whom you think will support you. That person may be able to support you if you 'come out' to others.

Liam

I think disclosure can be very helpful, but my advice would be to be careful who you disclose to. Be strategic – are they likely to be supportive? If they aren't friends, would your diagnosis be a useful thing for them to know in their dealings with you? What are the institution's policies and the country's laws around privacy in the workplace? For example, in England it is sufficient for the purposes of protections offered by anti-discrimination law for an employee to disclose to their immediate supervisor while asking them to keep the information confidential – e.g. they can't report it to HR without permission. I say all this in the context of a relatively new diagnosis and having a permanent contract. I don't know if I will be more open in the future with others about my diagnosis as I become more set in what it means to me, and I don't know if I would have disclosed if I were on probation.

Lisa

I don't think there's any point in disclosing unless and until you have done your diligence and seen what's on the other side. Most people have no clue what autism is. Telling them is the equivalent of saying "I'm a retard." That sounds harsh but I do think that is what people perceive. And then of course they reply with "You don't look like a retard. You don't act like a retard." Which of course we don't. What has been gained? Nothing. What we have to remember is that autistics have been around since the dawn of time. Every society and culture has had its own way of dealing or not dealing with certain behaviors or ways of seeing the world. We don't need to tell people we're different. They know it. Down to their DNA they know it. What we want them to know is that it's not catching or dangerous. But is that true? My buddy at work is 10 times smarter than the rest of us. The corporation could fire about 1,000 people and just keep her, and the job would be done better. Is that not a danger?

Marie

I believe I am too new to this to be in a position to offer advice. I would be eager to learn from others – especially those with a very late diagnosis or identification of autism. I'm also curious to learn whether others have encountered stereotypes or even bullying after disclosure.

Moon Man

One reason disclosure is important is that empowers the autistic person to present their authentic self. Additionally, when in the interview process, an early disclosure can serve as a screening tool – screening out situations where one would not be accepted for their autistic self. It is important to disclose oneself as autistic from an honest, strength-based, and realistic point of view as it pertains to a particular job opportunity. The autistic person should prepare to talk about how their autistic characteristics are a benefit to their candidacy. Solutions to needed accommodations should be presented in a clear and concise manner.

Morgan

In terms of advice, I'm not sure I have any . . .! I still feel like I'm not adult enough at this to offer advice to others, and everyone's context is so different.

Olivia

The staff disability network organised an online talk with someone from the National Autistic Society. At the end, I asked if they had any advice about disclosure. The speaker said – and I thought it was a very good point – that it needs reflecting on because once your line manager has been told, you can't take it back. Someone else in the meeting messaged me to say that they have disclosed and have been wrangling about reasonable adjustments for 6 months. I was so happy to see an autistic colleague; we've arranged a virtual chat for next week.

It made me feel so happy that I think I have been missing something I've never had – contact with other autistics.

Proline

I recommend that if you need some accommodations, it might be OK to disclose your disability. Also, if you are working in a state agency, it might be OK as well. If you don't like your work, it can be a lose-lose situation. If you don't disclose, you will be labelled as lazy, while if you do disclose, you will possibly be discriminated especially in a close-minded field like engineering.

Psyche

As the decision to disclose is so subjective, the only advice I could give to other autistic academics would be this: Only disclose if and when you want to, and you have to be prepared to possibly face discrimination as a result. If you don't feel comfortable with how autism sits with your own identity, I would recommend trying to not disclose, if possible, as it will also help to perpetuate the negative stereotypes around autism. You can ask for supports without having to disclose, such as saying that you need to wear sunglasses because you suffer from migraines, or that you need to have the window open because you have breathing difficulties, or that you need to wear headphones because you have tinnitus and loud noises make it worse. If you have atypical behaviours that are difficult to hide, then you could explain those in a different way. For instance, you could explain restless tapping with fingers as that you are learning to play a piece of music and are practising the rhythm, or that you have been advised to rock in your seat by a physiotherapist to deal with a muscle problem. If autism sits in your identity well and you're willing to take the risk, then maybe disclose openly to help normalise the idea of autistics in every workplace, and that autism can mean 'strengths' and not just 'deficits'. Be loud and proud when you have a skill or knowledge set that is impressive, such as ability to hyperfocus or retain every little piece of information about a particular subject, because you are autistic. And finally, all research concerning the welfare of autistic people should include actually autistic researchers who are involved at each stage of the process, to ensure they include the autistic voice.

Ruth

I don't feel particularly qualified to provide advice here.... I do, however, feel strongly that autism researchers (both quant and qual) should situate themselves as Autistic or non-Autistic. I also think that it's important as a teacher to be open if we are to claim that we are actively promoting inclusion in our classrooms. This is an area where my ideas are still developing and being challenged. My partner, also an Autistic academic, feels very strongly about being upfront about their Autistic, gender, and sexual identity, and they have challenged me quite a bit about this. I have realised that, while I'm openly Autistic, I don't feel as comfortable acknowledging the intersectionality of my identity. I think much of this is a hang-up from my early career, working in schools in the '90s, where boundaries were critical and people's views were very different at that time.

Saskia

I'm slightly ashamed to admit that I would not advise faculty to disclose until they're tenured. I want to be the kind of person who pumps her fist and says YES! Tell them you're autistic! But having watched human evil in action, I just can't. I'm a full professor and still only disclose on a one-on-one basis, if I feel comfortable with the person. I would never deny it – I won't lie – but I just don't bring it up at the group level because I'm dealing with enough dysfunction as it is. I don't need additional people messing with me.... My advice for those who wish to disclose is to get involved in initiatives, in department or out, where collaborative work has to happen, so people can see how good they are at the job. The reason I even have a chance at moving up in administration (something I'm not sure about, but I do love a new learning curve) is that people in my college worked with me on committees and saw over time how committed I am to ethical and thoughtful work toward a common goal. Our label sets people on guard, but our record of performance can overcome it.

Scarlett

Disclosure is such a complex thing to consider, and I don't actually know how someone should disclose. For me it's about being honest with myself and others and for that reason I am more than happy for my colleagues to know about my diagnosis. But honestly I don't know how you would go about disclosing to your colleagues. What tends to happen in my experience is disclosure happens in an ad hoc way, which is not very helpful. But as far as I have seen their really isn't a way to disclose to everyone all at once so that they are all on the same page. I would feel strange 'disclosing' to each of my colleagues individually, it just isn't relevant in most circumstances.... I think the decision to disclose would come down to the type of colleagues/boss that you have. However given some of the distinctly autistic-unfriendly characteristics that come with academic jobs (in my opinion) then disclosure may be the only way of managing it without continued negative impacts on your own health and well-being.

Scott

It depends. If the academics are working in the autism field, I would certainly advise disclosing. I have no regrets about my own decision, as an autistic autism researcher, to disclose my autism. On the other hand, there are other aspects of my identity that I seldom disclose. They aren't as relevant to my work, and aren't terribly central to my identity. I don't feel like I'm hiding a part of myself when I keep them to myself, nor do I experience much stress in doing so, because they aren't typically subjects that come up in my academic discussions. I suspect some people will be in a position where their autism is more like my [other aspects], so they might be perfectly comfortable keeping it to themselves.

Sophia

My personal experience doesn't really allow me to give any advice to other autistics people in academia. My person choice though was not to disclose because of the very strong intolerance towards autism in my country and especially in the intellectual world. I only have an example of a master student of mine who also is autistic and who did all he could to get support. Everybody knows about his autism and he only had bad consequences (colleagues trying to make sure he won't succeed, other students making fun of him). I have been supporting him and I am trying to fight for him to succeed but it is very hard and I don't feel quite honest not telling him that I am autistic as well. But I still have the feeling that I support him better in front of my other colleagues without them knowing that I am autistic.

Sunny

If it's safe – as in, you're not going to risk your employment, health, or life – do it. The more of us who do it, the more we normalize it and make it safer for others. The more of us who do it, the more those systems of oppression break down. Being open at work means having access to reasonable accommodations/adjustments that can help you be more successful in your career. Being open at work means not suffering the (increasingly well-documented in the scientific literature) negative impacts of camouflaging or pretending to be something you're not at work. It's just healthier to be in a work environment where you can be yourself and are supported fully in what you need to do your work – for everyone!!! Being visible, even if your research isn't directly related to autism, helps pave the way for the future generation to have an easier job. It's not all awesome and there will be a fight, but there's going to be a fight either way. So if you can, do it.

Trina

I wish I could offer advice, but since every situation varies, I really don't think I can. Some environments may be very hostile to autistic faculty/staff. I was very fortunate not to have that experience. I think each person must feel out the environment for themselves. If a person has been diagnosed after having already held a job and built a good reputation in that job, I would like to think that disclosing should not be that difficult. In a new job situation, I'm sure it would be a very different story.

APPENDIX B:

Self-Advocacy in the Workplace

Question: How can autistic employees self-advocate in the workplace without the fear of retribution or prejudice that unfortunately sometimes accompanies the revealing of an autism diagnosis?

Amy

There is strength in numbers, so maybe if there were an association of autistic faculty or employees or something like that. The only way to avoid undue retribution is to have accountability mechanisms that are either internal or external to the institution, and that keep the relevant people/offices/services in check with regard to ableist discrimination. This should include channels for autistics to file a formal complaint if the need arises.

Baz

Check if there are autistic support groups or disability support groups. Find out if there is a way to know if others are autistic to rally and stick together. If your workplace has HR (some smaller orgs or businesses might not) then approach them [to] ask about adjustments in the workplace. If you have awesome people in your workplace there should be an autism inclusion advocacy group! ☺ *Support from allied health professionals. Knowing and clearly stating your needs in a way that others will understand. Researching your rights and the workplace policies, knowing how to get what you need.*

Dave

First, please remember most people use language wrongly, and we have to translate what they say – when someone says, "I don't think you're autistic," or "you don't seem to be autistic," we tend to take their words literally and get offended. I submit to you it would be better to translate and answer that. I like to translate that to "I don't understand autism" and then I answer that statement, typically with, "yeah, I had a lot of misconceptions about autism myself. Some call it an invisible disability for good reason."

Second, it may help to first explore how open-minded an individual is about neurodiversity before deciding to disclose. Some folks are opposed to any other perspective or view, and it is difficult to have a meaningful discussion with such folks (and they are more likely to weaponize your disclosure and turn it against you).

Third, you don't have to go into specifics. Saying something like, "I have a medical condition that makes it difficult for me to function in harsh lighting" or "I was born without the instincts many take for granted in socializing, so sometimes I use language that may be perceived as offensive or hostile" may be a better way to ask for accommodations than disclosing your autism, which they are likely to not understand in most cases.

Ella

I haven't figured this out yet. In the past, people have already found me 'abrasive', 'opinionated', 'blunt', 'difficult', and 'aggressive', so I do my best to just be quiet now. Self-advocacy requires speaking out, and I'm less willing to do this now after a lifetime of experiences telling me it's rarely helpful for me.

Emma

I still struggle with self-advocacy in the workplace, particularly because the one time I did self-disclose, the end result was horrible. Part of me thinks it would be easier to just not disclose a diagnosis, but I know that can lead to burnout and depression. Knowing what I know now, I wouldn't disclose unless it was for the sole purpose of receiving accommodations. Last time I disclosed, I did so from the very beginning because I thought it would help with the transition from working at university to working at a company (albeit only for a 4-month contract). Instead, disclosing seemed to create more roadblocks because the people that I worked with had all these assumptions about me that weren't true, and it just made things more difficult to navigate.

Eva

Self-advocacy in the workplace and choice whether to disclose or ask for a specific small accommodation is dependent on the situation and person. For instance, I will simply say "visual impairment" if asking for airport assistance when traveling to conferences as "topographical agnosia" and "temporal lobe impairment" is a more challenging explanation and airport staff are unlikely to understand this or know that I often need to be escorted to my gate. In simple terms, it is a visual impairment, but based in the brain. Similarly, I have heard individuals say they cannot hear conversations when several people are speaking or there is a lot of background noise while not delving into potential neurological explanations. However, in other environments disclosure is necessary and may even be useful. For instance, as a qualitative autism researcher, it is an important aspect of my research to identify myself as a member of the specific minority group I am researching, and it adds to my credibility.

Evelyn

I'd recommend staff join workers' unions once they have a role. I wouldn't recommend disclosing up front until you know the employer won't change their mind about hiring you if they know you're autistic. Beggars can't be choosers and while a workplace that doesn't want autistic workers is not a good place to work and absolutely doesn't deserve us, autistic people struggle at the best of times to get jobs, let alone during financial crises or pandemics. We don't have much bargaining power or leverage to be selective about employment, all we can do is take what we're offered and use the security that provides to look for something better.

Flora

I don't think I have the answer to this question, nor am I sure it is possible!!

Isabella

I dunno. I keep thinking there has to be a better way to explain autism. Although you have to fight the preexisting stereotypes.

Jane

Focus on your needs. E.g. Wearing my cap = no headache (or less severe) = more productive.

If you don't feel comfortable talking initially – write an email before discussing.

Also goes back to disclosure & stereotypes – but need to have confidence to be able to advocate for yourself. I've had my diagnosis for 23+ years now, so I know who I am.

Kelly

Being diagnosed at 48 years old means that I spent almost a half century thinking I was not Autistic (living as an NT). What I learned while passing as an NT is that prejudice often results from the lack of education, and exposure. I know this from being a Black, Brown, and Indigenous woman as well. When I enter into a work environment where people had little exposure to racialized people, I experienced prejudice or curiosity and through education, experiences with an actual Black person etc., they were able to form an educated opinion that was often positive. I feel strongly that education and exposure to the benefits of Autistic people can be very helpful in creating a strong diverse environment.

Liam

If you know of other disabled colleagues who work under or at least know your manager, ask them if they know the manager's attitude/approach toward disability and reasonable accommodations.

Know your legal rights, and disclose in such a way that you convey you know them – e.g. if you don't work for HR, disclose to your line manager and say something like 'HR is legally obligated to do X', which both lets them know you know your rights and effectively gives the manager the option to kick the 'problem' upstairs.

Join a union if you have one and consult them for advice before disclosing

If there is a disabled employees network, check it out before disclosing to them – are they based in HR? If so, get a sense of what HR is like first, and remember that structurally they are not your friend regardless of how accommodating individuals within the department might be, so tread carefully.

While the onus is on the employer in the legal sense (at least under UK disability law), and you should not have to put in all the labor to make the university a tolerable place to work, the simple fact is that you're likely to get much better results for yourself if you disclose in a way that offers concrete and realistic solutions to minimize the possible perception that you're a management problem.

Louise

I don't have any good advice on how to self-advocate. For me, I'm pretty militant about it because I know that, despite my disabilities, I bring a lot of strengths to each job I do and I am valued. If individuals have experienced stigma or prejudice, or they have struggled to feel valued in previous jobs, then I imagine it would be much more difficult to self-advocate. I think that every organisation should have a neurodiversity co-ordinator who advocates for neurodivergent employees and promotes diversity of all types in the workplace.

Marie

This is something that I've struggled with and am eager to learn about, as I decide whether to disclose.

I have begun to talk about neurodiversity in general in class and among faculty. In several instances, I've been able to introduce others to the concept for the first time. I believe this may be the start of educating others at my institution.

Moon Man

Effective self-advocacy includes educating the individual(s) being advocate to why that need is being expressed, how it can be addressed, and what the benefits are to the person and workplace receive by providing the support.

For example, suppose an autistic person is overly sensitive to recessed lighting fixtures with bare lightbulbs glaring downwards and the individual realizes that wearing a baseball cap will mitigate the issue. The autistic person might explain that they need to wear a hat because the bright lights hurt their eyes. And if they wear this hat, they can be more productive – to the benefit of themselves and the organization at large.

Morgan

I have no idea honestly . . .!

Olivia

Hah! Good question. I don't even know. People seem to have a strange idea of what autism is, so perhaps if that were changed, there would be less stigma.

Proline

As far as self-advocacy is concerned, unfortunately, I have a very low bandwidth when it comes to ignorant people. In fact, I would, on any day, prefer to be physically assaulted rather than suffer mental health issue since I can withstand physical pain very well (I recovered within two days after my orchiectomy surgery, which most people take around two weeks to recover from). I would prefer to have an advocate with me at all times who would be ready to speak on my behalf if any awkward situation has to arise. In this way, my advocate will protect me and I don't have to feel alone as I generally find it easy to ask for help and would actually love it if someone helps me all the time, but I hate to be left alone since it triggers my BPD (Borderline Personality Disorder). In fact, I will never ever reject help from anyone when it comes to mental health advocacy or mental health issues.

Psyche

This is something I personally would love to know, as I have found it very difficult to self-advocate without retribution or prejudice! I suppose you can try not mentioning autism at all . . . for instance, my husband just tells people that he needs to wear a brimmed hat or turn lights off because he gets migraines. I tend to tell people that loud, sudden noises are painful for me because I suffer from tinnitus and the noises make it worse (also true). Since answering the last question for this study, I have left my position as research administrator for an autism specific preschool and have started relief teaching instead while I undertake my PhD which starts in January. I have not felt that I have wanted to tell the school in which I work that I am autistic as the reaction in my last workplace was so terrible. Luckily for me, however, my PhD supervisor is also autistic and was my inclusive practices lecturer for my Master of Teaching degree. He is very clued up about reasonable adjustments for autistic people, so I feel I can be open and honest about my requirements and asking for adjustments. I am so lucky to have found the perfect supervisor, so I'm sure that if there were more openly autistic academics, autistic students would feel more comfortable about advocating for themselves, and perhaps work environments would feel less upset about making adjustments.

Ruth

I don't have an answer for this. I think it would depend a lot on individual circumstances. An increasingly casualised workforce also makes things difficult. Perhaps those with tenure would be better placed to self-advocate. I've been fortunate in being able to establish my competence in certain areas and then being in a position to do things on my own terms in many ways. I've also had some great colleagues who have really helped. I'd imagine that, had I gone in when I was first contracted, and said, "I'm Autistic, and I want X, Y, Z," that people wouldn't have been so amenable and that may have been my last contract.

Saskia

I am torn here. A centralized ADA compliance office would let employees document diagnosis with the office, and then the office could call the department for accommodations, so the employee need not out themselves to the people in the department. So that would be a start. The reason I'm torn is that I am a tenured full professor, and hiding my autistic status doesn't help anybody. I am fairly certain that I will not be fired for it. If I don't have job security after outing myself, who does? So I feel an obligation to normalize neurodivergence by just talking openly about it. I have a colleague who talks openly about his ADD, and I have more and more students who are open. There's a generational change coming, and I welcome it. The more of us who are open about it, the harder it will be to deny the intellectual capacity and potential of neurodivergent people. So I feel like self-advocacy is more likely to be effective if other people are already open about their needs and their contributions. It's a group endeavor.

Scott

Yes, this is a very good question. I don't have a good answer. This is a systemic cultural problem, in some fields more than others.

Some required anti-ableism type trainings would help and I certainly believe such trainings should be offered, assuming that the trainings in question were developed by actually autistic and disabled people (as if they were developed solely by non-disabled people, or if they contain medical/pathology model assumptions about autism and disability, I suspect they could backfire and worsen the problem), but these certainly wouldn't be sufficient.

Even if someone doesn't simply look down on autistic and disabled people, in an academic environment where everyone usually has limited time and resources, the prospect of bringing on an autistic grad student, postdoc, or colleague would likely be intimidating and would make people worry that the person would end up causing more work for them or something. Having adequate resources to address disability barriers – which would require establishing something like the academic version of job coach I mentioned above, along with making sure student and HR disability offices are competent (and for grad students, not siloed but that one has clear responsibility) could help some with the latter fear, although not with all forms of prejudice.

Ultimately, some form of countervailing pressure to support disabled and neurodivergent academics in hiring decisions, grad school applications, grant applications, etc., may be necessary to overcome prejudices and increase numbers of openly autistic academics. We already know that subtle differences in our social mannerisms make others biased against us in any sort of social or interview setting, even if we don't disclose, so granting formal preference to applications by autistic people would simply tend to counteract this form of discrimination.

Such countervailing pressure wouldn't entirely protect autistic academics from being discriminated against in a given department or workplace after their hire. While a robust ombudsperson or semi-judicial process could help in some cases, usually discrimination is subtle and hard to prove.

Moreover, many ombudspersons or judicial offices at universities operate in a largely opaque and arbitrary manner, without the clear rights and processes that have been established in courts of law. As a result of this lack of due process, and based on some anecdotal cases I'm aware of, I believe that these bodies in fact tend to discriminate against autistic and disabled people. Thus, we must first of all ensure these formal bodies do no harm.

Sophia

My way to advocate in the workplace is to not self-advocate. Hiding my autism helps me be more effective to help others. I would love to self-advocate but the fear of prejudice is too strong and has been confirmed by the negative experiences other autistic professionals or students have had by exposing their autism. I try to camouflage self-advocacy in my research by reporting and spreading other autistic academic people's voices.

Sunny

So this is literally a core research question in my primary research agenda – I just submitted a grant proposal in fact on how to answer this LOL I think that there will need to be a risk/benefit assessment that will vary depending on a lot of things – the workplace culture, the employee's relationship with others in the workplace, the social culture, whether or not the employee has additional marginalized identities, the employee's past history of workplace trauma, how any legal protections for people with disabilities are interpreted or practiced, etc. I don't know that there is a pat answer to this. My feeling is that a flexible tool to assess the situation and then some pathways for how to respond based on the assessment is probably needed. I'd love to say there's "a way" to do this, but the reality is that we live in a world that includes a substantial amount of ableism, and for some the job is what's keeping their children alive and disclosure can be extremely risky. It's not an easy question.

Trevor

I think knowing your rights helps and I have found employers are more reasonable that many in the community realise. Also, don't be put off by any initial perceived resistance. I think it helps if the request is specific and solution focused and put in the context of improving your productivity then that is language managers understand. Also, having reasonable expectations and arrange for what you need with the minimum of inconvenience or expense for others in the workplace.

Trina

I have a difficult time with this idea of retribution, at least as an expectation. I lived in Australia in the early 2000's before I realized that I had autism. By and large, I do not think this fear of retribution is warranted there any more than it is in the US or Germany. As for prejudice, this is unfortunately a reality we must contend with in any social circumstance, as prejudice is an inevitable part of human nature. The social justice scholarship centering on autism as neurodiversity is long overdue, but it also has the power to perpetuate prejudice against those who are not like "us" by reducing them to a label of "neurotypical".

I think it's important to recognize that some people (be they colleagues or supervisors) may not believe us when we tell them we have autism. It is understandably surprising for people given that autism has been represented over the decades. The best way to advocate for ourselves is to be patient with those who do not understand our challenges, engage with them in a non-combative, non-judgmental and non-condescending way. The identity first mentality has its benefits, but it also polarizes us in situations where we really don't need to be polarized. I would like to see autistic academics rise above this fashionable tendency to presume that others are not enlightened or "woke" enough to support us when we need it. I speak to myself as well when I say that we all need to stop focusing so much on our own ideas of victimization and the systems of power that we perceive to be oppressing us. We must deal with people on an individual level by treating them the way we would want to be treated and give them the benefit of the doubt as much as possible.

APPENDIX C:

Additional Resources

Websites and Networks

Autism Training Academy

Founded by Dr T. C. Waisman, the Autism Training Academy supports and inspires our accomplished clients to expand their knowledge of autism and neurodivergence while giving them tools they can utilize to support all individuals in their particular environment. This is made possible through a variety of concise, online, asynchronous micro-trainings founded on research, gamification, and a universal design evidence-based framework that gives clients concrete skills and tools to actualize their learning. https://adaptcoach.com/autism-training-academy/

Autism in Adulthood

While there are a number of autism journals currently available, this journal is a standout given both its focus on adults and its involvement of autistic people in the review process. If your institution's library doesn't already subscribe to *Autism in Adulthood*, I strongly recommend that they do so. https://home.liebertpub.com/publications/autism-in-adulthood/646

Autistic Professor

www.autisticprofessor.com (the author's website)

Autistic Scholars International

This Facebook group, which is only for autistic scholars, was created by scholars from Australia, Canada, the United Kingdom, and United States.

It brings together English-speaking autistic scholars from around the globe in a safe space online, to discuss matters of importance to their work without risking unintended disclosure. The group's aims include undertaking research to benefit the worldwide community of autistic scholars.

The College Autism Network

The College Autism Network links varied stakeholders engaged in evidence-guided efforts to improve access, experiences, and outcomes for postsecondary students with autism. https://collegeautismnetwork.org

Frist Center for Autism and Innovation at Vanderbilt University

The Frist Center for Autism and Innovation, 'engineering technologies and transforming the workplace – inspired by neurodiversity', at the Vanderbilt University School of Engineering, brings engineers, business scholars, and disabilities researchers together with experts in neuroscience and education to understand, maximize, and promote neurodiverse talent. www.vanderbilt.edu/autismandinnovation/

Neurodiversity Hub

The purpose of this initiative is to create environments that will maximally facilitate these individuals to grow and achieve their full potential. It is about facilitating a community of practice for universities, colleges, employers, and service providers to work together to create these environments and opportunities for neurodivergent young adults. www.neurodiversityhub.org

Further Readings (Recommended by Participants)

The following list of further readings that may be of interest has been provided by some of the members of the group. This list is not meant to be comprehensive, but rather a starting point based on readings that these autistic academics have found valuable.

Advisory Committee to the Director's (ACD) Working Group on Diversity (2022). Advisory Committee to the Director Working Group on Diversity Subgroup on Individuals with Disabilities Report, National Institutes of Health (NIH).

Botha, M. (2021). 'Academic, Activist, or Advocate? Angry, Entangled, and Emerging: A Critical Reflection on Autism Knowledge Production'. *Frontiers in Psychology* **12**. https://doi.org/10.3389/fpsyg.2021.727542

Botha, M., and E. Cage (2022). '"Autism research is in crisis": A Mixed Method Study of Researcher's Constructions of Autistic People and Autism Research'. *Frontiers in Psychology* **13**. e2020049437F. https://doi.org/10.1542/peds.2020-049437F

Brown, H. M., P. S. R. Dwyer, D. L. Gassner, M. G. Onaiwu, S. K. Kapp, A. Ne'eman, J. G. Ryan, T. Waisman, and Z. J. Williams (2022). 'The Autism Intervention Research Network on Physical Health Autistic Researcher Review Board'. *Pediatrics* **149**(Supplement 4).

Brown, J. E. (2022). 'Pursuing a Scientific Career with ADHD'. *Nature Reviews Endocrinology* **18**(6): 325–326.

Castro, F., E. Stuart, J. Deal, V. Varadaraj, and B. Swenor, K. (2022). 'Disability Disparities in STEM: Gaps in Salaries and Representation for Doctorate Recipients with Disabilities in the U.S., 2019'. *medRxiv*: 2022.2012.2004.22283081.

Catala, A. (2022a). 'Academic Excellence and Structural Epistemic Injustice: Toward a More Just Epistemic Economy in Philosophy'. *Journal of Social Philosophy* April: 1–24. https://doi.org/10.1111/josp.12465

(2022b). 'Toward Greater Neuroinclusion in Philosophy'. *Blog of the APA*: https://blog.apaonline.org/2022/04/04/toward-greater-neuroinclusion-in-philosophy/.

(2023a). 'Epistemic Injustice and Epistemic Authority on Autism'. In *The Bloomsbury Guide to Philosophy of Disability*. Ed. S. Tremain. N.p.: Bloomsbury Academic: 241–261.

(2023b). 'Understanding Neurodiversity, Unlearning Neuronormativity'. *Blog of the APA*: https://blog.apaonline.org/2023/04/11/understanding-neurodiversity-unlearning-neuronormativity/.

(forthcoming). 'Becoming Who You Are: Hermeneutical Breakthroughs, Transformative Experience, and Epistemic Empowerment'. In *The Dynamics of Epistemic Injustice: Situating Epistemic Power and Agency*. Ed. A. Catala. New York: Oxford University Press.

Catala, A., L. Faucher, and P. Poirier (2021). 'Autism, Epistemic Injustice, and Epistemic Disablement: A Relational Account of Epistemic Agency'. *Synthese* **199**(3): 9013–9039.

Chellappa, S. L. (2022). 'Foster Neuroinclusivity at Scientific Meetings'. *Nature* **612**(7939): 211.

De Niz, M. (2022). 'Autism in Science: "Through the Looking Glass" and the Role of Empathy in the Equation'. *Journal of Cell Science* **135**(7).

den Houting, J., J. Higgins, K. Isaacs, J. Mahony, and E. Pellicano (2022). 'From Ivory Tower to Inclusion: Stakeholders' Experiences of Community Engagement in Australian Autism Research'. *Frontiers in Psychology* **13**. 13:876990. doi: 10.3389/fpsyg.2022.876990.

Dumonteil, J. (2020). 'Autistes: Entre situations de vulnérabilité et pouvoir d'agir?' [Autistic People: Between Situations of Vulnerability and Empowerment?] *Education et Socialisation*. https://doi.org/10.4000/edso.12673.

(2022). 'Enseignants autistes: L'aboutissement d'un parcours inclusif?' [Autistic Teachers: the Culmination of an Inclusive Path?] *Education et Socialisation*. https://doi.org/10.3917/chaso.kohou.2023.01.0132.

Guest, E. (2020). 'Autism from Different Points of View: Two Sides of the Same Coin'. *Disability & Society* **35**(1): 156–162.

Jones, S. C. (2021). 'Let's Talk about Autistic Autism Researchers'. *Autism in Adulthood* **3**(3): 206–208.

Milton, D. E. M. (2014). 'Autistic Expertise: A Critical Reflection on the Production of Knowledge in Autism Studies'. *Autism* **18**(7): 794–802.

Milton, D. E. M., and M. Bracher (2013). 'Autistics Speak but Are They Heard?' *Journal of the BSA MedSoc Group* **7**: 61–69.

Nuwer, R. (2020). 'Meet the Autistic Scientists Redefining Autism Research'. *Spectrum*. www.spectrumnews.org/features/deep-dive/meet-the-autistic-scientists-redefining-autism-research/.

Pellicano, E., W. Lawson, G. Hall, J. Mahony, R. Lilley, M. Heyworth, H. Clapham, and M. Yudell (2021). '"I Knew She'd Get It, and Get Me": Participants' Perspectives of a Participatory Autism Research Project'. *Autism in Adulthood* **4**(2): 120–129.

Pells, R., and A. Grant (2022). 'How Science Can Do Better for Neurodivergent People'. *Nature*. doi: 10.1038/d41586-022-04248-5. Epub ahead of print. PMID: 36460911.

Rodríguez Mega, E. (2023). '"I am not a broken version of normal": Autistic People Argue for a Stronger Voice in Research'. *Nature* **617**(7960): 238–241.

Schleider, J. L. (2023). 'The Fundamental Need for Lived Experience Perspectives in Developing and Evaluating Psychotherapies'. *Journal of Consulting and Clinical Psychology* **91**(3): 119–121.

Stark, E. A. (2022). 'Empowering Autistic Academics'. *Nature Human Behaviour* **6**(9): 1184.

StEvens, C. 'The Lived Experience of Autistic Teachers: A Review of the Literature'. *International Journal of Inclusive Education*: 1–15. https://doi.org/10.1080/13603116.2022.2041738

Swenor, B. K., B. Munoz, and L. M. Meeks (2020). 'A Decade of Decline: Grant Funding for Researchers with Disabilities 2008 to 2018'. *PLoS One* **15**(3): e0228686.

Thompson-Hodgetts, S. (2022). 'Reflections on my Experiences as a Non-Autistic Autism Researcher'. *Autism* **27**(1): 259–261.

Yerbury, J. J., and R. M. Yerbury (2021). 'Disabled in Academia: To Be or Not to Be, That Is the Question'. *Trends in Neurosciences* **44**(7): 507–509.

Zurn, P., J. Stramondo, J. M. Reynolds, and D. S. Bassett (2022). 'Expanding Diversity, Equity, and Inclusion to Disability: Opportunities for Biological Psychiatry'. *Biological Psychiatry: Cognitive Neuroscience and Neuroimaging* **7** (12): 1280–1288.

References

Anderson, A. (2021). 'Job Seeking and Daily Workforce Experiences of Autistic Librarians'. *The International Journal of Information, Diversity, & Inclusion* **5** (3): 38–63.

Anderson, A. H., M. Carter, and J. Stephenson (2018). 'Perspectives of University Students with Autism Spectrum Disorder'. *Journal of Autism and Developmental Disorders* **48**(3): 651–665.

(2020). 'An On-Line Survey of University Students with Autism Spectrum Disorder in Australia and New Zealand: Characteristics, Support Satisfaction, and Advocacy'. *Journal of Autism and Developmental Disorders* **50**(2): 440–454.

Anderson, A. H., J. Stephenson, M. Carter, and S. Carlon (2019). 'A Systematic Literature Review of Empirical Research on Postsecondary Students with Autism Spectrum Disorder'. *Journal of Autism and Developmental Disorders* **49**(4): 1531–1558.

Arnold, S. R. C., J. M. Higgins, J. Weise, A. Desai, E. Pellicano, and J. N. Trollor (2023). 'Towards the Measurement of Autistic Burnout'. *Autism*: 13623613221147401.

Arnold, S. R. C., Y. Huang, Y. I. Hwang, A. L. Richdale, J. N. Trollor, and L. P. Lawson (2020). '"The single most important thing that has happened to me in my life": Development of the Impact of Diagnosis Scale – Preliminary Revision'. *Autism in Adulthood* **2**(1): 34–41.

Aspler, J., K. D. Harding, and M. A. Cascio (2022). 'Representation Matters: Race, Gender, Class, and Intersectional Representations of Autistic and Disabled Characters on Television'. *Studies in Social Justice* **16**(2).

Badhwar, R. (2021). 'Special Needs, Disability Disabilities, and Cybersecurity: Often, a Great Fit'. In *The CISO's Transformation: Security Leadership in a High Threat Landscape*. Ed. R. Badhwar. Cham: Springer International Publishing, 73–76.

Barham, E., and C. Wood (2022). 'Teaching the Hidden Curriculum in Political Science'. *PS: Political Science & Politics* **55**(2): 324–328.

Black, M. H., R. Kuzminski, J. Wang, J. Ang, C. Lee, S. Hafidzuddin, and S. McGarry (2024). 'Experiences of Friendships for Individuals on the Autism Spectrum: A Scoping Review'. *Review Journal of Autism and Developmental Disorders* **11**: 184–209.

Black, M. H., S. Mahdi, B. Milbourn, M. Scott, A. Gerber, C. Esposito, M. Falkmer, M. D. Lerner, A. Halladay, E. Ström, A. D'Angelo, T. Falkmer, S. Bölte, and S. Girdler (2020). 'Multi-informant International Perspectives on the Facilitators and Barriers to Employment for Autistic Adults'. *Autism Research* **13**(7): 1195–1214.

Botha, M., and K. Gillespie-Lynch (2022). 'Come as You Are: Examining Autistic Identity Development and the Neurodiversity Movement through an Intersectional Lens'. *Human Development* **66**(2): 93–112.

Brown, N., and K. Ramlackhan (2022). 'Exploring Experiences of Ableism in Academia: A Constructivist Inquiry'. *Higher Education (Dordr)* **83**(6): 1225–1239.

Bury, S. M., R. L. Flower, R. Zulla, D. B. Nicholas, and D. Hedley (2021). 'Workplace Social Challenges Experienced by Employees on the Autism Spectrum: An International Exploratory Study Examining Employee and Supervisor Perspectives'. *Journal of Autism and Developmental Disorders* **51** (5): 1614–1627.

Bury, S. M., R. Jellett, J. R. Spoor, and D. Hedley (2023). '"It Defines Who I Am" or "It's Something I Have": What Language Do [Autistic] Australian Adults [on the Autism Spectrum] Prefer?' *Journal of Autism and Developmental Disorders* **53**(2): 677–687.

Byrne, J. P. (2022). 'Perceiving the Social Unknown: How the Hidden Curriculum Affects the Learning of Autistic Students in Higher Education'. *Innovations in Education and Teaching International* **59**(2): 142–149.

Cage, E., M. De Andres, and P. Mahoney (2020). 'Understanding the Factors That Affect University Completion for Autistic People'. *Research in Autism Spectrum Disorders* **72**.

Cage, E., and J. Howes (2020). 'Dropping Out and Moving On: A Qualitative Study of Autistic People's Experiences of University'. *Autism* **24**(7): 1664–1675.

Cage, E., and Z. Troxell-Whitman (2019). 'Understanding the Reasons, Contexts and Costs of Camouflaging for Autistic Adults'. *Journal of Autism and Developmental Disorders* **49**(5): 1899–1911.

Callus, A.-M. (2017). 'Making Disability Conferences More Actively Inclusive'. *Disability & Society* **32**(10): 1661–1665.

Cannizzo, F., C. Mauri, and N. Osbaldiston (2019). 'Moral Barriers between Work/Life Balance Policy and Practice in Academia'. *Journal of Cultural Economy* **12**(4): 251–264.

Christopher, S. (2019). 'Touch Hypersensitivity in Children with Autism: An Analysis'. *International Journal of Research and Analytical Reviews* **6**(2): 616–622.

Cook, J., L. Crane, L. Hull, L. Bourne, and W. Mandy (2022). 'Self-Reported Camouflaging Behaviours Used by Autistic Adults during Everyday Social Interactions'. *Autism* **26**(2): 406–421.

Cooper, R., and C. Kennady (2021). 'Autistic Voices from the Workplace'. *Advances in Autism* **7**(1): 73–85.

Cope, R., and A. Remington (2022). 'The Strengths and Abilities of Autistic People in the Workplace'. *Autism in Adulthood* **4**(1): 22–31.

Corden, K., R. Brewer, and E. Cage (2021). 'Personal Identity After an Autism Diagnosis: Relationships with Self-Esteem, Mental Wellbeing, and Diagnostic Timing'. *Frontiers in Psychology* **12**: 699335.

Cost, K. T., A. Zaidman-Zait, P. Mirenda, E. Duku, L. Zwaigenbaum, I. M. Smith, W. J. Ungar, C. Kerns, T. Bennett, P. Szatmari, S. Georgiades, C. Waddell, M. Elsabbagh, and T. Vaillancourt (2021). '"Best Things": Parents Describe Their Children with Autism Spectrum Disorder over Time'. *Journal of Autism and Developmental Disorders* **51**(12): 4560–4574.

Craig, J., and S. Baron-Cohen (1999). 'Creativity and Imagination in Autism and Asperger Syndrome'. *Journal of Autism and Developmental Disorders* **29**(4): 319–326.

Davies, J., B. Heasman, A. Livesey, A. Walker, E. Pellicano, and A. Remington (2022). 'Autistic Adults' Views and Experiences of Requesting and Receiving Workplace Adjustments in the UK'. *PLoS One* **17**(8).

(2023). 'Access to Employment: A Comparison of Autistic, Neurodivergent and Neurotypical Adults' Experiences of Hiring Processes in the United Kingdom'. *Autism* **27**(6): 1746–1763.

Davis, A., M. Solomon, and H. Belcher (2022). 'Examination of Race and Autism Intersectionality among African American/Black Young Adults'. *Autism in Adulthood* **4**(4): 306–314.

de Leon, F. L. L., and B. McQuillin (2018). 'The Role of Conferences on the Pathway to Academic Impact: Evidence from a Natural Experiment'. *Journal of Human Resources*: 1116-8387R.

Dwyer, P., S. M. Acevedo, H. M. Brown, J. Grapel, S. C. Jones, B. R. Nachman, D. M. Raymaker, and Z. J. Williams (2021). 'An Expert Roundtable Discussion on Experiences of Autistic Autism Researchers'. *Autism in Adulthood* **3**(3): 209–220.

Edelheim, J. R., K. Thomas, K. G. Åberg, and G. Phi (2018). 'What Do Conferences Do? What Is Academics' Intangible Return on Investment (ROI) from Attending an Academic Tourism Conference?' *Journal of Teaching in Travel & Tourism* **18**(1): 94–107.

Ekdahl, D. (2023). 'The Double Empathy Problem and the Problem of Empathy: Neurodiversifying Phenomenology'. *Disability & Society*: 1–23. doi.org/10.1080/09687599.2023.2220180.

Etzion, D., J. Gehman, and G. F. Davis (2021). 'Reimagining Academic Conferences: Toward a Federated Model of Conferencing'. *Management Learning* **53**(2): 350–362.

Ezerins, M. E., T. J. Vogus, A. S. Gabriel, L. S. Simon, C. Calderwood, and C. C. Rosen (2023). 'From Environmental Niches to Unique Contributions: Reconsidering Fit to Foster Inclusion across Neurotypes'. *Industrial and Organizational Psychology* **16**(1): 41–44.

Fabri, M., G. Fenton, P. Andrews, and M. Beaton (2022). 'Experiences of Higher Education Students on the Autism Spectrum: Stories of Low Mood and

High Resilience'. *International Journal of Disability, Development and Education* **69**(4): 1411–1429.

Ferrigno, S., G. Cicinelli, and R. Keller (2022). 'Bullying in Autism Spectrum Disorder: Prevalence and Consequences in Adulthood'. *Journal of Psychopathology* **3**.

Fontes, R., and M. Pino-Juste (2022). 'Portrayals of Autism and Social Awareness: A Scoping Review'. *Advances in Autism* **8**(3): 196–206.

Friedfeld Kesselmayer, R., C. M. Ochrach, B. N. Phillips, N. Mpofu, B. Lee, X. Chen, D. Geslak, and T. N. Tansey (2022). 'Autism Employment Initiative in a Global Business Management Consultancy Firm: A Case Study'. *Rehabilitation Counselors and Educators Journal* **11**(1).

Gaeke-Franz, B. (2022). 'Rejection or Celebration? Autistic Representation in Sitcom Television'. *Studies in Social Justice* **16**.

Gellini, H., and M. Marczak (2023). '"I always knew i was different": Experiences of Receiving a Diagnosis of Autistic Spectrum Disorder in Adulthood: A Meta-Ethnographic Systematic Review'. *Review Journal of Autism and Developmental Disorders*. https://doi.org/10.1007/s40489-023-00356-8.

Gesi, C., G. Migliarese, S. Torriero, M. Capellazzi, A. C. Omboni, G. Cerveri, and C. Mencacci (2021). 'Gender Differences in Misdiagnosis and Delayed Diagnosis among Adults with Autism Spectrum Disorder with No Language or Intellectual Disability'. *Brain Sciences* **11**(7): 912.

Ghanouni, P., T. Jarus, J. G. Zwicker, J. Lucyshyn, S. Chauhan, and C. Moir (2019). 'Perceived Barriers and Existing Challenges in Participation of Children with Autism Spectrum Disorders: "He Did Not Understand and No One Else Seemed to Understand Him"'. *Journal of Autism and Developmental Disorders* **49**(8): 3136–3145.

Gibbs, V., J. Hudson, Y. I. Hwang, S. Arnold, J. Trollor, and E. Pellicano (2021). 'Experiences of Physical and Sexual Violence as Reported by Autistic Adults without Intellectual Disability: Rate, Gender Patterns and Clinical Correlates'. *Research in Autism Spectrum Disorders* **89**: 101866.

Gierczyk, M., and G. Hornby (2021) 'Twice-Exceptional Students: Review of Implications for Special and Inclusive Education'. *Education Sciences* **11** DOI: 10.3390/educsci11020085.

Gill, C. J. (1997). 'Four Types of Integration in Disability Identity Development'. *Journal of Vocational Rehabilitation* **9**: 39–46.

Gillespie-Lynch, K., E. Hotez, M. Zajic, A. Riccio, D. DeNigris, B. Kofner, D. Bublitz, N. Gaggi, and K. Luca (2020). 'Comparing the Writing Skills of Autistic and Nonautistic University Students: A Collaboration with Autistic University Students'. *Autism* **24**(7): 1898–1912.

Goddard, H., and A. Cook (2022). '"I Spent Most of Freshers in my Room": A Qualitative Study of the Social Experiences of University Students on the Autistic Spectrum'. *Journal of Autism and Developmental Disorders* **52**(6): 2701–2716.

Goldblum, J. E., T. C. McFayden, S. Bristol, O. C. Putnam, A. Wylie, and C. Harrop (2023). 'Autism Prevalence and the Intersectionality of Assigned Sex at Birth, Race, and Ethnicity on Age of Diagnosis'. *Journal of Autism and Developmental Disorders*. doi: 10.1007/s10803-023-06104-5

Grant, A., and H. Kara (2021). 'Considering the Autistic Advantage in Qualitative Research: The Strengths of Autistic Researchers'. *Contemporary Social Science* **16**(5): 589–603.

Grenawalt, T. A., E. A. Brinck, R. Friefeld Kesselmayer, B. N. Phillips, D. Geslak, D. R. Strauser, F. Chan, and T. N. Tansey (2020). 'Autism in the Workforce: A Case Study'. *Journal of Management & Organization*. doi: 10.1017/jmo.2020.15.

Griffiths, S., C. Allison, R. Kenny, R. Holt, P. Smith, and S. Baron-Cohen (2019). 'The Vulnerability Experiences Quotient (VEQ): A Study of Vulnerability, Mental Health and Life Satisfaction in Autistic Adults'. *Autism Research* **12**(10): 1516–1528.

Griful-Freixenet, J., K. Struyven, M. Verstichele, and C. Andries (2017). 'Higher Education Students with Disabilities Speaking Out: Perceived Barriers and Opportunities of the Universal Design for Learning Framework'. *Disability & Society* **32**(10): 1627–1649.

Gurbuz, E., M. Hanley, and D. M. Riby (2019). 'University Students with Autism: The Social and Academic Experiences of University in the UK'. *Journal of Autism and Developmental Disorders* **49**(2): 617–631.

Habib, A., L. Harris, F. Pollick, and C. Melville (2019). 'A Meta-analysis of Working Memory in Individuals with Autism Spectrum Disorders'. *PLoS One* **14**(4): e0216198.

Hall-Lande, J., A. Hewitt, S. Mishra, K. Piescher, and T. LaLiberte (2014). 'Involvement of Children with Autism Spectrum Disorder (ASD) in the Child Protection System'. *Focus on Autism and Other Developmental Disabilities* **30**(4): 237–248.

Hamilton, L. (2019). 'Disability as a Social Construction: Investigating How Autism Is Represented in the Mainstream Media'. *Prism: Casting New Light on Learning, Theory and Practice* **2**(2): 20–38.

Hamilton, L. G., and S. Petty (2023). 'Compassionate Pedagogy for Neurodiversity in Higher Education: A Conceptual Analysis'. *Frontiers in Psychology* **14**. https://doi.org/10.3389/fpsyg.2023.1093290.

Hamzić, U., and S. Bećirović (2021). 'Twice-Exceptional, Half-Noticed: The Recognition Issues of Gifted Students with Learning Disabilities'. *MAP Social Sciences* **1**(1): 13–22.

Happé, F., and P. Vital (2009). 'What Aspects of Autism Predispose to Talent?' *Philosophical Transactions of the Royal Society B: Biological Sciences* **364**(1522): 1369–1375.

Harmens, M., F. Sedgewick, and H. Hobson (2022). 'Autistic Women's Diagnostic Experiences: Interactions with Identity and Impacts on Well-Being'. *Women's Health (London)* **18**: 17455057221137477.

Hase, A., M. Haynes, and G. Hasler (2023). 'Using Simple Economic Games to Assess Social Orienting and Prosocial Behavior in Adolescents with Autism Spectrum Disorder'. *Autism Research* **16**(6): 1199–1209.

Hayward, S. M., K. R. McVilly, and M. A. Stokes (2019). '"I Would Love to Just Be Myself": What Autistic Women Want at Work'. *Autism in Adulthood* **1** (4): 297–305.

Hernaus, T., M. Cerne, C. Connelly, N. Poloski Vokic, and M. Škerlavaj (2019). 'Evasive Knowledge Hiding in Academia: When Competitive Individuals Are Asked to Collaborate'. *Journal of Knowledge Management* **23**(4): 597–618.

Hickey, A., J. Crabtree, and J. Stott (2018). '"Suddenly the first fifty years of my life made sense": Experiences of Older People with Autism'. *Autism* **22**(3): 357–367.

Huang, Y., Y. I. Hwang, S. R. C. Arnold, L. P. Lawson, A. L. Richdale, and J. N. Trollor (2022). 'Autistic Adults' Experiences of Diagnosis Disclosure'. *Journal of Autism and Developmental Disorders* **52**(12): 5301–5307.

Hull, L., M.-C. Lai, S. Baron-Cohen, C. Allison, P. Smith, K. V. Petrides, and W. Mandy (2020). 'Gender Differences in Self-Reported Camouflaging in Autistic and Non-Autistic Adults'. *Autism* **24**(2): 352–363.

Hull, L., W. Mandy, M. C. Lai, S. Baron-Cohen, C. Allison, P. Smith, and K. V. Petrides (2019). 'Development and Validation of the Camouflaging Autistic Traits Questionnaire (CAT-Q)'. *Journal of Autism and Developmental Disorders* **49**(3): 819–833.

Humphrys, E., J. Rodgers, N. L. Asquith, S. A. Yaghi, A. Foulstone, R. Thorneycroft, and P. S. Cook (2022). '"To prove I'm not incapable, I overcompensate": Disability, Ideal Workers, the Academy'. *The Economic and Labour Relations Review* **33**(4): 698–714.

Hurley-Hanson, A. E., C. M. Giannantonio, and A. J. Griffiths (2020a). 'Leadership and Autism'. In *Autism in the Workplace: Creating Positive Employment and Career Outcomes for Generation A*. Ed. A. E. Hurley-Hanson, C. M. Giannantonio and A. J. Griffiths. Cham: Springer International, 215–236.

(2020b). 'The Stigma of Autism'. In *Autism in the Workplace: Creating Positive Employment and Career Outcomes for Generation A*. Ed. A. E. Hurley-Hanson, C. M. Giannantonio, and A. J. Griffiths. Cham: Springer International, 21–45.

Irish, J. E. N. (2020). 'Increasing Participation: Using the Principles of Universal Design to Create Accessible Conferences'. *Journal of Convention & Event Tourism* **21**(4): 308–330.

Irvine, B., and A. MacLeod (2022). 'What Are the Challenges and Successes Reported by Autistic Students at University?: A Literature Review'. *Good Autism Practice (GAP)* **23**(1): 49–59.

Jones, S. C. (2019). 'Autism, a Neurotype Not an Insult'. *Sydney Morning Herald*, 9 July.

(2022a). 'Autistics Working in Academia: What Are the Barriers and Facilitators?' *Autism* **27**(3): 822–831.

(2022b). 'Hey Look, I'm (Not) on TV: Autistic People Reflect on Autism Portrayals in Entertainment Media'. *Disability & Society*: 1–18.

(2023). 'Advice for Autistic People Considering a Career in Academia'. *Autism* **27**(7): 2187–2192.

Jones, S. C., C. S. Gordon, M. Akram, N. Murphy, and F. Sharkie (2022). 'Inclusion, Exclusion and Isolation of Autistic People: Community Attitudes and Autistic People's Experiences'. *Journal of Autism and Developmental Disorders* **52**(3): 1131–1142.

Jones, S. C., C. S. Gordon, and S. Mizzi (2023). 'Representation of Autism in Fictional Media: A Systematic Review of Media Content and Its Impact on Viewer Knowledge and Understanding of Autism'. *Autism* **27**(8): 2205–2217.

Kalmanovich-Cohen, H., and S. J. Stanton (2023). 'How Can Work from Home Support Neurodiversity and Inclusion?' *Industrial and Organizational Psychology: Perspectives on Science and Practice* **16**(1): 20–24.

Kapp, S. K. (2023). 'Profound Concerns about "Profound Autism": Dangers of Severity Scales and Functioning Labels for Support Needs'. *Education Sciences* **13**(2): 106.

Kasirer, A., E. Adi-Japha, and N. Mashal (2020). 'Verbal and Figural Creativity in Children with Autism Spectrum Disorder and Typical Development'. *Frontiers in Psychology* **11**: 559238.

Keashly, L. (2021). 'Workplace Bullying, Mobbing and Harassment in Academe: Faculty Experience'. In *Special Topics and Particular Occupations, Professions and Sectors*. Ed. P. D'Cruz, E. Noronha, L. Keashly, and S. Tye-Williams. Singapore: Springer Singapore, 221–297.

Keating, C. T., L. Hickman, J. Leung, R. Monk, A. Montgomery, H. Heath, and S. Sowden (2023). 'Autism-Related Language Preferences of English-Speaking Individuals across the Globe: A Mixed Methods Investigation'. *Autism Research* **16**(2): 406–428.

Kenny, L., C. Hattersley, B. Molins, C. Buckley, C. Povey, and E. Pellicano (2016). 'Which Terms Should Be Used to Describe Autism? Perspectives from the UK Autism Community'. *Autism* **20**(4): 442–462.

Laiduc, G., and R. Covarrubias (2022). 'Making Meaning of the Hidden Curriculum: Translating Wise Interventions to Usher University Change'. *Translational Issues in Psychological Science* **8**(2): 221–233.

Leedham, A., A. R. Thompson, R. Smith, and M. Freeth (2020). '"I was exhausted trying to figure it out": The Experiences Of Females Receiving an Autism Diagnosis in Middle to Late Adulthood'. *Autism* **24**(1): 135–146.

Lei, J., and A. Russell (2021). 'Understanding the Role of Self-Determination in Shaping University Experiences for Autistic and Typically Developing Students in the United Kingdom'. *Autism* **25**(5): 1262–1278.

Levitis, A., C. D. Gould van Praag, R. Gau, et al. (2021). Centering Inclusivity in the Design of Online Conferences: An OHBM–Open Science Perspective, *GigaScience* 10(8), https://doi.org/10.1093/gigascience/giab051.

Lilley, R., W. Lawson, G. Hall, J. Mahony, H. Clapham, M. Heyworth, S. R. Arnold, J. N. Trollor, M. Yudell, and E. Pellicano (2022). '"A way to be me": Autobiographical Reflections of Autistic Adults Diagnosed in Mid-to-Late Adulthood'. *Autism* **26**(6): 1395–1408.

Lindsay, S., and K. Fuentes (2022). 'It Is Time to Address Ableism in Academia: A Systematic Review of the Experiences and Impact of Ableism among Faculty and Staff'. *Disabilities* **2**(2): 178–203.

Lindsay, S., V. Osten, M. Rezai, and S. Bui (2021). 'Disclosure and Workplace Accommodations for People with Autism: A Systematic Review'. *Disability and Rehabilitation: An International, Multidisciplinary Journal* **43**(5): 597–610.

Lockwood Estrin, G., V. Milner, D. Spain, F. Happé, and E. Colvert (2021). 'Barriers to Autism Spectrum Disorder Diagnosis for Young Women and Girls: A Systematic Review'. *Review Journal of Autism and Developmental Disorders* **8**(4): 454–470.

Lopez, K., C. Nicolaidis, A. Garcia, T. C. Waisman, M. A. Cascio, and B. Feng (2022). 'An Expert Roundtable Discussion on Intersectionality and Autism in Adulthood'. *Autism in Adulthood* **4**(4): 258–264.

Lovelace, T. S., M. P. Comis, J. M. Tabb, and O. E. Oshokoya (2022). 'Missing from the Narrative: A Seven-Decade Scoping Review of the Inclusion of Black Autistic Women and Girls in Autism Research'. *Behavior Analysis in Practice* **15**(4): 1093–1105.

Lubin, J., and J. Brooks (2021). 'College Students with Autism: Navigating the Bumpy Road'. *College Student Journal* **55**(3): 318–324.

Macdonald, D., G. Luk, and E. M. Quintin (2022). 'Early Reading Comprehension Intervention for Preschoolers with Autism Spectrum Disorder and Hyperlexia'. *Journal of Autism and Developmental Disorders* **52**(4): 1652–1672.

Madaus, J., S. Reis, N. Gelbar, J. Delgado, and A. Cascio (2022). 'Perceptions of Factors That Facilitate and Impede Learning among Twice-Exceptional College Students with Autism Spectrum Disorder'. *Neurobiology of Learning and Memory* **193**: 107627.

Mantzalas, J., A. L. Richdale, A. Adikari, J. Lowe, and C. Dissanayake (2022). 'What Is Autistic Burnout? A Thematic Analysis of Posts on Two Online Platforms'. *Autism in Adulthood* **4**(1): 52–65.

Markel, K. S., and B. Elia (2016). 'How Human Resource Management Can Best Support Employees with Autism: Future Directions for Research and Practice'. *Journal of Business and Management* **22**(1): 71–85.

Martin, N. (2020). 'University through the Eyes of Autistic Students and Staff'. In *Neurodiversity Reader*. Ed. D. Milton. West Sussex: Pavilion Publishing, 287–308.

(2021). 'Perspectives on UK university Employment from Autistic Researchers and Lecturers'. *Disability & Society* **36**(9): 1510–1531.

Martin, N., C. Barnham, and J. Krupa (2019). 'Identifying and Addressing Barriers to Employment of Autistic Adults'. *Journal of Inclusive Practice in Further and Higher Education* **10**(1): 56–77.

Martin, V., T. D. Flanagan, T. J. Vogus, and D. Chênevert (2023). 'Sustainable Employment Depends on Quality Relationships between Supervisors and Their Employees on the Autism Spectrum'. *Disability and Rehabilitation* **45**(11): 1784–1795.

Mazumder, R., and S. Thompson-Hodgetts (2019). 'Stigmatization of Children and Adolescents with Autism Spectrum Disorders and Their Families: A Scoping Study'. *Review Journal of Autism and Developmental Disorders* **6** (1): 96–107.

McQuaid, G. A., N. R. Lee, and G. L. Wallace (2022). 'Camouflaging in Autism Spectrum Disorder: Examining the Roles of Sex, Gender Identity, and Diagnostic Timing'. *Autism* **26**(2): 552–559.

Mellifont, D. (2023). 'Ableist Ivory Towers: A Narrative Review Informing about the Lived Experiences of Neurodivergent Staff in Contemporary Higher Education'. *Disability & Society* **38**(5): 865–886.

Milton, D., E. Gurbuz, and B. López (2022). 'The "Double Empathy Problem": Ten Years On'. *Autism* **26**(8): 1901–1903.

Minio-Paluello, I., G. Porciello, A. Pascual-Leone, and S. Baron-Cohen (2020). 'Face Individual Identity Recognition: A Potential Endophenotype in Autism'. *Molecular Autism* **11**(1): 81.

Mittmann, G., B. Schrank, and V. Steiner-Hofbauer (2023). 'Portrayal of Autism in Mainstream Media: A Scoping Review about Representation, Stigmatisation and Effects on Consumers in Non-fiction and Fiction Media'. *Current Psychology*. https://doi.org/10.1007/s12144-023-04959-6.

Morgan, E. H., R. Rodgers, and J. Tschida (2022). 'Addressing the Intersectionality of Race and Disability to Improve Autism Care'. *Pediatrics* **149**(Supplement 4): e2020049437M.

Morrison, A. (2019). '(Un)Reasonable, (Un)Necessary, and (In)Appropriate Biographic Mediation of Neurodivergence in Academic Accommodations'. *Biography* **42**(3): 693–719.

Nagib, W., and R. Wilton (2020). 'Gender Matters in Career Exploration and Job-Seeking among Adults with Autism Spectrum Disorder: Evidence from an Online Community'. *Disability and Rehabilitation* **42**(18): 2530–2541.

(2021). 'Examining the Gender Role in Workplace Experiences among Employed Adults with Autism: Evidence from an Online Community'. *Journal of Vocational Rehabilitation* **55**: 27–42.

Navarro-Pardo, E., M. F. López-Ramón, Y. Alonso-Esteban, and F. Alcantud-Marín (2021). 'Diagnostic Tools for Autism Spectrum Disorders by Gender: Analysis of Current Status and Future Lines'. *Children* **8**(4): 262.

Nocon, A. S., A. Roestorf, and L. M. G. Menéndez (2022). 'Positive Psychology in Neurodiversity: An Investigation of Character Strengths in Autistic Adults in the United Kingdom in a Community Setting'. *Research in Autism Spectrum Disorders* **99**: 102071.

North, G. (2023). 'Reconceptualising "Reasonable Adjustments" for the Successful Employment of Autistic Women'. *Disability & Society* **38**(6): 944–962.

O'Connor, M., S. C. Jones, C. Gordon, and A. Joosten (2024). 'Exploring Environmental Barriers and Facilitators to Inclusion on a University Campus for Autistic Students'. *Autism in Adulthood* **6**(1): 36–46.

Patekar, J. (2021). 'The Perpetuation of Stereotypes in Croatian Public Discourse: "Autistic" as a Pejorative'. *Collegium antropologicum* **45**(4): 287–297.

Patton, E. (2019). 'Autism, Attributions and Accommodations: Overcoming Barriers and Integrating a Neurodiverse Workforce'. *Personnel Review* **48** (4): 915–934.

Penton, T., N. Bowling, A. Vafeiadou, C. Hammond, G. Bird, and M. J. Banissy (2023). 'Attitudes to Interpersonal Touch in the Workplace in Autistic and Non-Autistic Groups'. *Journal of Autism and Developmental Disorders* **53** (12): 4731–4743.

Petty, S., L. Tunstall, H. Richardson, and N. Eccles (2023). 'Workplace Adjustments for Autistic Employees: What Is "Reasonable"?' *Journal of Autism and Developmental Disorders* **53**(1): 236–244.

Pfeffer, R. D. (2016). 'Childhood Victimization in a National Sample of Youth with Autism Spectrum Disorders'. *Journal of Policy and Practice in Intellectual Disabilities* **13**(4): 311–319.

Phillips, B. N., T. N. Tansey, D. Lee, B. Lee, X. Chen, R. F. Kesselmayer, A. Reyes, and D. S. Geslak (2023). 'Autism Initiative in the Industrial Sector: A Case Study'. *Rehabilitation Counselors and Educators Journal* **12**(1). https://doi.org/10.52017/001c.37780.

Qeshmi, S. S., J. Batchelor, and G. Burch (2023). 'Autistic Employees, Cybersecurity, and Diversity: How the Three Intersect to Enhance Information Security and Privacy'. In SAIS 2023 Proceedings. 8. https://aisel.aisnet.org/sais2023/8.

Raso, A., A. Marchetti, D. D'Angelo, B. Albanesi, L. Garrino, V. Dimonte, M. Piredda, and M. G. De Marinis (2019). 'The Hidden Curriculum in Nursing Education: A Scoping Study'. *Medical Education* **53**(10): 989–1002.

Raymaker, D. M. (2017). 'Reflections of a Community-Based Participatory Researcher from the Intersection of Disability Advocacy, Engineering, and the Academy'. *Action Research (Lond)* **15**(3): 258–275.

Raymaker, D. M., M. Sharer, J. Maslak, L. E. Powers, K. E. McDonald, S. K. Kapp, I. Moura, A. F. Wallington, and C. Nicolaidis (2022). '"[I] don't wanna just be like a cog in the machine": Narratives of Autism and Skilled Employment'. *Autism* **27**(1): 65–75.

Raymaker, D. M., A. R. Teo, N. A. Steckler, B. Lentz, M. Scharer, A. Delos Santos, S. K. Kapp, M. Hunter, A. Joyce, and C. Nicolaidis (2020). '"Having All of Your Internal Resources Exhausted beyond Measure and Being Left with No Clean-Up Crew": Defining Autistic Burnout'. *Autism in Adulthood* **2**(2): 132–143.

Riccio, A., S. K. Kapp, A. Jordan, A. M. Dorelien, and K. Gillespie-Lynch (2021). 'How Is Autistic Identity in Adolescence Influenced by Parental Disclosure Decisions and Perceptions of Autism?' *Autism* **25**(2): 374–388.

Roberson, Q., N. R. Quigley, K. Vickers, and I. Bruck (2021). 'Reconceptualizing Leadership from a Neurodiverse Perspective'. *Group & Organization Management* **46**(2): 399–423.

Romualdez, A. M., B. Heasman, Z. Walker, J. Davies, and A. Remington (2021). '"People might understand me better": Diagnostic Disclosure Experiences of Autistic Individuals in the Workplace'. *Autism in Adulthood* **3**(2): 157–167.

Romualdez, A. M., Z. Walker, and A. Remington (2021). 'Autistic Adults' Experiences of Diagnostic Disclosure in the Workplace: Decision-making and Factors Associated with Outcomes'. *Autism & Developmental Language Impairments* **6**. doi: 10.1177/23969415211022955.

Russell, G., S. K. Kapp, D. Elliott, C. Elphick, R. Gwernan-Jones, and C. Owens (2019). 'Mapping the Autistic Advantage from the Accounts of Adults Diagnosed with Autism: A Qualitative Study'. *Autism in Adulthood* **1**(2): 124–133.

Scott, M., A. Jacob, D. Hendrie, R. Parsons, S. Girdler, T. Falkmer, and M. Falkmer (2017). 'Employers' Perception of the Costs and the Benefits of Hiring Individuals with Autism Spectrum Disorder in Open Employment in Australia'. *PLoS ONE* **12**(5): e0177607.

Scott, M., and F. Sedgewick (2021). '"I have more control over my life": A Qualitative Exploration of Challenges, Opportunities, and Support Needs among Autistic University Students'. *Autism & Developmental Language Impairments* **6**: 23969415211010419.

Shein, E. (2020). 'Hiring from the Autism Spectrum'. *Communications of the ACM* **63**(6): 17–19.

Shevchuk-Hill, S., S. Szczupakiewicz, B. Kofner, and K. Gillespie-Lynch (2023). 'Comparing Narrative Writing of Autistic and Non-Autistic College Students'. *Journal of Autism and Developmental Disorders* **53**(10): 3901–3915.

Smith, O., and S. C. Jones (2020). '"Coming Out" with Autism: Identity in People with an Asperger's Diagnosis after DSM-5'. *Journal of Autism and Developmental Disorders* **50**(2): 592–602.

Solazzo, S., N. Kojovic, F. Robain, and M. Schaer (2021). 'Measuring the Emergence of Specific Abilities in Young Children with Autism Spectrum Disorders: The Example of Early Hyperlexic Traits'. *Brain Sciences* **11**(6): 692.

Spurk, D., A. Hofer, and S. Kauffeld (2021). 'Why Does Competitive Psychological Climate Foster or Hamper Career Success? The Role of Challenge and Hindrance Pathways and Leader-Member-Exchange'. *Journal of Vocational Behavior* **127**: 103542.

Steenkamp, N., and R. Roberts (2020). 'Does Workload and Institutional Pressure on Accounting Educators Affect Academia at Australian Universities?' *Accounting & Finance* **60**(1): 471–506.

Taels, L., J. Feyaerts, M. Lizon, M. De Smet, and S. Vanheule (2023). '"I felt like my senses were under attack": An Interpretative Phenomenological Analysis of Experiences of Hypersensitivity in Autistic Individuals'. *Autism* **27**(8): 2269–2280.

Tan, C. D. (2018). '"I'm a normal autistic person, not an abnormal neurotypical": Autism Spectrum Disorder Diagnosis as Biographical Illumination'. *Social Science & Medicine* **197**: 161–167.

Taylor, E., R. Holt, T. Tavassoli, C. Ashwin, and S. Baron-Cohen (2020). 'Revised Acored Sensory Perception Quotient Reveals Sensory Hypersensitivity in Women with Autism'. *Molecular Autism* **11**(1): 18.

Taylor, N. C., and J. H. Johnson (2020). 'Challenges and Solutions for Autism in Academic Geosciences'. *Advances in Geosciences* **53**: 33–39.

Tomczak, M. T. (2022). 'How Can The Work Environment Be Redesigned to Enhance the Well-Being of Individuals with Autism?' *Employee Relations* **44** (6): 1467–1484.

Tomczak, M. T., and K. Kulikowski (2024). 'Toward an Understanding of Occupational Burnout among Employees with Autism: The Job Demands-Resources Theory Perspective'. *Current Psychology: A Journal for Diverse Perspectives on Diverse Psychological Issues* **43**: 1582–1594.

van den Bosch, K. E., A. Krzeminska, E. Y. Song, L. B. E. van Hal, M. M. Waltz, H. Ebben, and A. P. Schippers (2019). 'Nothing about Us, without Us: A Case Study of a Consumer-Run Organization by and for People on the Autism Spectrum in the Netherlands'. *Journal of Management & Organization* **25**(4): 464–480.

Vincent, J. (2020). 'Employability for UK University Students and Graduates on the Autism Spectrum: Mobilities and Materialities'. *Scandinavian Journal of Disability Research* **22**(1): 12–24.

Waisman, T. C., L. A. Alba, and S. A. Green (2022). 'Barriers to Inclusive Learning for Autistic Individuals'. *Pediatrics* **149**(Supplement 4): e2020049437Q.

Waisman-Nitzan, M., E. Gal, and N. Schreuer (2019). 'Employers' Perspectives Regarding Reasonable Accommodations for Employees with Autism Spectrum Disorder'. *Journal of Management & Organization* **25**(4): 481–498.

(2021). '"It's like a ramp for a person in a wheelchair": Workplace Accessibility for Employees with Autism'. *Research in Developmental Disabilities* **114**.

Warren, N., B. Eatchel, A. V. Kirby, M. Diener, C. Wright, and V. D'Astous (2021). 'Parent-Identified Strengths of Autistic Youth'. *Autism* **25**(1): 79–89.

Webster, A. A., and S. Garvis (2016). 'The Importance of Critical Life Moments: An Explorative Study of Successful Women with Autism Spectrum Disorder'. *Autism* **21**(6): 670–677.

Weiss, J., and M. Fardella (2018). 'Victimization and Perpetration Experiences of Adults with Autism'. *Frontiers in Psychology* **9**. doi: 10.3389/fpsyt.2018.00203.

Wen, B., H. van Rensburg, S. O'Neill, and T. Attwood (2023). 'Autism in the Australian Workplace: The Employer Perspective'. *Asia Pacific Journal of Human Resources* **61**(1): 146–167.

Whelpley, C., J. Bochantin, G. Banks, and R. Sandoval (2019). 'An Inductive Approach to Autism at Work: A Neurodiverse Perspective'. *Academy of Management Proceedings* **2019**(1): 15007.

Wilson, R. B., A. R. Thompson, G. Rowse, and M. Freeth (2023). 'The Experience of Seeking, Receiving, and Reflecting upon a Diagnosis of Autism in the UK: A Meta-synthesis of Qualitative Studies Conducted with Autistic Individuals'. *Research in Autism Spectrum Disorders* **103**: 102135.

Wodziński, M., M. Rządeczka, and M. Moskalewicz (2023). 'How to Minimize the Impact of Experts' Non-rational Beliefs on Their Judgments on Autism'. *Community Mental Health Journal* **59**(4): 756–769.

Wong, P. S., M. Donelly, P. A. Neck, and B. Boyd (2018). 'Positive Autism: Investigation of Workplace Characteristics Leading to a Strengths-Based Approach to Employment of People with Autism'. *Revista de Management Comparat International* **19**(1): 15–30.

Wood, R., and F. Happé (2023). 'What Are the Views and Experiences of Autistic Teachers? Findings from an Online Survey in the UK'. *Disability & Society* **38**(1): 47–72.

Woolard, A., E. Stratton, E. A. Demetriou, K. A. Boulton, E. Pellicano, N. Glozier, V. Gibbs, N. Rogerson, P. Quinn, I. B. Hickie, and A. J. Guastella (2021). 'Perceptions of Social and Work Functioning Are Related to Social Anxiety and Executive Function in Autistic Adults'. *Autism* **25**(7): 2124–2134.

Yến-Khanh, N. (2023). 'Representation of Autism in Vietnamese Digital News Media: A Computational Corpus and Framing Analysis'. *Communication Research and Practice* **9**(2): 142–158.

Index

In this index figures are indicated by *italics* and tables by bold type.